Cricket Ball

Cricket Ball

The Heart of the Game

Gary Cox

BLOOMSBURY ACADEMIC
LONDON • NEW YORK • OXFORD • NEW DELHI • SYDNEY

BLOOMSBURY ACADEMIC
Bloomsbury Publishing Plc
50 Bedford Square, London, WC1B 3DP, UK
1385 Broadway, New York, NY 10018, USA

BLOOMSBURY, BLOOMSBURY ACADEMIC and the Diana logo are trademarks of
Bloomsbury Publishing Plc

First published in Great Britain 2019

Cover design: Irene-Martinez Costa

Cover image © Lee Wakerley

Bloomsbury Publishing Plc does not have any control over, or responsibility for, any
third-party websites referred to or in this book. All internet addresses given in this
book were correct at the time of going to press. The author and publisher regret
any inconvenience caused if addresses have changed or sites have ceased to
exist, but can accept no responsibility for any such changes.

A catalogue record for this book is available from the British Library.

A catalog record for this book is available from the Library of Congress.

ISBN: HB: 978-1-3500-1458-9
       ePDF: 978-1-3500-1457-2
       eBook: 978-1-3500-1459-6

Typeset by RefineCatch Limited, Bungay, Suffolk
Printed and bound by CPI Group (UK) Ltd, Croydon, CR0 4YY

To find out more about our authors and books visit www.bloomsbury.com
and sign up for our newsletters.

For my mother Jane
who taught me the game

Contents of the Over

First Delivery: Loosener 1

    Animated inanimate object 1

    A regular Mad Hatter's tea party 4

    Watching cricket on the radio 15

Second Delivery: Cricket Ball Surveyed 21

    Ideal ball 21

    Real ball 26

    Perfect handful 34

Third Delivery: Cricket Ball Made 41

    What is a cricket ball? 41

    Evolution of the rolling globular body 62

    Coriaceus orbis 68

    Centres of excellence 76

Fourth Delivery: Cricket Ball Played 83

    Bowling overarm, not underarm or throwing 83

New ball, old ball, live ball, dead ball, no-ball, lost ball, swing ball, dot ball 89

Ball tampering 100

Fast bowling: pace is nothing without control 120

Length 128

Line 134

Bodyline 139

Spin bowling: the art of confusion 144

Fielding: the art of attentiveness 156

Transcendental ball 162

Fifth Delivery: Cricket Ball Pain 167

Comedy and tragedy 167

Pitches, padding and cane-handle bats 171

Death toll 181

Princes, umpires and pigeons 188

Sixth Delivery: Cricket Ball Fame 191

Great players, stats and performances 194

Botham rises from the ashes 212

Easeful Atlas 219

The Gatting Ball 232

The Strauss Ball 238

The Laker Ball 245

The Sobers Six Sixes Ball 247

Seventh Delivery: Umpire Miscounting and Other Ball Stories 255

Bibliography 275
Index 279

Before the fast bowler began his run he held the ball up and shook it at Cudjoe, and Cudjoe in turn held up his bat and shook it at the bowler. The fast bowler ran up and bowled and Cudjoe hit his first ball out of the world. It didn't seem to matter how many he made after that. The challenge and the hit which followed were enough. It was primitive, but as the battle between Hector and Achilles is primitive.

C. L. R. JAMES, *Beyond a Boundary,* pp. 10–11

First Delivery

Loosener

Animated inanimate object

I have long harboured a secret desire to write a book about the glorious game of cricket with a mildly philosophical spin. Like the guy in that excellent reggae song 'Dreadlock Holiday' by English art-rock band 10cc, cricket is not a game I merely like, I absolutely love it. So, when I decided to write a book about a single physical object, there was no question which object I would choose to write about.

I encountered no difficulty finding a whole book full of wonderful things to say about that most singular, iconic object, the cricket ball. Indeed, it often struck me that there was too much to say. The real challenge, apart from saying what needed to be said about the cricket ball's complex and exciting life, was knowing where to draw the line, the crease. Every object is at the centre of the universe, every sustained consideration of any object soon begins to drag the whole universe in. Not least, cricket is a universe in and of itself. This book is no narrow treatment of cricket or its ball. Quite the contrary, this zooming in on the ball – the essential and ever present heart of the game – opens up many new ways of thinking about the infinite cricket universe.

Writing this book has undoubtedly involved a prolonged preoccupation with the life of a single, apparently mundane thing, a mere ball. In one sense, the cricket ball is a mundane thing, commonplace and not particularly valuable in most cases, the kind of thing you find discarded at the back of a drawer, but a closer look soon reveals that the cricket ball is anything but dreary, anything but humble.

What you have here, amongst many other things, is an exploration of all aspects of the hidden and not so hidden life of the cricket ball – its being, its production, its history, its role in the game, its image, its status, its legend, its social, cultural and political significance, its future. Anything and everything really that a detailed telling of the cricket ball story can reveal.

The cricket ball is an extraordinary object that has led and continues to lead a remarkable and exciting life. The world would certainly be a far less interesting though safer place without the cricket ball in it. Its complex idiosyncrasies have determined the fates of many people. Each day around the world the cricket ball creates fools, villains and heroes. Occasionally it creates martyrs. It has ruined promising careers and destroyed lives. It has shamed entire nations while restoring the pride of others. It has more than once been the cause of diplomatic crises and legal wrangles, as this book will show. It is a most animated inanimate object; made to be in motion, the core of the action, always the focal point of the battle, demanding and absorbing desperate concentration and constantly creating controversy.

In his book *Science, Perception and Reality*, the American philosopher Wilfrid Sellars argues that all so-called inanimate objects are really 'truncated persons' (p. 13). We apply the category *person* to them, he argues, but only in a pruned, curtailed form. Most Western societies do not credit inanimate objects with full-blown personhood because they are not alive in the 'scientific' sense of the term. Yet so many objects feel full of personality, some of them more so than many living things!

Surely some objects also have a presence, exert a force in the world that is akin to being alive. Indeed, in animistic cultures, where the lines between life and 'non-life' are blurred, some objects are thought to be possessed of spirit and are credited with having life or even, in some cases, with being life-giving. I can't help feeling the cricket ball can be seen very much as a living energy, a vital, *animate* power beating away at the heart of the game.

If we view the cricket ball animistically, it can be said to have a very full and rich personality. It is a tough, energetic, artful, mischievous, hard-nosed character, unpredictable even enigmatic in its behaviour and given to extreme mood swings. Its element is surely fire. Like fire it is a good servant and a bad master.

I hope you enjoy reading my myriad thoughts and ideas on the cricket ball as much as I have enjoyed formulating them from a combination of close observation, detailed research, extensive statistics, strange stories, highly amusing hearsay and a lifetime spent musing and meditating on the great game. Whatever thoughts I have come up with, it was ultimately the cricket ball itself that inspired them. I hope that you never think about the cricket ball in the same way again. I certainly never will. Above all, I hope that I am making a small contribution to the already incredibly rich and forever ongoing biography of the matchless leathern orb.

A regular Mad Hatter's tea party

Before I proceed, a few thoughts on the game of cricket itself. The centuries-old bat and ball field game of cricket has a reputation for being horrendously complicated, yet the hundreds of millions of people who play and watch it throughout the world have no problem understanding it at all. Better to say then that cricket is complex rather than complicated once a person has become familiar with the basics. From an understanding of the basics a person who enjoys cricket will go on to realize that cricket is a game of infinite structural, logistical, legal, tactical, strategic, psychological, sociological, dramatic, artistic, aesthetic, ethical, philosophical and spiritual depth.

It seems to me that of all the popular field games, cricket is the most *complete* game, the truly beautiful game. To play it well, to play it beautifully, requires maximum reason and reflex, character and courage, all expressed through an enormously diverse skill set. And the greater the skill and the better the play, the more the game's infinite beautiful possibilities are revealed.

As C. L. R. James argues in *Beyond a Boundary*, perhaps the most profound and penetrating book on cricket ever written, 'The greatness of the great batsman is not so much in his own skill as that he sets in motion all the immense possibilities that are contained in the game as structurally organised' (p. 261).

Beyond a Boundary is also a masterfully subtle exploration of the complex relationship between cricket, ethics, colonialism, class, caste and race. A Trinidadian black man who became a leading Marxist activist, James analyses the complex racial and class discrimination that influenced the composition of cricket teams in the West Indies where he grew up. A player of considerable ability himself, he notes that discrimination in West Indian cricket was not just a problem of black–white segregation. There were exclusively white teams, prevalently white teams that admitted one or two black players of high social standing or famed ability, black teams with white captains and black teams, Maple for example, that had a limit on how black their players could be.

> One of these clubs was Maple, the club of the brown-skinned middle class. Class did not matter to them so much as colour. They had founded themselves on the principle that they didn't want any dark people in their club.
>
> *Beyond a Boundary*, pp. 66–7

It is difficult to do real justice to James's detailed socio-political analysis of West Indian colonial cricket in the space available to me, so I urge you to read him for yourself, but the great contradiction he highlights is that between the fair play and justice that were sacrosanct *within* the boundary of the field of play and the inequality and prejudice that prevailed *beyond* it. A great lover and philosopher of cricket, James is nonetheless prepared to praise the game on precisely those grounds where many have criticized it. 'Cricket,' he says, 'is a game of high and difficult technique. If it were not it could not carry the load of social response and implications which it carries' (*Beyond a Boundary*, p. 45). James has the subtlety to recognize that it is yet another testament to the power and greatness of cricket *as a game* that it can be so deeply implicated in the expansion, education, ideology, contradictions and controversy of the largest empire the world has ever known, when it is, after all, apparently, 'only a game'.

Although essentially a team game, cricket highlights individual strengths and exposes individual weaknesses like no other team sport. Football makes much of the penalty shoot-out, the way the shootout places an individual player on the spot to test his skill, nerve and character, but cricket is a penalty shoot-out all the time, a game in which the mettle of each player is inevitably, microscopically and lingeringly scrutinized to be found copious, sufficient or wanting.

> The batsman facing the ball does not merely represent his side. For that moment, to all intents and purposes, he is his side. This fundamental relation of the One and the Many, Individual and Social, Individual and Universal, leader and followers, representative and ranks, the part and the whole, is structurally imposed on the players of cricket. What other sports, games and arts have to aim at, the players are given to start with, they cannot depart from it.
>
> *Beyond a Boundary*, p. 259

Cricket is not a slow game, if slow implies sluggish, pedestrian and boring, but it is a measured and deliberate game that allows ample time for the subtle qualities of a person's character to emerge, and uses every trick to draw that character out. As the doyen of cricket writers Sir John Frederick Neville Cardus CBE says in his classic book *English Cricket*, 'It is because cricket does not always hurry along, a constant hurly-burly, every player propelled here and there by the pace of continuous action, that there is time for character to reveal itself' (p. 11).

Arguably, all other field games are simply incapable of matching the multi-faceted physical complexity, tactical intricacy and strategic subtlety of cricket. Football, by comparison, is scarcely more than brief periods of desperate hoofing with largely obvious tactics and little time for grand strategy, while baseball has scant subtlety or variety in its batting compared with the intricate defensive–offensive art and epic ergonomic endeavour that is cricket batting.

A baseball bat, like a softball bat, is essentially a club, a heavy stick with a thick end, used to bludgeon the ball, while a rounders bat is a mere cudgel. A cricket bat, on the other hand, in the hands of a skilled batsman, is a flat-fronted precision instrument capable of a huge range of strokes, an exquisite blade, a fine sword for resisting and subverting the myriad malign intentions of the bowler as expressed through the ball. None of this, of course, precludes the effectiveness of the cricket bat as a club on the right occasion. Cricket is a high art with stubbornly brutal and agricultural foundations.

Interestingly, English-born Henry Chadwick, the father of baseball in America, was also a huge cricket fan, yet despite his best efforts baseball took off in America and cricket did not. In his novel *Netherland*, about the cricket that is widely played in New York on terrible pitches by Southern Asians, West Indians and the occasional Dutchman, Joseph O'Neill writes, 'There's a limit to what Americans understand. The limit is cricket' (p. 243).

C. L. R. James argues that what would have been beyond the grasp of the Americans he watched baseball with when he was resident in the USA was not so much the technicalities of cricket, but its ethics, its code of honour and gentlemanly conduct. Despite hailing from the outrageously multi-segregated system described above, he was nonetheless deeply shocked by the uncouth attitude and behaviour of baseball spectators and players in the USA.

> I sat at baseball matches with friends, some of them university men, and saw and heard the howls of anger and rage and denunciation which they hurled at the players as a matter of course. I could not understand them and they could not understand me either – they asked anxiously if I were enjoying the game. I was enjoying the game; it was they who were disturbing me. And not only they. Managers and players protested against adverse decisions as a matter of course, and sometimes, after bitter quarrels, were ordered off the field, fined and punished in other ways.
>
> *Beyond a Boundary*, p. 57

Such behaviour is rare in the world of cricket, not only because civilized conduct and good manners generally prevail, even between the supporters of teams that are fighting each other to the death on the field, but because within cricket the ethic of respect for one's opponents is well understood and highly valued. A team is as good as the difficult opposition it can beat.

Perhaps what many Americans also fail to understand is that cricket is more than a sport; it is a *distillation* of the art of war. I stress 'distillation' because it is crass to suggest, as some have done, that cricket *is* warfare. If it is warfare, it is very metaphorical and sublimated warfare, although not, as my fifth delivery shows, combat devoid of danger. Claims like the one misattributed to the Duke of Wellington – 'The battle of Waterloo was won on the playing fields of Eton' – are problematic and controversial, but certainly some men have found personal qualities and practical skills honed in cricket invaluable in warfare: loyalty, humility, patience, controlled aggression, leadership, communication, cooperation, resource management, cunning tactics, grand strategy, meteorology, ejecting grenades from trenches double quick and, above all, keeping one's wits and composure when put on the spot.

The five-day Test match, four days in the case of women's cricket, is cricket's most celebrated and sacred format, played only between international sides with Test status as determined by the nearly all-powerful International Cricket Council (ICC). Test matches are certainly more of a war than a battle, with many distinct phases and countless individual battles and skirmishes within. The Test match easily surpasses three-dimensional chess in its strategic and psychological complexity, with the added bonus of having infinitely more physical action, spectacle and nail-biting tension. Cricket, in case you do not know, is essentially a pressure game.

Cricket only gets really complicated, ridiculously so, when an attempt is made to explain its complexities in mere words.

The explanation tends to make little or no sense without the proper cricket jargon, and the jargon tends to make little or no sense unless a person has already *observed* the various objects, actions and situations the jargon refers to within the context of an actual match.

The great difficulty, perhaps impossibility, of explaining cricket in mere words is humorously captured in the famous lines below, which are tenuously attributed to the Marylebone Cricket Club (MCC), based at Lord's Cricket Ground, St John's Wood, London, the traditional home and spiritual centre of world cricket. These lines, or similar, are very popular on tea towels for some reason. Please forgive the jingoistic title, which assumes that there are only two types of people in the world, English people and foreigners; that is, those superior beings who invented cricket and exported it throughout their once vast empire, and those mere mortals who received the divine blessings of its civilizing power. It ignores the fact that many foreigners now not only have a far better grasp of cricket than the average English person but are also far better at playing it.

Cricket Explained to a Foreigner

You have two sides, one out in the field and one in. Each man that's in the side that's in the field goes out and when he's out he comes in and the next man goes in until he's out. When a man goes out to go in, the men who are out try to get him out, and when he is out he goes in and the next man in goes out and goes in. When they are all out, the side that's out comes in and the side that's been in goes out and tries to get those coming in out. Sometimes there are men still in and not out. There are two men called umpires who stay out all the time, and they decide when the men who are in are out. Depending on the weather and the light, the umpires can also send everybody in, no matter whether they're in or out. When both sides have been in and all the men are out – including those who are not out – then the game is finished.

MCC: Attributed

For all its ins and outs, however, cricket is a very rational game with a law book that is a paragon of clarity and fairness. Yet cricket nonetheless preserves a surreal quality. I want to say an '*Alice in Wonderland* quality', but of course in that strange book they play croquet, a game that shares some of cricket's most basic and ancient DNA. The point is though, cricket, precisely as it is, would not be out of place in Wonderland because it is, in its way, completely absurd.

A regular Mad Hatter's tea party obsessed with tea and cakes. The first All-England Eleven even found it fitting to play in Mad Hatter-style top hats. White clothing unsuited to hiding grass and ball stains. At the centre of a large, oval field, two little constructions of sticks around which enormous efforts are interminably focused. The wheeling motion of the bowler's arms as he flings the blood-red ball up the track *ad infinitum* towards a padding encrusted batsman defending one set of sticks with his willow blade as though his life depended on it. His cricket life, of course, does depend on it. Strangely named fielding positions like silly point, long on and deep square leg. The fielders walking in each time the bowler performs his cartwheel or 'stooping very much as if ... "making a back" for some beginner at leap-frog' (Charles Dickens, *The Pickwick Papers*, p. 91).

The endless, breathing repetition of it all and the obsessive, hieroglyphic recording of every detail to produce a multi-faceted score sheet that appears to require a combined Mathematics and Egyptology PhD to fathom it out. Five days' play sometimes ending in a draw following gargantuan efforts by both teams, perhaps because two old men in white coats with several jumpers tied around their waists and several hats upon their heads have judged the daylight to be a tad dimpsy even when everyone, including them, could still see perfectly well.

But then cricket is a rich metaphor for life and death, and as such it reminds us that they too are absurd. Like cricket, nothing in life really makes any sense beyond the context, beyond the boundary, of whatever game, whatever language game, is being played. Cricket is no more absurd than any other activity on earth, and a lot more organized in its absurdity than almost every other activity on earth.

Fortunately, it is not the purpose of this little book to explain the game of cricket. I doubt that even a book of a million words could provide an adequate explanation. I doubt that cricket can be understood from an explanation of it delivered *a priori*, an explanation delivered independently of any empirical encounter with the game itself. If you know nothing about cricket whatsoever, have never watched or played it, have never *experienced* it, then you are, of course, still welcome to plough on with this book, but I strongly advise you to set this book aside for now and return to it later after you have acquired some non-theoretical cricketing experience.

Cricket is a vast, enchanted labyrinth with a literature to match. No other sport has anything like the enormous, diverse, brilliant and acclaimed penmanship that surrounds cricket. Why is this? Why is cricket writing such a rich genre, a thoroughly respectable branch of English literature?

A person does not have to be particularly meditative to enjoy cricket, the game attracts all sorts of people from all sorts of backgrounds, and everyone who enjoys it does so in their own way, but certainly the more deep thought a person invests in watching cricket the more it offers him or her and the more he or she gets out of it. Cricket, therefore, attracts thoughtful people, who are also often highly educated people, self-taught geniuses or products of the best schools, colleges and universities.

No doubt cricket is also placed in the life path of many advantaged people at an early age, given that the private education sector has always considered cricket, along with rugby, to be a game well suited to the broader education and character development of the upper classes. Anyway, as a spectacle, cricket tends to absorb 'big minds' regardless of their social background, while minds that are 'easily entertained' are bored to tears by it.

Now, a game that can go on for five days or longer – the last timeless Test in 1939 involved nine days' play spread over 12 days – is likely to afford a thoughtful person many opportunities to set his various musings down on paper. There is always so much to contemplate and analyse, be it tragic, amusing or darkly comical: the pavilion patter, the sightscreen sarcasm, the historical context, the complex human drama, the psychological and political warfare, the tough test of character, the titanic struggle, the total domination, the inevitable peculiar incident.

Nothing seems to lend itself more readily to the hilarious anecdote, humorous story or chucklesome poem than cricket. Many great writers from James Herriot to Julian Barnes, from Douglas Adams to John Betjeman, from Charles Dickens to G. K. Chesterton, have been unable to resist the rich comedy within cricket culture.

> And are the penmen players all?
> Did Shakespeare shine at cricket?
> And in what hour did Bunyan wait
> Like Christian at the wicket?
> When did domestic Dickens stand
> A fireside willow wielding?
> And playing cricket – on the hearth,
> And where was Henry Fielding?
>
> G. K. CHESTERTON, *Lines on a Cricket Match*

As an aspiring cricket writer myself, I have, of course, embellished this book with more than a smattering of droll cricketing yarns. They are, it seems, unavoidable. The best are utterly irresistible. Cricket writing is also popular, it has to be said, because newspapers want back-page copy, publishers want manuscripts with broad appeal and cricket pundits want the money. Most TV and radio cricket commentators have a regular column or two in the national press of the cricket-playing nations.

The men who bowl for England
Are sometimes known to tire,
And under-pitch and over-toss
And lack their early fire.
But those who write for England
Go on from strength to strength;
They send us for the 'close of play'
Ten thousand words each blessed day,
And never lose their length.

'Giglamps', 'The Men Who Play for England',
The Morning Post, c. 1934

Watching cricket on the radio

On a brief autobiographical note, I grew up with the game of cricket, a member of a cricket-obsessed family, and I have no recollection of ever having made any effort to learn the game as a child, as I had to struggle to learn maths or spelling at school for example. I simply became familiar with the basics of the game at an early age by process of observational osmosis, and came to increasingly appreciate its infinite depths as I grew older and more thoughtful. I now realize, having written this book, that describing cricket as a game of infinite depth hardly does justice to its complexities and subtleties. It is deeper even than that.

When I was young every moment of every five-day Test match played in England was available on the BBC, without adverts. Thirty seconds of viewing might be lost occasionally as the station switched coverage from BBC1 to BBC2. I learnt about cricket slumped in an armchair in the living room during school summer holidays, my mother frequently popping in from the kitchen to watch a particularly important or exciting passage of play or to explain some subtlety of the rules.

Like many boys, I was introduced to the men's Test cricket that is the main focus of this book by a woman who worshipped the game and had an extensive knowledge of it. I have scorecards my mother completed in the late 1940s, when she was just a teenager, of matches in England against India and Australia. In the summer of 1948 my mother saw the great Donald Bradman bat and the legends Ray Lindwall and Bill Johnston bowl. In that 34-match tour, which included five Test matches, Australia went undefeated.

The ending of the last Test match of the summer, which always used to be played at London's other great ground, the Kennington Oval, never failed to throw me into a pit of despair. It meant the long, lazy cricketing summer was over and a new school year was looming. It would begin with bullying PE teachers forcing me to play rugby.

I have always had more success as a cricket spectator than as a cricketer. I have watched thousands of hours of cricket in my life, mostly on TV. It never fails to intrigue and excite, or to frustrate and infuriate. Sometimes it requires nerves of steel just to go on watching. Anyone who followed the 2005 Ashes Test series will know exactly what I mean. There is an account of some of that series, namely the classic second Test at Edgbaston, in my sixth delivery: 'Cricket Ball Fame', in the section 'Strauss

Ball'. I recall Aussie super-pundit Richie Benaud saying that the 2005 Edgbaston Test was the best he had ever seen. I agree with him.

These days I watch a lot of cricket on the radio. The BBC *Test Match Special* commentary is so eloquent that, knowing the game as I do, I can picture the match in my head. As every *TMS* fan knows, there is always a wonderfully relaxed mixture of profound insight and dry humour, not always about the match itself. It is not surprising that one of the best-selling cricket books of recent times is *The Wit and Wisdom of Test Match Special*, compiled by Dan Waddell, a collection of fine quotations from a programme that celebrated its 60th anniversary in 2017 and is by far the longest running radio sports programme in the world.

> Brian Johnston: Fred, who do you think were the six
>   fastest bowlers since the war?
> Fred Trueman: There were me ...
> Brian Johnston: Oh, there must have been seven.
> > *The Wit and Wisdom of Test Match Special*, p. 71

There can be no better job in the world than that of a radio cricket commentator. Salaried, all expenses paid free entry to Test matches in some of the most exotic locations in the world, with the best seats in the house guaranteed. Sitting around all day making pleasant, droll, civilized conversation with colleagues – who are mostly good friends – about the glorious game and other multifarious matters arising, all the while eating scrumptious homemade cakes sent in by adoring listeners. The workaday reality cannot be too far from the romantic myth. Radio cricket commentators certainly always seem to be in excellent spirits as they practise their highly skilled craft.

John Arlott was a cricket commentator for the BBC for 34 years. He summed up the art of cricket commentary very well in an interview he once gave. His words also capture very well the way cricket lovers such as myself think about the game, the multiple contexts in which every cricket match simultaneously exists.

> One doesn't invent things about cricket commentary because you don't need to invent them. There is so much happening all the time. You've got two things ... three things. The actual mathematics of the game – they're essential, those you must keep up to date. Then you've got the mechanics of the play, which you're observing ... and you have the background of the play, the buildings outside, the people around the ground. And finally you have the history, of the whole game, not just this match. Sometimes the play itself is so dramatic that you have only time for the mathematics and the action ... nothing of the surrounding circumstances and nothing of back history. But on other occasions when the play is quiet, surroundings and history.
>
> *The Wit and Wisdom of Test Match Special*, pp. 254–5

As a player, well, I played as a boy. At school and every summer day in the park with my brother and our friends. Single wicket, every man for himself with the bat and everyone else fields. My brother was so much better than the rest of us that it was often us versus him in the end, the struggle to get him out. My brother went on to be a mainstay of a couple of local teams, a good all-rounder. I went on to be a philosopher.

I took the game up again for a while in my thirties with some initial success. I immediately became a sort of bowler because I could never get enough net practice to emerge as a batsman. In amateur practice at least, established batsmen net first. By the time the tailenders get a knock nobody wants to bowl to them for long. A bowling machine would have been useful.

I took wickets and was even made Man of the Match on one occasion when my economical bowling won the day. A lack of consistency, however, led me to increasingly distrust what I might deliver next until it ceased to be a pleasure to be called upon to bowl. The cricket ball certainly has the power to exalt and humiliate by turns.

I quit playing regularly after just a few years, though my kitbag is always packed and ready for when my arm is twisted to play in the occasional friendly match. Any man is better than no man when it comes to making up the numbers, especially when he has the sort of nice kit that will impress the opposition, at least in those moments before he starts playing. 'Once more unto the breach, dear friends, once more.'

Judging by the injuries I sustained during my relatively short time as a moderately serious adult player, even in the practice nets, including an ankle so badly bruised by a fast inswinging yorker that the bruise was visible on both sides of my foot, I would probably have had all my teeth knocked out by now, broken my nose or fractured my skull. I may even have been killed.

Make no mistake, the cricket ball kills, as my fifth delivery: 'Cricket Ball Pain' harrowingly reveals. I certainly have to acknowledge that writing this book about the cricket ball is, perhaps, a last, desperate, highly abstract attempt to gain some semblance of permanent mastery over the little red beast.

Anyway, this book is not about me. It is about the cricket ball, qua object, qua phenomenon, qua action, qua idea, qua symbol, qua history, qua legend, qua whatever I can squeeze from its mysterious nature for your illumination and entertainment.

Having only a carrier bag full of battered old cricket balls, I recently walked to my local county cricket club shop and dutifully purchased a brand-new and very expensive Dukes Special County 'A' cricket ball. I felt I needed this beautiful, proud, unforgiving object before me at all times as a guide to my thoughts and feelings and as a source of inspiration as I bowled the over that is this book.

Second Delivery

Cricket Ball Surveyed

Hard, crimson, leather-bound, deadly, the cricket ball is the swinging, bouncing, spinning heart of the magnificent game that gives it its name. Before placing it fully in motion let us polish that beautiful nut, cherry or conker on our lily-white trousers for a while and toss it from hand to hand feeling its weight and pent-up energy. Like Dickens's Mr Luffy, who 'applied the ball to his right eye for several seconds' while Dumkins 'confidently awaited its coming' (*The Pickwick Papers*, p. 91), let us take a little time to closely contemplate that sphere as an object, entity or thing; as a pure phenomenon.

Ideal ball

According to the ancient Greek philosopher Plato, the cricket ball has always been and will always be. Well, he does not actually say this, even though the ancient Greeks are believed to have played a bat and ball game similar to cricket, but it is directly implied by his grand theory of reality, his *theory of forms*, as put forward in his greatest philosophical dialogue, *The Republic*.

Plato argues that every particular thing in the physical world, every set of particular things, has a perfect, ideal counterpart in a timeless, non-physical, metaphysical world. These *ideal forms* of particular things are what is truly real. They have always existed and will always exist, regardless of whether or not there are any particular physical things corresponding to them. Particular physical things, argues Plato, are mere shadows cast by their perfect, timeless forms. For example, what is truly real is the form or idea of the perfect sphere. Actual spheres in the physical world only approximate towards this perfection. Unlike the perfect form of a sphere, actual so-called spheres are not even truly spherical, not really spheres at all.

So, according to Plato, this cricket ball I am holding in my hand is not truly or fully a cricket ball. It is only a shadow of, or an approximation towards, the perfect, timeless, metaphysical cricket ball that exists beyond the realm of space and time. The problem with the metaphysical cricket ball – and this objection exposes certain weaknesses in Plato's general theory – is that it would not be the perfect ball to play with. Impossible to bowl, catch or hit for six. Also, its timeless, incorruptible nature would prevent it from ageing, from undergoing any wear and tear. Even if it could be played with, it would remain forever brand new, forever maximally hard.

A new ball in cricket is often desirable, particularly to the bowling side. It can, for example, be bowled faster than an old ball and is therefore often more intimidating to the batsman. It has the speed to beat him and tie him in knots as he strives to hit it cleanly and safely. But a new ball is not always best. Depending on the bowler, the state of the pitch and the weather conditions, an older ball might do more, turn more, swing more, spin more, making it harder for the batsman to play than a new ball. So, in some matches an older ball is the more perfect ball, at least for the bowling side, a ball more suited to achieving the objectives of the bowling side, which is to prevent runs and take wickets.

This being so, there would have to be a perfect form of cricket ball for every stage of wear and tear that the cricket ball undergoes during its life. A perfect new ball, a perfect old ball, a perfect still shiny on one side and so more likely to swing in the air ball and so on. Now, a possibly infinite range of different types of metaphysical cricket ball is a far cry from the existence of one, supreme, perfect, metaphysical cricket ball that is the very essence of cricket ballness itself. For Plato's theory to work there would have to be such a ball, a ball that somehow perfectly captured all the characteristics of all the different types of cricket ball, all the different grades and ages of the cricket ball. A ball that was both a perfect new ball and a perfect old ball all at the same time.

To Plato's credit, he began to recognize as he grew older and even wiser that his theory of forms was subject to precisely this kind of difficulty. His more impertinent followers asked him, and so he asked himself, such questions as, is there an unchanging form of change, or a perfect, infinitely beautiful form of ugliness?

Later philosophers have trapped Plato's theory of forms in difficulties by asking, for example, what is the perfect leaf like?

The perfect leaf, as the essence of leafness, would have to capture all the essential characteristics of every type of leaf. But leaves vary so much in appearance and structure that it is impossible to imagine anything that is somehow all leaves at once. We are attempting a similar sort of trap for his theory of forms with the example of the cricket ball. Bowling him an unplayable philosophical delivery that forces him onto the back foot. Howzat?

Moving swiftly on from Plato, but sticking with idealism for a moment, the eighteenth-century Irish philosopher Bishop George Berkeley – not to be confused with the English cricketer, George Fitz-Hardinge Berkeley – argues that there are no physical things, that everything is a collection of ideas that must appear to a mind in order to exist. This view, expressed in Berkeley's magnum opus *Principles of Human Knowledge*, is often summed up in the Latin phrase *esse est percipi* (to be is to be perceived). So, the cricket ball is not a thing existing in its own right, but a collection of appearances – roundness, redness, hardness and so on – that must appear to a mind in order to have any reality whatsoever.

This seems to imply that when the cricket ball is hit out of the field of play into the long grass and no one can see it, and the entire fielding side are frantically searching for it, it is not only lost but has, until it is found, ceased to exist. Fortunately, the situation is not quite so drastic because, according to Berkeley, the cricket ball continues to exist because God perceives it. God, being God, perceives everything all the time, including the cricket ball the players have lost, which, for God, can never be lost. Incidentally, being omnipresent, God would make an excellent fielder, except that it is debatable whether or not he has any hands.

It is easy to imagine an honest, down-to-earth, cricketing chap mocking the idealism of Berkeley, or anyone who espouses it, by saying, 'So, you won't mind if I throw this cricket ball at your head. If it is just a collection of ideas it won't hurt you.' Actually, the original version of this tale related to a philosophy student who tried to explain Berkeley's philosophy, with reference to a house brick, to a bunch of bricklayers he worked with on his summer job. They spent the rest of the summer jokingly threatening to throw house bricks at his head.

Such mockery is misplaced, of course, because a cricket ball thrown at the head would certainly produce bruising and pain, phenomena that can themselves be described as appearances to a mind. When asked what he thought of Berkeleyan idealism, the writer Samuel Johnson contemptuously kicked a stone and hurt his foot, declaring, 'I refute it thus' (James Boswell, *Life of Johnson*, p. 333). This stubbing of his toes, however, was not actually a refutation because, according to Berkeley, the stone, Johnson's foot and the pain in Johnson's foot were all just ideas in Johnson's mind.

Berkeley's idealism may be wrong. There may, after all, be a physical world out there entirely independent of anyone's mind. This does not mean, however, that the way the world appears to us is the way it is in itself, independent of our perceptions of it. The cricket ball we perceive may not exist in itself. What is out there may be just a lump of matter, a collection of atoms, rather than a cricket ball as such.

In a very real sense, the cricket ball is a cricket ball *for me*. I collect all its various appearances together and say, this is a cricket ball. It surely does not do this for itself because the cricket ball does not have self-awareness, despite what animists claim about inanimate objects possessing a spiritual essence. Not least, I place the cricket ball in its context and define it by its use, whereas the lump of matter itself has no awareness of the context and use that make it what it is for me.

Real ball

The seventeenth-century English philosopher John Locke was a realist. He argues, in opposition to idealism, that there is a physical world out there made ultimately of tiny particles that exist independently of anyone's mind. He nonetheless holds that we do not perceive the world as it is in itself. Not least, we do not perceive collections of atoms or organizations of molecules but *things*. We perceive what the English philosopher J. L. Austin, in his book *Sense and Sensibilia*, wittily referred to as 'familiar objects – moderate-sized specimens of dry goods' (p. 8); cricket balls for example.

Locke pondered what belongs to objects themselves and what belongs to our perception of them, to our relationship with them, and eventually came up with his famous and very useful distinction between primary and secondary qualities (*An Essay Concerning Human Understanding*, Bk 2, Ch. 8, Para. 15, p. 73).

Primary qualities or properties, although perceived, belong to objects themselves. Secondary qualities or properties belong only to our perceptions of objects and do not exist in objects themselves. The primary qualities that belong intrinsically to that lump of matter we call a cricket ball are extension, figure, solidity, number and motion. The secondary qualities that belong to the way we perceive the cricket ball are colour, taste, smell and sound.

Extension refers to the fact that the cricket ball is extended in space, it occupies a certain amount of space, a cricket ball-sized handful of space in fact. If it did not occupy a certain amount of space it would not exist.

Figure refers to its shape. If the cricket ball occupies a certain amount of space it must have a certain shape. An object cannot have no shape. The cricket ball does not just look spherical to me, it is spherical in and of itself.

Solidity refers to the resistance the cricket ball has to any other object occupying the same space as it is currently occupying. If the extension of the cricket ball is its occupation of a certain amount of space, the solidity of the cricket ball is the way in which it occupies space.

Locke gives his consent for the term 'impenetrability' to be used in place of the term 'solidity'. (*An Essay Concerning Human Understanding*, Bk 2, Ch. 4, Para. 1, p. 61). The cricket ball is solid in the sense that it cannot be easily penetrated. It is far less penetrable than a cloud, for example, though far more penetrable than a diamond. It can be penetrated by a bullet – though I have never seen a cricket ball shot with a gun – but the fact that it would need a bullet, a crossbow bolt or a bandsaw to penetrate it emphasizes just how solid it is in the ordinary sense of the term.

Number refers to the fact that one cricket ball is one cricket ball in and of itself and not two or more. What I clearly perceive as one cricket ball is indeed one whole thing, even though it is, in another sense, a collection of parts. More on the parts and composition of the cricket ball in due course. We shall also see in due course that although one cricket ball is one cricket ball, there is a sense in which it becomes many cricket balls as it is delivered again and again in different ways. Nothing encapsulates the mystical notion of the many in the one and the one in the many better than the cricket ball.

Motion refers to the fact that the cricket ball can be moved. This potential for movement belongs to the cricket ball as it is in itself and not merely to a person's perception of it. This is not to say that the cricket ball is capable of movement without being acted upon from outside, simply that movability is one of its intrinsic properties. It would certainly be impossible to play cricket if the cricket ball was an immovable object, but then there really is no such object. As any astronomer will tell you, everything is in motion all the time.

As you may have already gathered, the primary qualities of the cricket ball are really the primary qualities of all objects, the fundamental characteristics of any object whatsoever, as distinct from, for example, a concept. A concept does not have extension, figure or solidity, and as such is totally useless for playing cricket with. This book, as a kind of symbolic over, may be delivering concepts, but a bowler must deliver a ball. So, what about the secondary qualities of the cricket ball?

There is something about the atomic structure of the dye used to colour the cricket ball I am holding in my hand that makes me see it as red in ordinary light. I could equally be holding a cricket ball that looks white in ordinary light, or indeed one that looks pink or orange in ordinary light, but that is beside the point right now. Taking the cricket ball that most commonly looks red as our example, it can be said that it is not red in itself. It merely looks red in ordinary sunlight to a person who does not have red–green colour blindness. Change the light and so on and the ball will look a different colour. In complete darkness, or when nobody is perceiving it, the cricket ball has no colour.

Some philosophers say that secondary qualities are subjective, that they are entirely in the eye of the beholder, but this is not quite right. There is something about the composition of this cricket ball that makes me see it as red under normal conditions, rather than blue or purple. The redness, however, is not in the cricket ball itself but in my perception of it. The redness is a feature of my relationship with this cricket ball, a relationship between an object with a certain atomic structure and a conscious being with eyes of a certain kind.

How would this 'red' cricket ball look to me if I had the eyes of a cat or a bee? Cats do not see the same richness of colours that humans generally see, and bees can see ultraviolet but not red. Suppose I had monochrome vision, the cricket ball would still look extended and spherical but its colour would 'be' dark grey.

As with colour, any taste the cricket ball has is not a property of the ball itself but something produced in a perceiver by chemicals on the surface of the ball that are accessible to the tongue. To me, this brand-new cricket ball does not have much taste, only a tasteless sort of taste, perhaps very slightly bitter and waxy.

Someone with a more sensitive tongue might detect tastes that I am unaware of, tastes that therefore do not exist for me as such, at least with regard to this cricket ball. Perhaps to them it tastes salty.

An older cricket ball, a much-used cricket ball – you can lick one if you want to – is presumably going to have a much richer taste to most people. The taste of the stale sweat of 11 active players, the taste of the saliva the bowlers use to polish it up, a slight taste of grass or even willow and linseed oil, pounded into its surface by repeated strokes of the bat. Exactly how the ball tastes will be a matter of taste, although it will have no taste to those unfortunate people who have no sense of taste.

Much the same can be said for the smell of the cricket ball as can be said for the taste of the cricket ball. To me, and to most people, this new cricket ball has that rather pleasant leathery smell. This is not surprising as the ball's outer covering is made of leather. Like Fonzie, the cricket ball wears a leather jacket. But once again, the leather smell does not belong to the ball itself as shape belongs to the ball itself.

The surface of the ball is clearly emitting molecules that my nose detects and that I then identify as the smell of leather. However, these molecules, by themselves, are not the smell of leather. For there to be the smell of leather, these molecules must act on a functioning nose that belongs to a consciousness. In the absence of a nose and a consciousness the cricket ball would still emit the same molecules but there would be no smell because smell is smell *for me*.

To further emphasize the point that the smell of the cricket ball is a secondary property of the cricket ball, simply consider that the way leather smells to you may not be the way leather smells to me. A moment ago, I used the phrase, 'rather pleasant leathery smell', but what actually is that smell? A chemist may be able to identify the chemicals that cricket ball leather emits, but nobody can ever know that one person's private sensation of smelling cricket ball leather is the same as another person's.

Interestingly, some people do not find the smell of leather pleasant, rather they find it an unpleasant, musty smell. Does this indicate that leather does not smell the same to them as it smells to me? If it is always a matter of a person's entirely private experience – try *describing* the smell of leather – then there is no way to answer this question.

Finally to sound. The various sounds the cricket ball makes when it is rubbed on the bowler's trousers, struck by the cricket bat or clatters into the stumps are not primary qualities of the ball, but secondary qualities that arise through a person's perception of the ball. Following our by now familiar pattern of reasoning, it can be said that the physical properties of the ball, in conjunction with the physical properties of the bat, help to produce that unmistakable crack of willow on leather. By itself, however, willow striking leather only produces vibrations in the air. These vibrations alone do not amount to sound. They only amount to sound when they reach a functioning ear attached to a consciousness. No ear and consciousness, no sound.

When the cricket ball is struck in a match where all the players and all the spectators are stone deaf, does the contact between ball and bat make a sound? Answer, no. The contact merely makes vibrations in the air. Whereas the shape of the cricket ball belongs to the cricket ball regardless of me, the sound of the cricket ball being struck by the cricket bat belongs to me in my relationship to the ball and the bat.

Regardless of whether or not cricket balls are real or ideal, collections of ideas or mere shadows cast by the one, true, perfect, timeless and unchanging metaphysical cricket ball, regardless of which properties belong to the cricket ball as it is in itself and which to the perceiver of the ball, it is possible to treat all the appearances or properties of the cricket ball as equally real. Reality can be equated with whatever properties appear to us, and whatever properties appear to us can be granted the same reality status. This is the approach of a branch of philosophy called *phenomenology*. It explores the nature of phenomena as they appear to us without concerning itself with what may or may not lie behind those appearances.

To the ordinary, non-philosophical observer, the colour, taste, smell and sound of the cricket ball are all as real, all as much part and parcel of the cricket ball itself, as its extension, figure, solidity, number and motion. They are all equally appearances *to* an observer, all equally features or aspects of that complex phenomenon we call 'cricket ball'.

It may be the case that the cricket ball does not actually exist because the external world to which it supposedly belongs does not actually exist. There is no way of proving that the external world is out there as it appears to be. Many philosophers have tried and failed to prove the existence of the external world, including René Descartes, who tries unsuccessfully in his *Meditations on First Philosophy* to prove the existence of God so that he can make God the guarantor of the existence of the external world. Descartes' reasoning is that if a morally perfect God exists then he would not deceive me into thinking the external world is out there if it is not.

If, in the end, all I am aware of is sensations, then it may be the case that these sensations correspond to nothing at all. The entire external world, including the entire game of cricket and all its paraphernalia, may simply be a figment of my imagination. What is called *solipsism* may be true, the view that only one's own mind exists and that there is nothing beyond it.

The great Scottish philosopher David Hume argues in his masterwork *A Treatise of Human Nature* that we never have access to anything but *impressions* of an external world. Therefore, we can never know that there is anything beyond these impressions giving rise to them. In short, we can never know that there is an external world. Furthermore, according to Hume, all our ideas and imaginings are based on these impressions and are never derived from anything else.

Hume advises that as we can never know there is an external world, the sensible thing to do is to abandon trying to prove it and simply assume that it exists. We all do this anyway, in our normal, everyday, practical, non-philosophical lives, unless we are completely insane. We can then get on with the job of exploring our impressions of the world in an orderly, scientific manner. Science – except maybe the far reaches of quantum physics – does not question the very existence of the external, physical world. Science accepts as an article of faith that the world is out there doing its own thing, having cricket matches and all the rest of it. Science then dedicates itself to the far more useful job of investigating the nature of the world and predicting its behaviour.

Having taken a whirlwind tour through a range of philosophical views regarding the fundamental reality and nature of the cricket ball, I am now going to adopt the practical, empirical, scientific approach to the cricket ball recommended by Hume. Cricket balls exist – get over it! And if they do not, who cares, especially when they certainly damned well seem to exist.

There is, after all, good common sense in Samuel Johnson's stone-kicking refutation, and in the summer-long ribbing the bricklayers gave the philosophy student. I still have a photograph of my horrifically bruised ankle and I have absolutely no ordinary, non-philosophical doubt that the yorked cricket ball that struck it so hard was utterly, painfully, existentially real.

Perfect handful

Cricket balls these days come in a variety of colours to serve different cricket formats and training purposes. More about cricket ball colours in the next chapter. The most common, typical, archetypal cricket ball, however, remains resolutely deep red; a beautiful, assertive crimson, the colour of dried blood or cranberries. Joseph O'Neill perfectly describes the cricket ball as a 'gigantic, meteoritic cranberry' (*Netherland*, p. 6).

If the archetypal cricket ball is crimson red, Cardus's 'crimson rambler', the *perfect* archetypal cricket ball is a brand-new, unplayed crimson cranberry, its hard, tight, leather surface polished to a deep, light-reflecting lustre. The surface, the patina, invariably bears a club's or manufacturer's logo in imitation gold leaf, along with the weight of the ball in imperial measure. Usually 5½ ounces (155.9 g) for a men's cricket ball, and never more than 5¾ ounces (163.0 g). Women's and junior cricket balls weigh half an ounce or so less. Beneath the indication of weight will often be found the words, 'Conforming to MCC regulations', emphasizing that the ball is subject to, and somehow under the protection of, the lengthy, detailed, rational, ethical and sacred MCC Laws of Cricket.

While I am giving you the weight of the ball, I must give you the size as well, as I would not want you to picture an object as small as a cranberry or a cherry, or indeed as large as a red-giant sun. A men's cricket ball has a circumference of 9 inches or slightly less. That is, between 224 and 229 mm, or 224 and 228.6 mm for those who like to be precise with their imperial to metric conversion. Women's cricket balls range between 210 and 225 mm in circumference, while junior cricket balls range between 205 and 225 mm in circumference.

When a boy becomes 14 he is expected to use a man-size cricket ball. In cricket, the ball determines that a 14-year-old boy is already a man. Cricket is a tough, sometimes brutal game, and anyone who plays it needs to grow up fast.

Setting aside ounces, inches and millimetres, the idea is that the sphere should rest comfortably and securely in the palm of the hand, the fingers extending comfortably and securely around it. Too big and the fingers cannot get around the sphere adequately to take a firm grip. Too small and the fingers, or, more pointedly, the fingernails, poke into one another over the ball as it lies uncomfortably and insecurely on the palm. In other words, the cricket ball, adjusted in size and weight to take account of age and gender, is the perfect handful for holding, throwing and catching.

Place the cricket ball in your hand, as I am now doing while I sit at my desk, and you immediately feel that perfection, that snugness. It was made for your hand, but it is as though your hand was made for it. There is no need to squeeze it to feel that you have a firm hold. You can easily raise it out of your palm with the tips of your fingers and thumb, rotate it in various directions on those tips, then allow it to roll neatly into your palm again.

After gripping it firmly for a while, there is a desire to throw it up and catch it, just to feel it settle decisively in your hand once more. There is a definite desire to throw it, to release its power; your power. It makes you want to be in the great outdoors, in a large field, so you can throw it as far as you can.

This cricket ball is by far the most beautiful and potent object on this desk among pens, paper, books, mugs, an ugly black paper puncher and a phone recharging cable. Unlike them, it demands to be outside as insistently as a cat at a locked cat-flap. It constantly tempts me to throw it through my plate-glass window. I hurriedly put it down.

The cricket ball is a pleasure to hold not only because of its size but because of its texture. Hard though it is, especially if it hits any part of your body at speed, it would be wrong to describe it as *rock* hard. It does not have the cold, hard, totally unyielding surface of a stone, but a very slightly yielding surface or casing of cowhide. What you touch when you hold the cricket ball is animal skin. Smooth, shiny, taut, sexy animal skin when new, which becomes rougher, duller and slightly spongier with use.

So, to hold the cricket ball is to place skin on skin, to caress and fondle skin. The cricket ball is far more animal or vegetable than mineral; an organic object that might have been born or grown on a tree, though what kind of mother or tree would produce a cricket ball I dread to think. Cricketers seldom if ever liken the cricket ball to a rock or a stone. Rather, it is affectionately likened to a nut, cherry or conker.

A conker is the large lustrous seed of the horse-chestnut tree. Although browner than the cricket ball the conker is like a little cricket ball when first released from its green, spiky casing. One reason, perhaps, why children love conkers and collect them so keenly. So, cricket balls, if they could be grown, would grown on something like the horse-chestnut tree.

A poet might even describe the cricket ball as an internal organ; a very round, very hard, very muscular heart. The cricket ball is visceral.

Though smooth and shiny the cricket ball is not slippery in the hand. The leather facilitates a certain soft friction against the skin. Grip is also greatly facilitated by the ¾-inch wide, slightly raised primary seam, comprising six rows of up to 80 tight white stitches that run around the ball's equator. The cricket ball may be closer to the planet Mars in colour, but in shape it is more akin to the planet Saturn with its unmistakable rings.

The cricket ball also has two secondary seams, known as quarter seams, that run in straight lines from the primary or equator seam across the poles of the ball and back again to the primary seam. The quarter seam across the north pole of the ball is at right angles to the quarter seam across the south pole of the ball. Unlike a planet, however, the cricket ball does not have an actual north or south pole.

The cricket ball has no real top and bottom, no head and tail, other than the head and tail arbitrarily defined by the gold-leaf logos stamped upon it. The two quarter seams reveal that the casing of the ball actually comprises four segments of leather tightly sewn together. Each segment has the same shape as the skin of a quarter of an orange when the juicy part of the orange has been eaten.

Unlike the primary seam, the quarter seams are not raised and are made to be as unobtrusive as possible. As the cricket ball deteriorates, however, the quarter seams begin to open up slightly giving it interesting aerodynamic properties that it did not previously possess. A good bowler will exploit these properties to his advantage. Players sometimes deliberately pick or bite at the quarter seams to open them up. This is one aspect of the illegal practice of ball tampering that is considered in detail in my fourth delivery: 'Cricket Ball Played'.

Apart from holding the various constituents of the cricket ball tightly together, the primary seam in particular gives the ball many possibilities of movement both in flight and off the pitch that it would not otherwise possess. A bowler who aligns the seam upright, towards the batsman, and pitches the ball on its seam so that its line deviates after pitching, is often called a seam bowler. As almost all fast bowlers employ the seam in this way, the term 'seam bowler' – sometimes shortened to 'seamer' – has become more or less synonymous with the term 'fast bowler'.

Every good bowler exploits to the utmost the possibilities of movement provided by the primary seam, and the position of the primary seam at any point during a good bowler's delivery is never a matter of indifference to him. A great bowler can exploit the seam in its relationship to atmospheric and pitch conditions to the extent that what he achieves in terms of movement of the ball appears to defy the laws of aerodynamics, or reveals that there are subtle laws of motion presently unknown to physics. More of this when we come to look at the cricket ball in play and at particularly great bowlers.

So much for the cricket ball contemplated as a phenomenon, surveyed as though it has always been, a God-given object that fell from the sky at the beginning of time. To get a deeper understanding of the cricket ball we need to recognize that it is, of course, a man-made object, an artefact, the product of a manufacturing process that evolved over a long period of time, a process with a rich and splendid history. Shortly, I will explore how the cricket ball is made, and how it has been made in the past. This will take us beyond the familiar shiny leather and seamed surface of the cricket ball into its mysterious depths and hidden guts.

What is inside the cricket ball? We might be forgiven for thinking that such a fiery object contains boiling magma beneath its thin crust, a molten mantle, like the Earth. Certainly, like the Earth, the cricket ball has different layers of highly compacted material beneath its surface and even a central core. Not surprisingly, cross-section diagrams of the Earth look similar to cross-section diagrams of the cricket ball.

I once read a very interesting little book called *Golf Ball* by Harry Brown. Did you know that there is always a golf ball in flight somewhere in the world? I wonder if there is also always a cricket ball being bowled somewhere in the world. Brown tells how, as a boy, he clamped a golf ball in a vice and cut it in half with a hacksaw to find, as he says, 'a lot of things inside' (*Golf Ball*, p. 3). As a boy myself, I conducted a similar operation with an old cricket ball and also found a lot of things inside.

I seem to recall that unlike a golf ball, with its seamless, highly resilient, almost indestructible resin shell, an old cricket ball will reveal the secrets of its composition and construction without the aid of anything so drastic as a hacksaw and a vice. Getting inside a tight, new, virgin cricket ball, on the other hand, would surely require at least a hacksaw, and would certainly be an interesting if sacrilegious exercise. YouTube contains various clips of a crazy Australian carving up expensive, new Kookaburra cricket balls with an electric bandsaw. See: 'I Just Cut Open a $120 USD Kookaburra Cricket Ball – See What's Inside'.

I recall that with a little effort, and perhaps the aid of a pair of pliers, a particularly ancient and baggy cricket ball can be torn and peeled apart at the seams like some weird, rindy, old Edam. I am going to repeat that strangely satisfying cricket ball disassembly and disembowelment operation right now in preparation for the next chapter. I am going to remind myself how it felt to perform that ball-breaking, investigative butchery and exactly what it was that I discovered within.

Third Delivery

Cricket Ball Made

What is a cricket ball?

I lacked the audacity, the gall, the financial wealth, to cut into a brand-new Dukes Special County 'A' cricket ball. Instead, I delved into my carrier bag of old cricket balls and selected the one that already had the most opened seams. I took it to the garden shed. At first I selected a pair of pliers for the autopsy but found that even where I could pinch a little leather it was impossible to tear it away from the rest of the ball, so tightly was everything sewn together. The ball I recall simply pulling apart as a boy must have been particularly damaged and loosened in its construction, a testament to how much we must have played with it.

I resorted to Harry Brown's hacksaw, though not the vice. I do not have a vice, only advice. Fortunately, unlike a golf ball, a cricket ball is big enough to grip with the fingers of one hand while you hacksaw it with the other. The hacksaw severed the stitching along one of the quarter seams and part of the primary seam enough for me to lift one of the quarter segments of leather. The leather was thicker than I imagined, no less than 3 mm, with another smaller, thinner piece of leather of the same shape and colour glued and stitched to its underside, smooth side down, facing the core. Each of the four segments of leather had the same thinner piece of leather attached to its underside.

Beneath the leather, wound around the core, I found a layer of soft, loosely spun, grey-brown flax twine. There was not as much of this twine as I thought there would be. I seem to remember lots of string when I took that cricket ball apart as a boy; it was the feature that most surprised and intrigued me. The core itself was a ball of relatively hard, brown cork/rubber, flecked with white. Cork/rubber is a composite substance made from a mixture of cork and rubber that has a wide range of uses from flooring to gaskets.

This roughly spherical core was flattened around its equator, giving it the shape of a very fat capsule. I attempted to cut the core in half with a handsaw but a coping saw proved far more effective, mainly because it was easier and safer to grip the core with my fingers while I cut through it with a small coping saw than it was to grip it with my fingers while I tried to cut through it with a large handsaw. The sawing produced a fine, soft, brown sawdust.

The core had no inner core. It was the same dull brown cork/ rubber all the way through. No void, no fluid-filled chamber, no deeply embedded diamond heart, no miniature cricket ball with the same construction *ad infinitum*. Clearly, like most things, what makes the cricket ball exciting is not what it is made of but what it does. I found taking it apart intriguing but all I have now, apart from a much improved knowledge of its construction, is a plastic margarine tub full of torn, eviscerated cricket ball, bits of leather and flax twine, two halves of a cork/rubber core and a certain amount of cork/rubber dust. Unlike my pristine, shiny new cricket ball that seems to breathe life and vitality, this is an emaciated, dismembered cricket ball corpse lying in a margarine tub coffin.

I have since discovered that the cricket ball I took apart was a relatively low-quality one, hence the small amount of flax and the single cork/rubber core. Had I cut into what is one of the world's best cricket balls, the elite Kookaburra Turf, the premier product of the Melbourne-based Kookaburra Sports Equipment Company, which retails at well over $100 and is used in most international cricket matches, particularly in the southern hemisphere, I would have discovered the same basic materials but a far more sophisticated construction.

The Kookaburra Turf cricket ball has a small cork/rubber nucleus surrounded by no less than five, thin, tightly packed layers of cork, each layer surrounded by a tightly woven quilt of soft worsted yarn. The worsted yarn, a type of wool yarn, is superior to the cheap flax twine found in inferior balls. The leather cover is made from four segments of pre-stretched, first grade, alum tanned steerhide, precision stitched together with the strongest, finest quality, white linen thread. The lacquer that coats the entire surface of even the good-quality, sub-$100, three-cork-layer Kookaburra Regulation ball, including its seam, is cleverly kept off the linen seam of the Kookaburra Turf, making the seam more abrasive.

The Kookaburra Turf is a sexy object, a dream to bowl, hit and catch. It is, however, seldom bowled, hit and caught by anyone but professional cricketers as only they can afford to play with it.

Other top-quality cricket balls are available, most notably those manufactured by Dukes & Son of England, a company with a 250-year history whose matchless Special County 'A' cricket ball, described by them as 'The best of the best!', is used in all UK and West Indies Test matches. Just as Carlsberg is probably the best lager in the world, so the Dukes Special County 'A' is probably the best cricket ball in the world. If anyone can be said to have invented and perfected the formal cricket ball as we know it today, it is Dukes. If you want a Special County 'A', and who would not, the red one is yours for a RRP of just £115. The pink version has a RRP of £125. Discounts are available. The Special County 'A' is often sold as a collector's item. No one is bowling and batting mine, which is a shame in a way.

Dukes recently sent 50 dozen cricket balls to Australia at the request of Cricket Australia after top-level umpires Down Under voiced concerns about the durability of the Kookaburra. ('No Ashes but cricket ball maker Dukes up for a match with Kookaburra', *Telegraph*, 5 January 2014). The Dukes ball, skilfully hand stitched in Pakistan before being flown back to London to be shaped, polished, treated and stamped, was well received by Australian players and umpires during trials.

The current owner of Dukes, Indian-born Dilip Jajodia, expressed high hopes that Dukes could break Kookaburra's monopoly of professional cricket Down Under. A Kookaburra spokesman was unavailable for comment. He might have said that the great rivalry between Australian and English cricket clearly exists even at the level of the cricket ball itself.

Test matches in India are played with the Indian-made Sanspareils Greenlands (SG) cricket ball. The SG has a more pronounced seam than the Dukes or the Kookaburra, resulting from the thicker thread used in its construction. SG, Kookaburra and Dukes cricket balls, as well as those made by the many other cricket ball manufacturers that exist – Surridge, Readers, Oxbridge, Slazenger, Upfront, Gray-Nicolls and so on – are available these days in a variety of colours to suit a variety of cricketing purposes.

The traditional red cricket ball is still used in the vast majority of local, village and school cricket matches played around the world. It is also used in men's and women's Test matches and first-class cricket matches. Today, first-class cricket is any match of a sufficiently high standard scheduled to last three or more days in which both sides must have the opportunity to play two innings each. What constitutes 'a sufficiently high standard' is decided by the national governing body or the ICC on the basis of certain well-established criteria.

A first-class match must be played between two teams of 11 players at an approved venue on natural turf in strict accordance with the Laws of Cricket. First-class matches are generally played between professional sides, such as county sides, or between a county side and an international side, but some top amateur sides, such as certain university sides, also play first-class matches.

In England and Wales men's County Championship matches, for example, are scheduled to last four days, while women's County Championship matches are 50-over one-day matches. It is only the shorter duration of the women's County Championship matches that prevents them from being officially described as first-class matches, in all other respects they are played to the same high first-class standards. Women, of course, play officially first-class cricket in the form of four-day Test matches.

Women's Test cricket is played in strict accordance with the Laws of Cricket, with various clearly defined variations as set out in the ICC document 'Women's Test Match Playing Conditions'. These variations concern such matters as the size and weight of the ball, the dimensions of the cricket field and the number of overs to be bowled per hour. As the women's field is somewhat smaller than the men's, 55 to 70 yards from the centre of the pitch rather than 65 to 90 yards, and bowling run-ups tend to be shorter, women Test players are expected to bowl 100 overs per day rather than the 90 overs per day of men's Test cricket. The brisk pace of women's cricket certainly contributes to its high entertainment value.

The most widely used non-red ball in modern cricket is the white ball. The white cricket ball was introduced when one-day matches began to be played at night under floodlights. It is far more visible under artificial light conditions than a traditional red ball which appears brown and can therefore be indistinguishable from the pitch. Recall Locke's philosophical point about colour being a secondary property that is not in the object itself.

The combination of white ball and floodlights removes one of the great limiting factors of cricket: players leaving the field due to bad light. The white ball allows matches to be played at any time, usually day into evening, weather permitting. Day–night matches have done wonders for the commercial prospects of cricket by increasing the number of spectators who attend matches or pay to watch them live on TV. This in turn has made cricket a more attractive proposition to advertisers and sponsors. The white ball has brought more money into cricket than any other innovation ever made within the game itself.

All professional one-day and Twenty20 matches are now played with a white ball regardless of floodlight use. The Kookaburra Turf white ball is used in all one-day international matches (ODIs) and Twenty20 international matches. Great ball, great monopoly, a monopoly that Dukes are keen to break.

Manufacturers, mainly Kookaburra for obvious reasons, insist that, in terms of performance, the white cricket ball is identical to the red cricket ball. They insist that both red and white cricket balls are made with exactly the same materials in exactly the same way, except that the leather of the red ball is coloured red while the leather of the white ball is coloured white, but here may lie a significant difference.

Differences in the processes required to achieve the different coloured leathers may be enough to account for what many players claim: that the white ball swings more than the red ball, that the white ball is harder than the red ball yet deteriorates more quickly. So far, experiments to scientifically prove or disprove that there is a difference in performance have produced inconclusive results.

Kookaburra have quite sensibly argued that there is only a *perceived* difference in ball performance rooted in the different playing conditions presented by red and white ball formats and the different player psychologies those formats give rise to. For example, in claiming that white balls are harder, some professional players have cited the fact that white balls break more bats. But perhaps it is simply the case that more bats are broken hitting white balls because white ball formats, especially Twenty20, tend to require a batsman to risk his wicket smashing the ball for six, whereas red ball formats, Test matches and first-class matches, tend to require a batsman to bat more defensively and to score more cautiously through temperate strokeplay.

One enduring drawback of the white cricket ball, unlike the red cricket ball, is its propensity to become dirty very quickly, or to be more precise, to show the dirt. An ostensibly white ball, liberally stained greenish-brown, can be difficult for players, particularly batsmen, to see clearly. The latest solution to this problem in ODI matches is to use two white balls in an innings, each one bowled from a different end. The respective umpire must remember to put the white ball he is in charge of away in his pocket at the end of an over before he walks away from the bowler's end towards square leg.

Cricket balls coloured luminous yellow and orange have been experimented with in the professional game in place of the white ball, all with the aim of improving visibility. Unfortunately, as the process used to colour these balls causes them to wear differently to the white ball, their regular use is not currently permitted. Cricket's governing bodies are highly resistant to changes in cricket equipment that introduce unwanted variables into the game that ultimately result in changes in overall player performance.

The key word is *consistency*, such that performance figures from one time and place should be comparable to those from another, otherwise any clear notion of the *same game* becomes problematic. In terms of the ball, a type or make of ball should not make it easier or harder for players to take wickets and score runs than any other type or make of ball that is or has been used in the same modern game.

One ball that has been used in professional matches and continues to be experimented with is the pink ball, a very attractive-looking ball that seeks to combine the best of white and red. The advantages of the pink ball, above and beyond it looking so pretty, are that it has better visibility under floodlights than the red ball, and, unlike the white ball, does not show the dirt. It is also distinguishable from the white clothing players must wear in Test matches. Whites must be worn in Test matches for quasi-religious reasons relating to aesthetics and tradition. Every cricket lover understands such practices and never scoffs at them. Whites also keep a player cool by reflecting sunlight.

Several top-class day–night matches have been played with a pink ball, including the first day–night Test match which took place between Australia and New Zealand at the Adelaide Oval from the 27 to 29 November 2015. The pink Kookaburra Turf balls used in that match performed well, although the novelty of pink ball conditions certainly seemed to favour the fielding side with the match lasting just three of the five scheduled days and only three batsmen scoring 50 or over. Peter Nevill top scored with 66 in Australia's first innings, while New Zealand opener Martin Guptill had the honour of being the first ever Test batsman to be dismissed by a pink ball when he was trapped leg before wicket (lbw) by Josh Hazlewood having scored just one run.

Test cricket's first 'magenta moment', which Australia won by three wickets, attracted a crowd of nearly 124,000 as well as large TV audiences and was declared a success by both captains. The general consensus following this historic Test match was that the pink ball Test is not yet the finished product but that the format, along with the ball itself, can and will be further refined and is definitely here to stay. The match certainly seemed to confirm what many suspected, that day–night Test cricket is a highly marketable product; an attractive spectacle that attracts big crowds of spectators, many of them not free to attend cricket matches during the earlier part of the day.

The first Kookaburra Turf pink ball used in the 2015 Adelaide Test match was immediately worth a fortune, with the other three pink balls used – none of the four innings exceeded 80 overs – immediately becoming highly collectable too.

Ideally, the ICC would like to have all Test matches played with a pink ball – or possibly a greeny-yellow ball, as has recently been suggested – so that the use of floodlights can finally put an end to the problem of bad light interrupting play and impacting on results. 'The long term solution to the problem of bad light curtailing finishes to Test matches, despite floodlights, could be the permanent use of a different coloured ball' (Mike Atherton, 'ICC looks to yellow ball after another dark day for Test format', *The Times*, 19 October 2015).

Atherton wrote his article in *The Times* a couple of days after the 2015 Abu Dhabi Test between Pakistan and England ended in a draw due to bad light. England were cut off just 25 runs short of their target with six wickets in hand and eight scheduled overs remaining. Indeed, enough overs for England to undergo a spectacular collapse! Stranger things have happened in cricket.

Fully replacing the traditional, archetypal red cricket ball with a ball of another colour, be it pink, yellow, greeny-yellow or whatever colour the technicians dream up next, would be a huge break with tradition, and it will not be a decision that the ICC and the MCC will make lightly, if at all, especially when the performance of the pink ball has already been called into question.

Brydon Coverdale, writing for superb, all-things-cricket website ESPN Cricinfo, points out that bowlers have so far been unenthusiastic about the performance of the pink ball in its various trials, claiming that it does not swing and goes soft too quickly. Batsmen have also complained about the ball's rapid softening, claiming it limits their ability to score. ('Pink balls could lead to very, very boring cricket', ESPN Cricinfo, 30 June 2014.)

The first pink ball day–night Test in England began at Edgbaston on the afternoon of Thursday 17 August 2017. I was pleased to be among the huge, expectant crowd that attended the first day of this historic match between England and West Indies. The pink ball in use during this match was a Dukes, and there was much comparison between it and the Kookaburra which has a flatter primary seam. Would the prouder seam of the Dukes pink ball cause it to swing? Like the Adelaide day–night Test, the Edgbaston day–night Test lasted just three of the five scheduled days, but arguably the pink ball and the pink ball conditions had very little to do with the brevity of the match.

With big name West Indies players like Chris Gayle, Dwayne Bravo and Marlon Samuels playing in the lucrative Twenty20 Caribbean Premier League, a somewhat second-string West Indies side were annihilated by an England line-up that boasted such formidable players as Alastair Cook, Joe Root, Ben Stokes, Moeen Ali, Stuart Broad and James Anderson. England won the toss and batted first. After losing a couple of early wickets, perhaps due to the pink ball still having maximum shine on it, Cook and Root settled in to gorge on the largely mediocre and consistently inconsistent West Indies bowling, not to mention the general lack of West Indies fielding pressure. The cry of 'village', implying that the quality of the West Indies fielding was more village amateur than national-level professional, was often heard from the more rumbustious parts of the Birmingham crowd as schoolboy fielding errors repeatedly enhanced the run rate. Respect for one's opponents in cricket does not preclude banter on the right occasion.

Captain Root made 136 runs in 189 balls, 88 of these runs coming from fours, before he was finally bowled by Kemar Roach. Meanwhile, opener Cook, as cautious and elegant as ever, batted throughout the first day and well into the second, amassing 243 runs in 407 balls before finally succumbing lbw to Roston Chase, at which moment England declared on 514–8.

In response, West Indies could muster only 168 all out although, notably, middle-order batsman Jermaine Blackwood survived 79 not out. Obliged to follow on, West Indies collapsed again scoring a miserable 137 all out. England won by an innings and 209 runs. To put the huge disparity of performance into perspective, the entire West Indies team batted twice for a total of just six and a half hours, while Cook batted for nearly ten hours on his own. As to records broken, West Indies lost a record 19 wickets in a single day.

So, the big story of this match before it began was that it was the 'UK's first day/night test match'. These words are printed on the ticket. By the end, the big story was the plight of West Indies cricket, with the 2017 Test team having to suffer a host of mercilessly unfavourable comparisons with the mighty and terrifying West Indies cricketing gods of old.

Remarkably, only a few days later in the second Test at Headingley, played with a red ball, largely the same West Indies line-up proved to be light years better than the zombies that rocked up at Edgbaston. They put in a formidable and transformative performance to beat England by five wickets with less than five overs remaining in what was a thoroughly thrilling and memorable match.

As for the Edgbaston Test, if the pink ball favoured the batting side it did so only in the hands of the West Indies. If the pink ball favoured the fielding side it did so only in the hands of England. The competition was just not close enough for any peculiarities in the behaviour of the pink ball to be revealed. That the pink ball did not appear to contribute anything perverse to play itself may well be good news for the pink ball, as its performance may be said to have been on a par with that of the red ball. Then again, had it been a red ball match it would have been a daytime-only match, without floodlights, it would have started earlier, it would have been, as the saying goes, a whole different ball game, so all but the most absurdly hypothetical comparisons are impossible.

What was far clearer was that the day–night format only added excitement to this particular Test match by way of anticipation. Granted, evening TV audiences in the UK were able to tune into live Test cricket, but at the ground itself, despite the historical novelty of the situation, there was, certainly by the evening of the first day, a widespread feeling that the experience would have been better had the match started in the morning and ended at the traditional time with the lengthening of the shadows and the sinking of the sun. By the evening of the first day, with Cook having broken the will of the West Indies and England calmly amassing a huge total, the crowd had more or less had enough of sitting in the relative cold and damp. People wanted to go home for their supper well before 90 overs were bowled and many did so. There were more empty seats than crowd visible during the last few overs.

At so-called lunch on the second day – the end of the first session was at 4 p.m., closer to tea time – BBC *Test Match Special* commentator Jonathan Agnew and top cricket analyst Simon Hughes had an in-depth discussion about the pink ball. I offer you the following summary of the key points of their fascinating conversation.

Surely, the pink Dukes ball and the red Dukes ball are identical except for their colour? Well, they are identical beneath their leather surface and they are stitched together in exactly the same way. Even the leather used for each type of ball is made from exactly the same top-quality cowhide. Crucially, however, the process of colouring leather red is very different from the process of colouring leather pink.

Red ball leather is aniline leather. That is, the leather has been dyed with soluble dyes without using a polymer topcoat of insoluble pigments. The deep crimson colour of the traditional red cricket ball is produced by penetrating the aniline leather with grease polish. It is this polish that players seek to draw out and maintain by further polishing the ball; by moistening it with saliva and sweat and rubbing it on their clothes. Polishing one side of the ball while allowing the other side to deteriorate and roughen causes the ball to swing in the air, producing a range of advantages for the bowler and various difficulties for the batsman. More on the technicalities of swing bowling in the next chapter.

Pink ball leather, meanwhile, is pigmented leather, it has a polymer topcoat of insoluble pigments that is lacquered to a shine. Once this shine begins to wear off during play it cannot be maintained by the on-field polishing process so effective in the case of the red ball. There is no grease to draw out of the pink ball leather, and even if there were grease in the leather, it could not pass through the topcoat. Similarly, saliva and sweat cannot penetrate into the leather through the topcoat. As has been noted by players and pundits alike, trying to polish the pink ball is like trying to polish plastic.

Greasing the red ball deepens its colour as the grease penetrates and enriches the leather, whereas the pink ball cannot be greased. According to Simon Hughes, attempting to grease the pink ball causes it to go a dirty colour and hence to lose its all-important vivid pinkness. It should be noted that greasing any cricket ball once it is in play, other than with saliva and sweat, is not allowed. Much more in the next chapter on what is and is not allowed to be done to the ball during play.

So, if the pink ball cannot be polished and maintained like the red ball it seems reasonable to conclude that as it ages its aerodynamic properties are likely to become different from those of the red ball. If swing is largely produced by one side of the ball being kept shiny and the other side being allowed to become rough, then the pink ball will never swing to the extent to which the red ball can be made to swing. To repeat Brydon Coverdale's point, bowlers claim that the pink ball does not swing. Other observers have noted that if the pink ball swings at all, it swings when it is shiny and new. It is at least interesting, or perhaps not, that in the 2017 Edgbaston day–night Test, England were 39–2 against the new pink ball after just 7.3 overs. But seriously, there has simply not been enough pink ball Test cricket played around the world, in widely different circumstances, for anything like a clear picture of the idiosyncrasies of the pink ball to emerge. The jury is still out and will, I suspect, be out for many years.

The ICC are certainly keen to have a pink ball that everyone is happy with. The future of cricket itself is not riding on a viable pink ball, but a certain more lucrative future definitely is. It is surely highly desirable to have Test matches that are not plagued by bad light as they are at present, with umpires fiddling with light meters, players repeatedly heading to the pavilion and matches ending prematurely in a draw when there would otherwise almost certainly have been a decisive result. The elimination of bad light is undoubtedly the main advantage of the pink ball Test format, but audiences may never appreciate this, not knowing the bad light frustrations that they have been spared.

Some traditionalists argue that it is sacrilegious to minimize the role of God Almighty in his own game. Arguably, good light and bad light are part of the intimate relationship cricket has always had with the elements. Perhaps the game will lose something vital, something spiritual, if it is further divorced from its agricultural roots.

Besides the range of leather and cork balls that are or have been permitted in formal matches played according to the Laws of Cricket, there exists a range of leather and cork balls for training and practice purposes. Practice balls are more cheaply made than proper match balls: second-grade leather, fewer stitches in the seam, a single cork/rubber core rather than the several layers of cork found in the best balls.

The ball I took apart was actually a practice ball, a cricket ball that might find its way into a very amateur match, but not a ball up to the standard required for a more serious match. No self-respecting, adult cricket team would provide such a ball for a match. I guess I have owned that ball since I was a boy. I had little or no money back then so it would have been the cheapest cricket ball in the shop. I may even have stolen it from school. Schools buy cheap cricket balls by the bucket load, literally.

Some practice cricket balls are two coloured, red and white, red and yellow and so on, a different colour each side of the primary seam, allowing the bowler to see more clearly the way the ball is swinging and spinning in flight and to perfect those subtle movements to his advantage. The batsman also learns to read and handle swing and spin by playing against two coloured balls in the practice nets.

The ultimate leather and cork, two-coloured practice ball is the red and white, entirely handmade, wonderfully named Upfront Opttiuuq Whispering Death Cricket Ball. The ideal ball, its advertising boasts, for developing a range of bowling skills: leg spin or off spin, outswing or inswing. Certainly, the Whispering Death is the must-have training accessory for the player who has the best of everything in his kitbag and wants to impress his team-mates in the practice nets.

'Whispering Death', incidentally, is also the nickname of West Indies fast bowler Michael Holding, as well as the title of his first autobiography. 'Whispering' recalls Holding's smooth, near silent run-up, while 'death' recalls the deadliness of the balls he bowled. More on Michael Holding and West Indies fast bowling in due course.

If we take 'cricket ball' to mean any ball that is used to play or practise some form of cricket or other, then beyond the world of the formal, regulation leather and cork cricket ball is a universe of cricket balls that are generally made of softer materials. Some of them, like the Incrediball or Aeroball, have a hard core but a relatively soft outer casing. The main training advantage of the Incrediball is that it has more or less the same bounce as a standard cricket ball but won't knock your teeth out if one happens to hit you in the face.

There is also the Gray-Nicolls Wonderball, made of PVC foam with a seam comprising six rows of stitches. It weighs the same 5½ ounces as a standard men's cricket ball and is available in all the aforementioned colours and combinations of colour. Most of the other major cricket ball manufacturers make something similar: the Kookaburra Softaball, the Dukes Soft Impact ball and so on.

A cheap and popular alternative, not only to cork and leather but also to PVC foam, is the soft plastic windball. Readers make a very popular bright orange windball with a seam that is part of the same moulding, while Lord's sell the Lord's Glitter Windball in a range of colours including green. Lord's even sell a blue windball, badged with the Middlesex County Cricket Club three scimitar logo. Middlesex play most of their home games at Lord's – although the ground is owned by the Marylebone Cricket Club – and their official club colour is blue. Windballs are as much about novelty, fun and advertising as they are about playing cricket. We are now a long way from those very serious, elite pieces of kit, the Dukes Special County 'A' and the Kookaburra Turf.

The main reason for the existence of soft replica cricket balls is, of course, safety. Not surprisingly, they are most often found where children are playing some type of cricket – Kwik cricket, French cricket – or being coached in the basics of the formal game. More generally, they are used by anyone who wants to practise cricket or play an informal cricket match without having to wear the protective gear – pads, gloves, helmet – that it is highly advisable to wear whenever playing or practising with a cork and leather ball.

There exists such a wide range of objects called cricket balls that it is possible to question what a cricket ball actually is. Is it really fair to say that the Kookaburra Turf is a cricket ball and the Lord's Glitter Windball is not, if both are used to play cricket in some form? Really, what makes a ball a cricket ball is not its possession of certain physical features, but that it is used to play or practise any game that can be broadly defined as cricket.

A game that can be broadly defined as cricket is arguably any game that uses any type of ball whatsoever, a flat-faced bat of any material, as opposed to a round bat – although the flatness of the bat's face is debatable – and some kind of wicket to aim the ball at, be it free standing, marks on a wall or simply the batsman's legs. The basic objective of all cricket would seem to be keeping the ball off the wicket with the bat. Scoring and other refinements belong only to certain types of cricket, such as the highly sophisticated game played in accordance with the MCC Laws of Cricket. It is the regulation ball of that type of cricket, formal cricket, that is the main concern of this book.

So, any ball used to play cricket is a cricket ball, be it normally, usually, ostensibly, officially a round stone, a piece of wood, a conker, a snooker ball, a baseball, a rounders ball or even a football. An entertainingly silly game of cricket can be played with a football. Anything goes. A tennis ball used to play cricket is certainly a cricket ball, and as everyone knows, a tennis ball is a pretty good ball to play an informal, reasonably safe game of cricket with, though perhaps it is a little lacking in weight.

Interestingly, the Anand & Anand company of India make what they call the Guru Cricket Tennis Ball in a variety of colours including, of course, cricket ball red. The Guru, like any other tennis ball, is a hollow rubber ball coated with fibrous felt. It is, however, heavier than an ordinary tennis ball. It is this extra weight that makes it a good ball for playing street cricket.

Street cricket is hugely popular in Southern Asia and is often played with a tape ball. A tape ball is a standard tennis ball wrapped up in a tight layer of usually red electrical tape. The tape gives the tennis ball extra weight, speed and distance, but does not make it so hard that it becomes dangerous in a street setting. It is the tape ball that the Guru Cricket Tennis Ball is trying to emulate. The windball has been described as 'the Western tape ball' by Southern Asians who view their homemade tape ball as a far superior product.

The tape ball originated in Pakistan where there are tape ball leagues. Many of Pakistan's great fast bowlers began their cricketing life as toddlers learning to deliver the tape ball in the street. The homemade tape ball is as true a cricket ball as the factory-made Kookaburra Turf, though I cannot see the MCC or the ICC giving the tape ball their approval to be used in Test matches any time soon, not least because it would perform very differently from the Test match-standard leather and cork ball and would certainly not last 80 overs without repeated repair.

Another cricket ball worthy of note, if only for its novelty value, is the Platypus Speedball Cricket Ball, an Incrediball with a built-in speed sensor. 'How fast can you bowl?' asks the advertising. The Platypus is only available in orange, must only be used to measure bowling speed and should never be hit with a bat.

Lastly, in our journey through the infinite variety of the cricket ball, the most expensive and the most useless cricket ball ever made is the Gitanjali Gems diamond-studded cricket ball complete with solid gold seam. Several of these $68,500 balls were made by the Mumbai-based jewellery giant and presented to the best players in the 2007 Cricket World Cup. Is this lovely object a cricket ball or merely symbolizing a cricket ball? Well, it is obviously an ornament, and a clever marketing stunt on the part of Gitanjali Gems, but if you were rich enough to make the experiment you could at least try to play cricket with it. Like the Platypus, it should never be hit with a bat, but it could be. Diamonds strewn across the pitch. The umpires would have a fit.

To summarize: Philosophically and existentially, a cricket ball is any lump of matter used to play any game that can be broadly defined as cricket. Officially, a cricket ball is a very specific lump of matter, one that meets with MCC and ICC regulations. Within the world of formal, regulation cricket, these august institutions, in consultation with all the national cricket boards, decide what constitutes reality.

Having looked at the regulation cricket ball as it is today and at some of the many other types of modern ball that bear a family resemblance to it in form or function, let us now penetrate even deeper into the heart of the cricket ball by examining the history of its development and manufacture; the way the cricket ball has evolved over time along with the age-old game of cricket itself.

Evolution of the rolling globular body

Once upon a time, hard though it is to imagine, cricket did not exist. It gradually evolved in England from the sixteenth century onwards from a range of simpler games each of which contributed some element to it. The origins of these simpler games are lost in the mists of time. They are so fundamental, these simpler games, that they must have been invented repeatedly, particularly by those most imaginative and creative of creatures, children at play.

People have always challenged themselves to hit an object away with a stick and since recorded history began there have been references made to a variety of games involving this skill. With regard to these early games we cannot always speak of bat *and* ball because often the object struck was not a ball, not a globular body that rolls, but a mere piece of wood; a short length of stick. As Hugh Barty-King points out in his excellent book *Quilt Winders and Pod Shavers: The History of Cricket Bat and Ball Manufacture*, in England and Scotland the object struck was most often called a cat, the striking implement a dog: 'The first Cricket ball was a cat; the first cricket bat a dog' (p. 9).

One cat and dog game, Cat in the Hole, involved one player trying to get the cat into a hole cut in the ground while another player defended it with the dog. As an essentially blocking and holing game, Cat in the Hole did not require a ball, although it was more exciting to play with a ball because a ball could be rolled along the ground at the hole and so on. Interestingly, cricket evolved, at least in part, from games that involved a striker keeping a ball out of a hole with a stick, while golf evolved from games that involved a striker getting a ball into a hole with a stick.

Barty-King makes the point that 'There are no true spheres in nature' (*Quilt Winders and Pod Shavers*, p. 14), so if players wanted to play Cat in the Hole with a ball they had to make one.

Rough balls were carved from box, holly or yew wood, while large rounded knots found in several types of tree including birch were removed and further shaped. Meanwhile, lightweight balls were woven from wicker. Enterprising individuals with access to the raw materials could fashion a soft ball by making a leather pouch, stuffing it with cloth, hair, feathers or sawdust, then sewing it up. Stuffed balls of various kinds have been made since ancient times.

Finding it impractical to dig a hole in the uneven, upland ground where they grazed their sheep, shepherds playing cat and dog preferred to aim at a hurdle gate in the sheep pen, known as a wicket, using a ball of matted wool. The word 'wicket' derives from the Anglo-Saxon 'wican', meaning 'to give way', the wicket being where a sheep pen gives way to allow sheep in. The shepherds defended the wicket from the ball of matted wool with a stick or a crook.

Another precursor of cricket was stool ball in which one player aimed a ball at a stool defended by another player, the object being to beat the defender and hit the stool. In the context of the game, one type of little wooden stool used was called a cricket, and certainly the Dutch word for a long, low, kneeling stool used in church is 'krickstoel'. The stool might stand or be laid down with the seat as the target. Defence of the stool might be made with the hand only or with a stick. When the stool was hit the defender was replaced by another, perhaps after one hit, perhaps after three hits.

As with any informal game, stool ball had no fixed rules beyond those the players agreed to while playing, and certainly there were regional variations in the way the game tended to function. Importantly, stool ball allowed plenty of scope for innovations, some of which naturally tended in the direction of cricket. For example, dismissing the defender by catching the ball off his hand or his stick and obliging the defender to run to another point and back after striking the ball, thus exposing the stool to attack.

One story Barty-King mentions is that of a nursemaid who turned a small stool upside down and laid a comb across two of the legs to serve as a wicket bail. She then invited the child in her care to bowl at this wicket with a ball of rags while she defended it with a hairbrush (*Quilt Winders and Pod Shavers*, p. 11). This is certainly an interesting version of stool ball but probably one derived from cricket rather than a precursor of it, as cricket was already well established in the mid-nineteenth century when this nursemaid's little game took place. But who knows, perhaps this little game had already been passed down through countless generations of nursemaids.

The development of Cat in the Hole, particularly as a game that allowed more participants, saw several of the key features of cricket as we know it today emerge. More holes allowed more players to take part and the practice of defenders exchanging holes by running between them began.

If the defender of a hole missed the cat or ball bowled by the first bowler, who was obliged to stand a certain distance away when he bowled, a 'second bowler' was allowed to receive it and attempt to place it in the hole while the defender vigorously defended the hole with his dog or bat.

Many a second bowler's hand must have been broken by the dog or bat as he attempted to do this. The solution was to allow the defender to pop his dog or bat into a space on the ground between the hole and a line eventually named the 'popping crease'. A batsman must still ground his bat behind the popping crease to avoid being run out or stumped. The second bowler was, of course, the forerunner of the wicket-keeper and the dismissal that risked a broken hand before the introduction of the popping crease was the forerunner of the stumping.

Introducing more fielders meant some players were too far away from the holes to see them clearly. The unsatisfactory solution was to mark the holes with a tree stump. 'But the stump got in the way, and they replaced it with two stumps, one on either side of the foot-wide hole, bridging them with a small stick' (*Quilt Winders and Pod Shavers*, p. 15). The holes persisted for some time before the stumps themselves eventually became the target.

A third stump, a middle stump, was introduced in 1775 following complaints of unfairness from famous bowler Lumpy Stevens. While playing for Kent against the legendary Hambledon Club, a name synonymous with the early development of cricket, Lumpy repeatedly bowled through the stumps of star batsman John Small without hitting them. As a consequence, Hambledon went on to win. It was Small himself, a hugely influential figure in the game, who then obligingly enshrined the three-stump wicket within the Laws of Cricket.

As for the length of a cricket pitch, this was standardized somewhat earlier than the use of the middle stump. Different distances were experimented with by the foremost clubs until, in the second half of the seventeenth century, according to the cricketer and author John Nyren, the length of a cricket pitch was fixed at 1 chain or 22 yards (20.12 metres) between the wickets.

John Nyren was the son of Richard Nyren, captain and stalwart of the Hambledon Club in the latter part of the eighteenth century. John Nyren grew up at the Bat and Ball Inn opposite Broadhalfpenny Down, Hampshire, the original home of the Hambledon Club. With a pedigree like that John Nyren must have had cricket ball dye running through his veins. In 1833 Nyren wrote *The Young Cricketer's Tutor* with the help of the renowned Shakespearian scholar Charles Cowden Clarke, teacher of the poet John Keats.

Referring, in his book, to an old manuscript containing cricket recollections and hints for players, Nyren says, 'From the authority before me, it appears that about 150 years since [1683] it was the custom, as at present, to pitch the wickets at the same distance apart, namely 22 yards' (quoted in Barty-King, *Quilt Winders and Pod Shavers*, p. 17).

Certainly, this distance was enshrined in the Code of 1744, the earliest known Laws of Cricket drawn up by the influential London Cricket Club, an organization founded by the Noblemen's and Gentlemen's Club of Pall Mall. Members of this rich and powerful social, sporting and gambling club also founded the Jockey Club and augmented the Hambledon Club. The London Cricket Club was, in some respects, the forerunner of the MCC.

The distance between bowler and batsman, certainly in the modern game, is significantly less than 22 yards. For his part, the batsman stands some way in front of his wicket, usually at the popping crease, which is sometimes referred to as the batting crease in the context of batting. In the modern game the popping crease is 4 feet (1.22 metres) in front of the bowling crease, the back edge of which runs through the centre of the wicket.

For his part, the bowler is permitted to bowl as far forward as the popping crease at his end. Indeed, he is permitted to slightly exceed the popping crease so long as part of his front foot is *behind* the popping crease when he releases the ball. Interestingly, until 1967 a bowler had to have part of his back foot behind the bowling crease when he released the ball, hence the name 'bowling crease'. Guidance notes to the Laws of Cricket say, 'The bowling crease is now redundant for bowling purposes'. The bowling crease is now effectively the popping crease.

The increasing sophistication and standardization of cricket during the seventeenth and eighteenth centuries extended to the cricket ball itself. Players and followers of the game demanded an ever more standardized, specialized, expertly crafted cricket ball of apposite roundness, resilience, durability, size and weight.

Coriaceus orbis

The gradual refinement and standardization of cricket rules and equipment accelerated greatly from the mid-seventeenth century onwards as the aristocracy became increasingly involved in the game. Driven from London by Cromwell's closure of the court and the Puritans' general disapproval of fun and gambling, aristocrats found themselves exiled to the home counties of England and in search of a diversion, particularly one they could place bets on. Their attention was soon drawn to the bowling, batting and catching games their servants and tenants played so enthusiastically on village greens.

As people of wealth and power for whom it was essential to keep up appearances, the aristocrats taking up cricket demanded state of the art equipment and were prepared to pay for it. As a player, his lordship wanted the best kit, the latest kit, as did the professional and semi-professional players who began to appear. In the latter part of the seventeenth century and the earlier part of the eighteenth century these were usually working-class men sponsored by aristocrats to help develop the game and provide challenging competition. By the 1770s the Hambledon Club was paying match fees to its professional players. All this encouraged craftsmen towards increasing specialization and refinement in the arts of bat and ball making. The days of homemade cricket equipment were numbered.

As gamblers, the aristocrats demanded standardization in the sport, an end to too many variables influencing outcomes for a reasonable bet to be placed. His lordship would not, for example, stake 10 guineas on a certain bowler he fancied if he feared the bowler's next performance would be completely undermined by the ball being very different from previous balls used.

The weight of the ball in particular was recognized as an extremely important factor influencing play. The Code of 1744 specified that the ball must be between 5 and 6 ounces. Balls were weighed to check that they were the right weight and those that were underweight were soaked in water to make them heavier. In 1774 the weight tolerance was narrowed to between 5½ and 5¾ ounces.

The use of wooden balls in cricket died out long before 1774. The *coriaceus orbis*, the leathern orb, appeared around the beginning of the eighteenth century and soon became the norm. The phrase *coriaceus orbis* comes from *In Certamen Pilae* (*On a Ball Game*), a Latin poem written in 1706 by English schoolmaster and vicar William Goldwin. The poem also mentions the *pila lubrica*, the greased ball. It became common practice to grease the ball with deer fat to improve its performance and protect the leather. *On a Ball Game* contains the first full description of a cricket match in English literature. It is, therefore, the earliest know piece of cricket writing.

Despite the grease, the leather cover provided 'a nice texture for friction and grip' (*Quilt Winders and Pod Shavers*, p. 29). Also, very importantly, a ball with a leather cover sewn around a core of cork and wool was far better for striking in terms of its resilience than a wooden ball. The leather helped dampen the harshness of contact between bat and ball. The leather cover was invariably dyed red from the earliest times as a matter of convention, long before rules governing the colour of the cricket ball were introduced. Not least, red was a cheap and effective colour for dyeing leather that stood out well against grass and did not show the dirt.

When considering the history of the development of the cricket ball, and particularly the development of the all-important primary seam, it is vital to mention the remarkable story of Stonyhurst Cricket.

In 1582 a Jesuit priest established a school in France for the sons of English Roman Catholics oppressed under the Protestant reign of Elizabeth I. Over 200 years later, in 1794, the school moved to Stonyhurst Hall near Preston, England, and established itself as Stonyhurst College.

Untouched by developments in the English game, the school preserved a form of Elizabethan cricket in which a ball was bowled along a hard, gravel pitch, a massive 30 yards in length, at a stone wicket 17 inches high by 13 inches wide. An over consisted of 21 balls bowled as fast as possible in quick succession with no waiting for the batsman to be ready. The game continued to be played in Stonyhurst's parallel universe until 1860 when it finally gave way to the London Cricket played according to MCC rules.

During its two centuries in France the school perfected a strong but not too hard ball with a thick seam ideally suited to the version of cricket it played. The rules specified that the ball was to be bowled as fast as possible always on the seam. Regarding the manufacture of the Stonyhurst ball, Barty-King writes:

All the balls used in Stonyhurst Cricket were partly made by the boys themselves. They made the interior which consisted of a core of list – cloth, that is – tightly covered with worsted soaked in glue which was then rapidly dried before a fire. In latter days they made the core with a nucleus of hard 'India-rubber', as it was then always called. The core, which had been made by the boys in this way, was then passed to the school shoe repair shop, where trained shoemakers covered it with two half-circles of thick, hard leather, the edges of which, with their inner surfaces laid together, were stitched through and through with wax-end – thread coated with cobbler's wax. The seam thus formed made a raised belt round the ball, like the ring of the planet Saturn.

Quilt Winders and Pod Shavers, p. 22

In 1760, the Duke family, under the company name of Duke & Son, formally established a workshop at Redleaf Hill, Penshurst, Kent, for the manufacture of the finest quality cricket balls. The growing popularity and formality of cricket demanded a dedicated workshop producing a specialized product. Hitherto, Dukes had been leather bootmakers with a sideline in cricket balls. In 1775, Duke & Son presented their first treble-sewn cricket ball to a 13-year-old, cricket-mad George Prince of Wales, who in 1820 became George IV and granted Duke & Son a royal warrant.

Some cricket experts, such as the well-known cricket writer Earnest Ward, consider the Dukes treble-sewn ball to be the first true cricket ball, arguing therefore that Dukes invented the cricket ball. In terms of the raised seam sewn through and through with wax-end, Stonyhurst may have beaten Dukes to it, but significantly, the Stonyhurst ball did not have the cork core of the Dukes ball.

Also, as Barty-King points out, 'treble sewn' may well refer to a ball with three sewn seams: a primary seam, not so raised as the Stonyhurst primary seam, and two quarter seams (*Quilt Winders and Pod Shavers*, p. 30). As this is essentially the modern cricket ball, Dukes may, with reasonable certainty, be said to have invented the modern cricket ball. There are certainly no better candidates that anyone knows of.

In 1811 the artist and member of the Royal Academy Joseph Farington visited the Dukes workshop while staying with a friend nearby. Farington's diary entry for the 21 October 1811 reads:

> The great secret of it is to wind the thread round an *octagon* piece of cork which forms the Kernel of the Ball. This art He [Timothy Duke I] does not disclose but to His own family & now had a Son, a lad [Timothy Duke II], working with Him. When the Ball is perfectly formed with Cork and thread, He delivers to men who work in a room adjoining and they put on the Leather cover which is made of *Bull Hide.* . . . The price of a ball of the best kind is Seven Shillings.
>
> *The Farington Diary*, Vol. VII, 10 June 1811–18 December 1814, Ch. XVII, 'A Holiday in Kent'

Interestingly, master cricket ball maker Timothy Duke I was the great-grandfather of the novelist H. G. Wells. H. G. Wells's father, Joseph Wells, grandson of Timothy, was a gardener and professional cricketer who played for the West Kent Club from 1857 to 1869 and, at the height of his career in 1862–3, for Kent County Cricket Club itself. In *Experiment in Autobiography*, H. G. Wells tells how on 26 June 1862 his father 'clean bowled four Sussex batsmen in four successive balls, a feat not hitherto recorded in county cricket' (p. 41).

Joseph Wells inherited a china shop in Bromley from which he also sold cricket equipment, including the balls now made by his cousin John Duke, son of Timothy Duke II. The smashingly inharmonious juxtaposition of china and cricket balls and bats was not good for trade and the Wells family were constantly on the brink of destitution, their next meal often dependent on the sale of a Dukes ball or a set of stumps.

As Farington also notes in the aforementioned diary entry, 'He [Duke] has only one Competitor in England for the reputation of making the best Balls'. The competitor referred to is most likely John Small of Petersfield, Hampshire, born 1737, whose name has already cropped up in connection with the introduction of the middle stump in 1775. Small made excellent cricket balls and bats at his linen draper's shop in Petersfield. His shop sign read:

Here lives John Small
Makes bat and ball
Pitch a wicket, play at cricket
With any man in England.

> Quoted in GEOFFREY MOORHOUSE, *The Best Loved Game: One Summer of English Cricket*, p. 164

Little is known about Small's ball-making process but it may well have been the same as the Stonyhurst process, at least early on. He certainly learnt leather craft from his father who was a London saddler, and some accounts have it that he was once a cobbler.

Small was a stalwart of the famous Hambledon Club that did so much to develop the modern game and establish its laws before the rise of the MCC. A renowned professional cricketer, arguably the greatest batsman of the eighteenth century, Small was the first player to master the newly introduced straight bat.

In September 1771, in his capacity as chief cricket bat maker to the Hambledon club, Small co-signed what became perhaps the most famous ruling in the history of cricket after Thomas 'Daddy' White of Reigate, often confused with 'Shock' White of Brentford, while playing for Chertsey against Hambledon at Laleham Burway, Surrey, strode to the crease with a vast bat far wider than the wicket. What is now Law 6.1 limits the width of a cricket bat to 4¼ inches.

White's main objective may well have been to stress that it was absurd to have no rule limiting the width of bats and that it was unacceptable to allow their width to be governed by mere notions of gentlemanly conduct. The noble Hambledon Club were far from amused by White's flippancy – certainly an early example of bringing the game into disrepute, or perhaps repute – but it clearly did the trick. Admittedly, this is a bat rather than a ball anecdote but one that no historian of cricket can ever resist.

John Small junior inherited his father's business and continued with it. John Small senior, however, also sold the secrets of his ball craft, and at least some of his tools, to Robert Dark, born 1802. Robert was the brother of James Henry Dark, born 1795, proprietor of Lord's Cricket Ground from 1835 until he sold the lease to the MCC in 1864 for £12,500. Small had made sure that the secrets of his technique would live on amongst men who were at the very epicentre of English cricket. Despite Dukes being so dominant everywhere else, certainly in southern England, the family connection meant that for many years Robert Dark had a monopoly on cricket balls used at Lord's.

Centres of excellence

The cricket ball reached near perfection quite early on in the development of cricket and has not changed much since the Dukes treble-sewn ball of 1775. The modern cricket ball is still essentially that ball, albeit with the various sophisticated refinements that are found in the most expensive contemporary balls, such as the multiple cork layers of the Kookaburra Turf. The cheap ball I gutted is almost certainly inferior to the Dukes ball of 1775.

The cricket bat, on the other hand, quite apart from 'Daddy' White's monster, underwent continuous change from the eighteenth to the twentieth century, developing from a crooked bat to a curved bat and then on through various types of straight bat. This continuous change was due almost entirely to the cricket ball, or rather, to changes in the way the cricket ball was bowled – a theme explored in my next delivery.

By the early part of the nineteenth century the essentials of cricket were well established: popping crease, length of pitch, three stumps in a wicket, width of bat, construction of ball. The game soared in popularity as a result. As the century progressed, cricket became the game of empire, a reminder of home and a focus for expatriate social occasions. More controversially, it became, in the eyes of patronizing and bigoted colonialists, a supposed means of teaching 'the natives' about rules, fair play and the essence of stiff-upper-lip Britishness.

The old, established cricket ball manufacturers struggled to meet demand for a product with such a generally short lifespan. New workshops sprang up like daisies, particularly in the adjacent towns of Southborough and Tonbridge in Kent, close by the Dukes long-established centre of excellence at Penshurst. Craftsmen with cricket ball-making skills were concentrated in the area; there was plenty of scope for outsourcing and an established supply chain of raw materials. Southborough and Tonbridge became cricket ball Mecca. To this day the Southborough coat of arms depicts a red roundel representing the leathern orb that contributed so much to the town's development and prosperity.

Dukes workshop in the garden was bursting at the seams. New premises were needed and in 1841 they moved five miles away to a purpose-built factory at Chiddingstone Causeway near Penshurst Railway Station. The highest standards were maintained and in 1851 Dukes won a first prize medal for excellence at the Great Exhibition. By this time Dukes were making a range of cricket equipment, including bats.

Dukes' only real rival in excellence at that time, Robert Dark, died in 1873, but not before passing on the skills he had learnt from the legendary John Small to a new generation of makers, most notably Thomas Twort of Speldhurst near Tonbridge, born in 1828. Originally a saddler, who was particularly adept at the fine stitching of leather, Twort turned his hand to the art of cricket ball making after learning all he could from Dark at Lord's.

Twort set up business in Southborough around 1851, stitching covers for other makers, including the Lion Cricket Ball Works established in the town by Leonard Woodhams some five years earlier. In 1853, Twort joined forces with John Martin to acquire a workshop on Southborough's London Road and began making his own balls. During the years that followed, Twort & Martin became two separate companies, then John Martin became John Martin & Son. Meanwhile, several other workshops sprang up in the town, including John Sales (1874), Parker & Mercer (1874), Henry Parker (1882) and George Avery (1891).

A scrupulous and temperate man who was determined to become a master cricket ball maker, Twort kept meticulous notes and diagrams of all he had learnt from Dark. He also kept detailed accounts from which we learn, for example, that he spent £2.2s on a crate of 'cricketz ball' that, cut up, provided a guide to his earliest efforts. On the subject of 'Making Red Colour' he writes: 'Two quarts of water; ¼ lb Brazel Chips; 1 teaspoonful of Brown Indies Lake; 1 oz of Termeriac; one piece of Alum (size of walnut), a few hops; all to be boiled up together for one hour' (quoted in *Quilt Winders and Pod Shavers*, p. 70). Tworte's spelling is idiosyncratic but by 'Brazel Chips' he means chips of brazilwood which yield a red dye called brazilin. By 'Brown Indies Lake' he means a brown pigment of lac dye: flakes or powder made from Indian gum lac, a dark red resin produced on certain trees by the sting of certain insects. By 'Termeriac' he means turmeric: a spice related to ginger used to flavour and colour curries. No wonder cricket balls are such hot stuff. 'Alum' is spelt correctly, but in case you do not know, alum is hydrated potassium aluminium sulphate (potassium alum), a naturally occurring mineral with many uses including the tanning of leather. In Twort's recipe, however, alum is functioning as a mordant: a substance used to set dyes on fabrics. Hops are primarily used as a flavouring agent in beer but can also be used to make a brown dye. Hops were abundant in Kent and still are.

As to the making of the ball's quilted core, Twort writes:

Take worsted and corke scolded in water; take one inch square [cubed] of the hardest corke dry, then thin squares 1/8 thick wound round with four cord worsted, then weges – thin cork to make the round, fasen off and hammer now.

Quoted in *Quilt Winders and Pod Shavers*, p. 71

Clearly, we have the layers of cork and worsted that are still found in every quality cricket ball. It is interesting that there is a final layer of thin cork 'to make the round'. A 1956 Pathé film of the Twort process, which remained essentially unchanged 100 years later, shows Charlie Tingley, a quilt winder with 30 years' experience, skilfully winding the worsted thread around the cork cube to make a tight ball that is then hammered in a wooden mould to perfect the shape ('Cricket Balls 1956', British Pathé, YouTube). Regarding the hammer, a type of lump hammer, Twort writes, 'the wheit of the quilt hammer 3 pounds cast' (quoted in *Quilt Winders and Pod Shavers*, p. 70).

Perhaps to conceal trade secrets, the Pathé film does not show the addition of the other pieces of cork, which can nonetheless be seen stacked on Tingley's workbench. After hammering the cores, Tingley weighs them then passes them through a thick wooden ring to check the size.

The Pathé film also shows the leather cover being attached. Two caps of leather made from four quarters of leather sewn along the quarter seams are placed over the quilt. The leather has to be incredibly tight, so the caps are made too small to entirely cover the quilt. The caps are squeezed and stretched over the quilt with a vice that applies a pressure of several tons, enough to close the gap and to cause the edges of the caps to rise together in a small ridge for sewing.

Although there may be small differences between manufacturers in terms of materials used, the exact composition of the quilt, methods of sewing, finishing processes, final coatings and so on, this is essentially how quality cricket balls are still made everywhere and will, presumably, always be made. Much of the process, it has to be said, has been mechanized. Kookaburra, for example, make no secret of the fact that their quilts are now wound by machine. The fact that every machine winding is identical to every other makes for near perfect consistency between balls. Even as I dare to suggest this I can hear old Charlie Tingley turning in his grave. Cricket ball makers are now largely trained machine operators rather than skilled craftsmen.

The hand-sewn seam is still the ultimate mark of excellence in a cricket ball – a hand-sewn seam does not flatten so much during play – and Kookaburra still at least *finish* the sewing of their very best cricket balls by hand. The Dukes ball is hand sewn in factories near Lahore in Pakistan before being returned to the Dukes factory – now in London – for finishing. It is part of the mystique and folklore of the cricket ball that it is born of deep and ancient hand craftsmanship, so it is not surprising that many manufacturers, particularly the older ones, are a little cagey about the extent to which their balls are now machine made.

In an effort to reduce costs in a market where the only thing heavier than demand is competition, cricket ball companies, now generally subsidiaries of large multi-national sports equipment corporations, are increasingly moving part or all of their operation to Southern Asia. One reason for the heavy competition is that making even the best cricket balls, although clever, is not exactly a technologically exclusive rocket science. Having said this, there are some very shoddy cricket balls on the market. You get what you pay for and serious cricketers avoid like the plague all but the most established brands.

Most Southern Asian seam sewers are highly skilled and Southern Asian appreciation of quality control is generally as deep as you would expect in a region of the world where cricket is virtually a religion. So long as the seam is hand sewn and the raw materials are of the finest quality, it seems fair to say that a largely machine-made cricket ball, made by a good company, performs just as well as a handmade cricket ball, perhaps better. Machines are nothing if not consistent.

The cricket ball has travelled a long way since the days of the early pioneers, Duke, Small, Dark and Twort, a long way from its birthplace, the villages and sleepy corners of England's home counties. Yet it is still a product the founding fathers would immediately recognize as their own, albeit with a critical eye. What would certainly please them is the way their leathern orb, more or less perfected in the eighteenth and nineteenth centuries, admirably bears the huge strains daily placed upon it by the fast and furious modern game.

It is time to turn our attention to the cricket ball in action, to the cricket ball in play.

Fourth Delivery

Cricket Ball Played

Bowling overarm, not underarm or throwing

In a cricket match the cricket ball is repeatedly delivered into action by the bowler bowling it. But what is this peculiar activity that repeatedly brings the cricket ball to life? In the simplest terms, bowling involves swinging an arm from behind the body to a point in front of the body before releasing the ball from the hand. The swinging action imparts motion to the ball and propels it forward towards the batsman. This equally describes underarm, roundarm and overarm bowling.

In the early days of cricket only underarm bowling was allowed. The ball had to be delivered from a point below the bowler's waist otherwise it was deemed a no-ball. To guarantee that the ball was delivered underarm the laws of the time even insisted that the back of the bowler's hand must not be uppermost when the ball was delivered.

The fact that the ball was always delivered underarm, along the ground, explains why cricket bats were still shaped rather like hockey sticks during the first half of the eighteenth century. As Cardus says, 'A curved bat, with the weight concentrated at the bottom, was necessary as a counter to the ancient underhand bowling, quick and along the ground, almost "grubs"' (*English Cricket*, p. 9).

As the eighteenth century progressed bowlers endeavoured to get more out of their underarm deliveries. They lobbed the ball through the air, pitching it on a length, so that it would rise unpredictably from the ground in front of the batsman. As a response, the familiar, straight, flat-faced cricket bat began to emerge from the 1760s onwards as an implement far better suited to dealing with the rising ball.

Only so much could be achieved with underarm bowling, however, and by the late eighteenth century many bowlers were bored with it. They wanted to deliver the ball with greater speed, improve its flight through the air and have it pitch up more sharply; most of all, they wanted to increase their chances of dismissing the batsman. By the 1780s some bowlers, such as Thomas 'Old Everlasting' Walker of Kent, were experimenting with roundarm bowling, delivering the ball by swinging their arm around their body below the height of their shoulder.

John Willes, also of Kent, rehearsed the roundarm style with his sister, Christiana, while their dog fielded. Some accounts have it that Christiana invented the roundarm style because the voluminosity of her dress prevented her from bowling underarm. The wits of the day joked that the three of them 'could beat any eleven in England' (*Quilt Winders and Pod Shavers*, p. 54). Willes was no-balled at Lord's in 1822 for bowling roundarm, prompting him to mount his horse in a huff and ride away vowing never to play cricket again. Some umpires were more tolerant of the new practice than others, but only ultra-conservatives were prepared to openly deny that roundarm made the game more exciting. Finally, in 1828, with so many bowlers defying the rules and bowling roundarm, the MCC legalized it.

Some bowlers immediately began to push at the new legal limit set at shoulder height, raising their arm higher than their shoulder in delivering the ball, hence bowling overarm. In the decades after 1828 the arm crept higher and higher above the shoulder towards the vertical. Some umpires tolerated the practice, some did not, but it was here to stay and was finally fully legitimized by the MCC in 1864. Cardus identifies the emergence of overarm bowling during the middle of the nineteenth century as the true beginning of the modern game, 'the most important bridge passage in cricket's symphonic progress' (*English Cricket*, p. 13).

Underarm bowling remained part of formal cricket, but by the start of the twentieth century it was rarely seen. Trevor Molony, who played three matches for Surrey in 1921, is thought to have been the last professional lob bowler or 'lobster'.

The last underarm delivery seen in formal cricket was bowled at Melbourne on 1 February 1981 by Trevor Chappell of Australia, under the orders of his brother, captain Greg Chappell, to prevent New Zealand batsman Brian McKechnie hitting the six his team needed to tie a Benson & Hedges World Series ODI.

The delivery, which remains one of the most controversial balls in the history of the game and a sore point between the two great cricketing nations of Oceania, left spectators booing and commentators diving for the law book to see if it was actually legal. Prior to the delivery, even some of the Australian players expressed concern about its legitimacy and acceptability. Legendary Australian wicket-keeper Rodney Marsh, for example, shook his head and shouted the words 'No mate!' to his captain and the bowler.

The umpires, who were informed of the bowler's intention to bowl underarm, judged the delivery to be legal and Australia won the match. McKechnie, who simply blocked the grub contemptuously with his bat, making no attempt to score, threw his bat away in disgust as he walked off.

New Zealand captain Geoffrey Howarth walked on to the pitch to protest to the umpires that underarm bowling was not allowed in domestic Benson & Hedges competitions in England – where he played much of his cricket for Surrey – on the grounds that nothing should be permitted that prevents a match from flowing freely. Unfortunately, this rule had not been included in the Australian Benson & Hedges World Series Cup regulations.

Former Australian captain and ultimate cricket expert Richie Benaud, who was commentating on the match for Australia's Channel Nine, did not mince his words when he said, 'I hope they put it [the rule] in by tomorrow morning, otherwise there will be a lot of criticism for what was a disgraceful performance out there today. . . . One of the worst things I have ever seen done on a cricket field.' New Zealand Prime Minister Robert Muldoon was even more outspoken when he referred to the delivery as 'an act of true cowardice', adding that it was 'appropriate that the Australian team were wearing yellow'.

Although strictly legal, at least in the match in question, the underarm delivery had clearly become underhand, an action that was against the spirit of the game because it no longer had any place within the game other than as a cynical act. It was all a far cry from a time in merry old England when bowling anything other than orthodox underarm was illegal and dishonourable. The MCC Laws of Cricket now clearly state: 'Underarm bowling shall not be permitted except by special agreement before the match' (Law 24.1b). 'Underarm bowling' here refers to all bowling where the arm does not exceed shoulder height during the delivery, hence it includes roundarm bowling.

Whatever else can be said about bowling, and a great deal can be said, bowling is absolutely not throwing. Fielders are allowed to throw the ball. The bowler, in his capacity as bowler, is definitely not allowed to throw the ball and never has been allowed.

Throwing involves partially or completely straightening the elbow joint in the act of propelling an object from the hand. In overarm bowling, the only form of bowling now permitted in formal cricket, the bowler is not allowed to partially or completely straighten his elbow joint during a delivery once his arm has reached shoulder height and before the ball is released. As Law 24.3: Definition of a Fair Delivery – The Arm, clearly states:

A ball is fairly delivered in respect of the arm if, once the bowler's arm has reached the level of the shoulder in the delivery swing, the elbow joint is not straightened partially or completely from that point until the ball has left the hand. This definition shall not debar a bowler from flexing or rotating the wrist in the delivery swing.

The final sentence about the wrist is important, as the art of bowling, particularly spin bowling, would be hugely impeded if bowlers were not allowed to impart various magical motions to the ball with a flick of that most articulate of joints.

So, contrary to popular belief, a legitimate delivery does not have to involve the bowler's arm being straight or indeed going through the vertical. During the last part of the delivery swing the arm can be a bent arm but it must not *straighten*, and it can be as near to horizontal as being above the shoulder allows.

Over the years many professional players have been 'called for throwing' by umpires who declare the thrown delivery a no-ball. Repeat offenders are reported to the ICC for having a suspect action. Further investigation leads to bowlers either being cleared or banned. Bowlers who can prove after remedial work that their action is no longer illegal are reinstated, while others never recover and their professional bowling career ends. Being called for throwing, or chucking as it is commonly called, is therefore a serious and controversial matter.

On a final note, just in case you thought you had fully understood the bowling/throwing distinction, the ICC, since 2005, have allowed bowlers 15 degrees of elbow extension after it was established that most bowlers' arms straighten to some extent during the latter part of the delivery swing as a result of the irresistible physical forces passing through the arm at that moment. Why 15 degrees? Well, an expert panel of former international cricketers judged that 15 degrees is the limit beyond which straightening becomes visible.

The bowling/throwing issue is far from settled and, I suspect, never will be, especially with spin bowlers in particular frequently inventing new actions that come under scrutiny as suspect. More about spinners shortly.

New ball, old ball, live ball, dead ball, no-ball, lost ball, swing ball, dot ball

As you may have already gathered, in cricket, a ball is not only the physical ball but each occurrence of the ball bowled, as in 'The third ball of the over was a bouncer'. To prevent confusion, commentators usually refer to the ball being bowled as a delivery. Modern cricket always proceeds with an over of half a dozen deliveries delivered from one end of the pitch or wicket by the same bowler, before another bowler delivers another half-dozen from the other end. An over, by the way, is called an over simply because the umpire calls 'Over' when it is over.

A no-ball, resulting from a throw or a foot fault or an unreported change of bowling arm or one of many other illegalities, some of which extend to certain actions by fielders, is part of an over, yet not part of an over. An additional ball must be delivered to make up for this bad egg in the half dozen. A no-ball remains the same physical ball yet it takes on a diminished status for the bowling side. It loses its capacity to dismiss the batsman, except to run him out. To the batting side a no-ball is a ball of increased value, it is worth one run gratis, two in some forms of competition, and can be slogged with impunity.

At the end of every ball or no-ball the same physical ball undergoes a temporary death. It becomes a dead ball as it crosses the boundary or settles into the gloves of the wicket-keeper, if he is not pursuing a stumping or a run-out, or settles back into the hands of the bowler, if he is not pursuing a run-out. The dead ball is instantly resurrected to a living ball once more, to a ball in play, when the bowler begins his run-up or, if he has no run-up, his bowling action.

A lost ball is a dead ball, probably because it has crossed the boundary. A ball lost or unable to be recovered within the field of play becomes a dead ball when any fielder calls 'Lost ball'. It is hard to imagine a ball being lost within a modern, mown, manicured cricket field. Then again, even today, not all cricket matches are played on cropped, immaculate greens, and certainly in the past scrubby outfields that could conceal a ball forever were commonplace.

The invariable routine that is the basic life and death of the cricket ball involves it being delivered, being hit or missed by the batsman and being fielded in some way before being returned to the bowler for the next delivery. This routine of the ball is nothing less than the essential, repetitive mechanism by which the game of cricket proceeds, its metronomic mainspring. To view cricket superficially is to see only this routine and not the myriad intricacies it contains. To view cricket superficially, as a mere visual spectacle, is to be unaware both of the ball-by-ball, ever-changing tactical and strategic situation or state of play of a match and the multi-layered intricacies of human psychology involved. Many people who claim cricket is boring are, arguably, simply not looking at it properly, not paying close enough attention to it, not thinking.

> Cricket is structurally perfect. The total spectacle consists and must consist of a series of individual, isolated episodes, each in itself completely self-contained. Each has its beginning, the ball bowled; its middle, the stroke played; its end, runs, no runs, dismissal. Within the fluctuating interests of the rise or fall of the game as a whole, there is this unending series of events, each single one fraught with immense possibilities of expectation and realization.
>
> *Beyond a Boundary*, p. 260

One factor that makes the life of the cricket ball infinitely more changeable than the repetitive bowler–batsman–fielder cycle into which it is forever locked is the way the physical state of the ball gradually alters as the game progresses, such that it is not really one ball throughout its life but a series of different balls each offering various possibilities to both bowler and batsman. Add to this changing state of the ball the great variety of ways in which it can be delivered by the bowler, all of which aim at bamboozling the batsman, starving him of runs and taking his wicket, and you have a large chunk of what makes the tick-tock game of cricket so deeply intricate and engaging.

Other balls do not have the complex life a cricket ball has during play. A cricket ball may endlessly do the same round – bowler, batsman, fielder – but as it goes around and around it is always gradually transforming, wearing, developing different aerodynamic properties, different properties of bounce, turn, swing and spin that bowlers and batsmen will try to exploit to their advantage. A football has to be the right size, correctly inflated and so on, but as an object it is instantly replaceable. If Ronaldo boots the football high into the stands the players do not wait for the crowd to return it; the ball-boy simply throws another one into the match. Tennis balls have to be the right specification, even the right temperature, but several are available in a match at any one time and the whole batch is soon replaced.

The cricket ball, by contrast, is one ball managed and worked on for many overs. In a Test match a cricket ball must last for 80 overs within an innings, unless it is lost, simply falls apart or becomes so misshapen as to be unplayable. Even then, the umpires, in consultation with the captain of the fielding side, must choose a ball of roughly equal wear and tear to the original from a box of balls kept for the purpose. The box will contain balls that have undergone different amounts of wear: balls that are marked as 30 overs old, balls that are marked as 40 overs old and so on.

What the fielding side certainly do not get before 80 overs is a brand-new ball. The ball, therefore, must be cared for, its wear and tear carefully managed to the advantage of the fielding side. It must be repeatedly daubed with saliva and sweat and these bodily fluids must be rubbed deep into its leather surface by polishing it vigorously on the trousers or shirt. The entire fielding side will become obsessed with this activity, each fielder giving the ball a spit and polish whenever possible before returning it to the bowler. The entire fielding side will become blooded by the ball, their once gleaming whites stained with streaks and patches of red.

Usually, a fielding side will strive to minimize wear and tear of the ball. This is largely done by keeping the ball off the ground as much as possible where it will get scuffed and even wet if the playing surface is damp. A fielder who has gathered the ball and is not seeking to run a batsman out is expected to return the ball to the wicket-keeper or bowler through the air and not along the ground. Unless a fielding side is specifically trying to roughen the entire surface of the ball for some tactical reason, they should always pass the ball cleanly from hand to hand through the air. Not least, keeping the ball off the ground is professional and aesthetically pleasing. It looks good and provides constant catching practice.

The best way to minimize wear and tear on the ball is to prevent the batsman from hitting it. A ball that is repeatedly smacked for six is going to suffer more wear and tear than a ball that constantly evades the batsman's bat and ends up in the gloves of the wicket-keeper, leather cushioned by leather.

It is of course inevitable that a cricket ball will wear during a match, this is its unavoidable fate. It will roughen, soften and somewhat lose its shape. This deterioration is by no means always a bad thing because, depending on conditions, an older ball might well 'do more' than a new ball. The fastest bowlers will squeeze less speed out of an older ball than they managed to when it was a new ball, it being less smooth, hard and spherically compact, but the course of the older ball through the air and off the pitch will often be far less predictable and therefore far more difficult for the batsman to read accurately.

The life of a cricket ball is one of closely managed decline. Fielding sides often allow the ball to roughen and deteriorate on one side of the primary seam while they constantly and enthusiastically polish and preserve it on the other. By this process they craft an asymmetrical ball, a swing ball, the weapon of choice of the swing bowler.

When this asymmetrical ball is bowled the shiny side moves through the air with less friction than the rough side which drags. When bowled fast with the seam upright and aligned more or less towards the batsman the drag causes the ball to swing sideways in the air as it hurtles up the pitch. The batsman will not face a delivery travelling in a straight line from the bowler's hand but a delivery that either swings away from his body towards the off side – an outswinger or away swinger – or a delivery that swings towards his body as it curves and curls in the direction of the leg side – an inswinger.

The swing bowler achieves outswing to a right-handed batsman by placing the rough half of the ball on the left and aligning the upright seam slightly to the left. He achieves inswing to the right-handed batsman by placing the rough half of the ball on the right and aligning the upright seam slightly to the right. Note that in terms of the way the ball is aligned in the bowler's hand the outswinger to the right-handed batsman will be an inswinger to the left-handed batsman, while an inswinger to the right-handed batsman will be an outswinger to the left-handed batsman.

The problem for a batsman facing the outswinger is that he has to go after or chase the ball with his bat as the ball swings away from him. A gap is opened up between bat and body through which the ball may pass and hit his wicket. Failure to judge the amount of outswing correctly will result in the batsman striking the ball with only the inside or outside edge of his bat. An inside edge may result in the ball deflecting onto his wicket – playing, dragging or chopping on – while an outside edge may well carry to one of the slip fielders or the wicket-keeper and be caught.

Achieving an outside edge that carries to the slips is the primary objective of the outswing delivery and a bowler bowling outswingers will want a good number of fielders in his slip cordon. The outside edge to slip off the outswinger is one of the most common forms of dismissal in modern cricket.

In an ODI match between Australia and Zimbabwe at Harare in 1999 Australia fielded nine slips, or to be precise eight slips and a gully, the gully fielder being an extension of the slip cordon who stands almost square of the batsman. In fact, looking at the images, it could be argued that Australia fielded two or even three gullies, and therefore six or seven slips, but this is a matter of debate. It was certainly a highly unusual field, as it left no fielders, other than the bowler and the wicket-keeper, to field anywhere else on the field, and the wicket-keeper, of course, was not far away from first slip. Clearly, at that point in the match,

Australia felt they could afford to risk giving away easy runs because they were extremely confident that the batsman would soon succumb to the outswinger by outside edging the ball.

The main danger for a batsman facing the inswinger is that of being hit on the pads and being dismissed lbw. In trying to avoid being dismissed lbw, by getting his legs out of the way, the batsman may allow the ball to find the gap between his bat and his legs. It is highly likely that the ball will then go on to hit his wicket.

An inswinger can be particularly devastating when combined with a yorker, a delivery that pitches on or near the batsman's popping crease, right under his bat, in the so-called block hole, or even on his toes. Such a delivery can be a nightmare for a batsman to defend against especially when it comes as a surprise delivery after a series of outswingers. A batsman who is dismissed by a yorker, or fails to connect his bat with it, is described as having been beaten by the yorker or yorked. A yorker that does not beat the batsman is called an attempted yorker. An attempted yorker is a yorker that does not 'york' the batsman. More about the yorker shortly in the section on length.

A great sultan of swing, such as England's current all-time leading wicket taker James Anderson, varies the amount of swing he puts into his deliveries and switches unpredictably between outswing and inswing, all with the aim of confusing, beating and dismissing the batsman. As far as possible, the swing bowler conceals the way he is holding the ball so as not to give the batsman any clues as to what kind of delivery, what kind of swing ball, he is about to deliver next.

Much has been made in recent years of the phenomenon of *reverse swing*, where the ball swings *towards* the shiny or smooth side of the ball and *away* from the rough side. Reverse swing is not yet fully understood and there are various theories, but it is certainly seen to happen when particular atmospheric, pitch and ball conditions apply. What are we to make of a phenomenon that seems to contradict all that has been said so far about swing?

Well, the most sensible explanation seems to be that reverse swing is not actually contradicting established swing theory, but rather that reverse swing happens in much the same way as conventional swing when a number of factors cause the shiny or smooth side of the ball to drag through the air more than the rough side.

Although highly desired by bowling sides because of its legendary capacity to confuse batsmen expecting at best no swing and at worst conventional swing, reverse swing is elusive. If it happens at all during a Test match, it tends to start happening when the ball is middle-aged, around 40 overs old. By this time, the shiny or smooth side of the ball can become so impregnated with legal saliva and sweat, and illegal lip gloss, sunblock, hair gel, sugar solution and so on, that it becomes significantly heavier than the rough side which has, of course, been left to wear away and dry out. It is widely recognised that reverse swing is more likely to occur when conditions are dry and the pitch is hard, both factors that accelerate the erosion of the uncared for side of the ball.

Furthermore, the various liquids that have been rubbed into the smooth side of the ball can expand it such that it presents a greater surface area and therefore greater air resistance than the rough side of the ball. Finally, the smooth side, although certainly smooth, may no longer be flat, but undulating and even bumpy due to non-uniform expansion. At a reasonably fast speed these undulations can trap air and create turbulence, further increasing the drag on the smooth side of the ball.

Reverse swing has a lot to do with the amount of turbulence a bowler can create on the smooth side of an ageing ball through the speed at which he bowls it, the way in which he angles the primary seam and how and where he causes the primary seam to pitch. Although reverse swing, like conventional swing, requires a reasonably fast speed, it is noted by some bowlers that reverse swing takes effect if the ball slows down by a particular amount as it nears the batsman. It is widely recognised that reverse swing tends to take place later in the ball's flight than conventional swing, another reason why batsmen find reverse swing so difficult to read. It must be said that a cricket ball always slows down during a delivery, something which is considered in the section on fast bowling, but a good bowler can use seam position, angle of pitch and so on, to influence the *rate* at which the ball slows down.

It has been argued that the reverse swinging asymmetrical ball described above can only be crafted by subjecting the smooth side of the ball to illegal moisturizers of various kinds. Hence, reverse swing remains controversial, often raising suspicions of *ball tampering*. Much more on ball tampering shortly.

In contemplating the various guises of the cricket ball we must not overlook the dot ball. A dot ball is a legitimate delivery from which no runs are scored and no wicket is taken. A dot ball is a delivery viewed from a scorer's point of view; a ball reduced to, or at least represented by, a mere pencil dot on a scorecard. Yet the dot transcends the scorecard to haunt the ball itself, such that a bowler may be described as having bowled a dot ball, or praised for his economy in having bowled a whole string of dot balls.

A dot ball is usually a good thing for the fielding side as it is a thwarting of the batting side's primary objective of scoring runs. Usually, a dot ball builds pressure on the batsman to do his job; it frustrates him and inclines him towards future error. Sometimes, however, in unlimited overs cricket, in a situation where the most the batting side can hope to achieve is to play out time for a draw by mounting an heroic rearguard action, a dot ball is a good thing for the batting side and a frustrating thing for the fielding side.

For a batting side in this situation, a dot ball is one step closer to a draw that will save the match and perhaps the series. For a fielding side in this situation, a dot ball is a failure to take a step towards victory by taking a wicket. In this scenario, each dot ball is a frustration to the fielding side that inclines them towards future error.

A dot ball is a delivery without the physical consequence, the visual spectacle, of runs or a wicket, but in the context of any match it is certainly not a non-event. The spectator who considers the dot ball to be a non-event is stuck at the level of visual spectacle, unable to understand or appreciate that every dot ball is of tactical and strategic significance. The phenomenon of the dot ball reveals very well that cricket concerns so much more than what is actually seen with the eyes. There is always a vast conceptual reality in cricket accessible only to the mental faculties of the sufficiently initiated.

Ball tampering

Having considered legal ways of altering the condition of the cricket ball, legitimate ways of keeping half its surface smooth and shiny while allowing the other half to deteriorate, we must, before exploring other types and styles of bowling, consider illegal ways of altering the condition of the cricket ball, so called *ball tampering*.

Like accusations of throwing the ball rather than bowling it, accusations of ball tampering are serious and controversial. Ball tampering is cheating and players found guilty of ball tampering have been fined, banned from the game for lengthy periods and eternally shamed.

Pakistani player Shahid Afridi was banned for two international Twenty20 matches in 2010 for biting the ball. Bizarrely, sections of the Southern Asian press argued that he was merely smelling the ball, an activity normally reserved for philosophers contemplating its secondary qualities.

At least one whole Test match was thrown into organized chaos and prematurely ended as a consequence of the bitter disagreement that the imposition of ball-tampering penalties gave rise to, and in March 2018 Australian cricket was rocked by what was arguably the most blatant, premeditated and conspiratorial ball-tampering incident in Test match history. More on all that in due course, but first let us get clear about the exact nature of ball tampering.

Law 42.3: The Match Ball – Changing its Condition, makes it clear that players may polish the ball so long as no artificial substance is used, they may remove mud from the ball under the supervision of the umpire and they may dry a wet ball with a towel. That is it. Any other action that seeks to deliberately change the condition of the ball is ball tampering.

It is legal to polish the ball with plain saliva but not with saliva sugared by sweets or chewing gum. It is legal to polish the ball with sweat but not lip gloss, suntan lotion, sunblock, hair gel or any other unguent a cricketer may feel the need to rub into his person ahead of a long session in the field. Although it is illegal for these substances to be used to condition the leather surface of the ball they are in reality regularly used, if a little furtively, without sanction or even complaint from the batting side. Both sides get the advantage of these polishes.

In reality, their use is impossible to police. For example, players standing under a baking sun all day can hardly be ordered not to wear sunblock, and inevitably it will mix with their sweat and find its way onto the ball. In his autobiography *Coming Back to Me*, former England opening batsman Marcus Trescothick, 'the man in charge of looking after the ball when we were fielding' (p. 95), extols the virtues of saliva sugared by Murray Mints as an excellent ball polish. 'It had been common knowledge in county cricket for some time that certain sweets produced saliva which, when applied to the ball for cleaning purposes, enabled it to keep its shine for longer and therefore its swing' (p. 96).

Trescothick reveals that initially he copied Warwickshire's Asif Din and used extra strong mints, but found them too dry to suck on all day. He also reveals that it was the task of England's Operations Manager, Phil Neale, to make sure the dressing room was liberally stocked with Murray Mints at all times (p. 96). Intriguingly, Trescothick adds that Murray Mints 'didn't work as well on the Kookaburra balls used overseas as the Dukes we used back home' (p. 96). As connoisseurs of quality cricket balls, we wonder why.

Could the difference actually have been due to climatic and atmospheric factors rather than to the balls themselves? Before a fair comparison could be made, a proper, controlled scientific study into Trescothick's hypothesis would have to test the performance of both makes of ball polished with a Murray Mint and saliva solution, both overseas and in the UK.

More serious than sugaring or creaming the ball is deliberately rubbing it on the ground with the hand or foot or deliberately scuffing it with an implement. Such actions are prohibited under Law 42.3(b). England bowler Stuart Broad was accused of deliberately scuffing the ball with his boot spikes in the third Test against South Africa at Cape Town in 2010. The accusation came in a South African press conference but the team did not press charges and no punishment was imposed.

Broad later defended himself, arguing that he would need the skills of a Premier League footballer to quickly trap the ball under his foot in such a way as to be sure of adding further wear to the non-polished side (*Telegraph*, 9 January 2010).

One of the best-known ball-tampering incidents of all time, largely because the minutiae of it has become the cricket equivalent of the theological debate about how many angels can dance on the head of a pin, did not involve rubbing the ball on the ground but, in a sense, rubbing the ground on the ball. This is the famous 'Dirt in the Pocket' affair, in which England captain Mike Atherton was caught on camera on Saturday 23 July 1994, on the third day of the first Test against South Africa at Lord's, placing a substance onto one side of the ball and then rubbing it in against his trousers. It later emerged that the substance was dirt which Atherton insisted he kept in his trouser pocket primarily for the purpose of drying his hands.

The incident seemed particularly scandalous against the match's highly political and diplomatic backdrop: the ending of Apartheid, South Africa's recent readmission to international cricket – having been banned since 1970 – and their first Test match at Lord's since 1965.

As Atherton wrote in his diary – entries from which are quoted in his autobiography, *Opening Up* – on the evening of the 23 July he was summoned to the office of the match referee, Peter Burge. Atherton decided to take his trousers along as evidence.

Burge shows the TV pictures to me and asks the umpires whether the condition of the ball has been changed. They say no and are asked to leave. Burge rambles on about how he has seen an increase in ball tampering in recent years, and that the usual practice on the sub-continent is to use resin in the quarter seam to make one side of the ball heavier. He asks me three questions: 'Have you an explanation for your actions?' 'Did you have resin in your pocket?' 'Did you have any other artificial substance in your pocket?' To the first I say that I was drying my sweaty hands, to the second and third I reply, 'No.'

p. 108

Atherton's first answer was true as far as it went, his second was true and his third was false. He was now also guilty of lying to the match referee. Reflecting on the incident in the main text of his autobiography, Atherton does not deny that he was in the wrong but he nonetheless seeks to play down the seriousness of the incident, describing it as 'a storm in a teacup' (*Opening Up*, p. 108). Of course, in the grand scheme of the universe, it was a storm in a teacup, but still no small matter within the grand scheme of the cricket universe.

Defending himself, Atherton says, 'I was not altering the condition of the ball, however; I was trying to *maintain* its dry and rough condition' (p. 109). This is reasonable mitigation to some extent in that the umpires confirmed that the condition of the ball had not been changed. Atherton was still, however, in breach of the Laws of Cricket for 'trying to maintain' the condition of the ball in the way that he did.

Atherton was subsequently fined £2000 for having dirt in his pocket and for not mentioning it was in his pocket when Burge first asked him to clarify the incident. The fine was a way of punishing Atherton for his actions without actually finding him guilty of ball tampering, which would have meant suspending the young captain for two matches and seriously damaging his career and reputation in the process.

> Later Burge admitted that had he known about the dust he would have suspended me and I would, in all probability, have lost the captaincy. I would, I think, have had no option but to take the matter to a court of law.
>
> *Opening Up*, pp. 109–10

That would have been a most interesting legal case. The law of the land conducting a close examination of the Laws of Cricket. Atherton says his defence would have been the umpires' assertion that 'the condition of the ball had not been altered in any way' (p. 110).

Nonetheless, a court of law would surely have upheld a decision to suspend him made on the grounds that he intentionally applied an artificial substance to the surface of the ball. As for the captaincy, it is the gift of the selectors. Atherton could not have served as captain while serving a suspension and would not have had an automatic right to return to the captaincy having served a suspension. Fortunately, all this is hypothetical as matters did not reach such a confrontational and litigious state of affairs.

If, as Atherton told his diary, he was merely *drying* the ball – 'I use the dust to keep my hands and the ball dry three or four times' (*Opening Up*, p. 107) – he should have used a towel as permitted under Law 42.3(a)(iii). It appears, however, that his intention in that moment of madness went well beyond merely drying the ball. He used an artificial substance to roughen, or at least attempt to maintain the roughness of, one side of the ball.

It has been argued that dirt is not an artificial substance and can, therefore, be used to *polish* the ball. The weakness of this defence is that even if we accept that dirt is not an artificial substance, it could never be used to *polish* a cricket ball but only to roughen it.

The strongest argument against Atherton appears to be that even though he was not rubbing the ball on the ground or, indeed, the ground on the ball – the ground being a place not a substance – he was using dirt he had gathered from the ground as an implement (implementing it) to interfere with the surface of the ball. A clear breach of Law 42.3(b). By placing the dirt in his pocket he transformed it into an artificial substance which he then used to change the condition of the ball. A clear breach of Law 42.3(a)(i).

Atherton tells how in panicking before the 'stern and headmasterly' Burge (*Opening Up*, p. 109) he convinced himself 'that dust was not an illegal or artificial substance' (p. 109). This is probably the closest he comes to a full admission of cheating, although he once again plays matters down when he suggests that using dirt was not as serious as using other artificial substances. '[I] assured him that no resin, iron filings, bottle-tops or any other instruments had been used' (p. 109). This is a fair point, and therefore further reasonable mitigation, in so far as using dirt from the field of play does not involve anywhere near so much dastardly premeditation as bringing along a pocket full of iron filings and resin or indeed sandpaper.

What is certainly not debatable, a simple matter of fact rather than a complex matter of linguistics, jurisprudence, ethics and philosophy, is that England gained no significant advantage from Atherton's actions. South Africa won the match by 356 runs with a day to spare. But that is not the point. As moral philosophers often note, a key characteristic of ethical considerations is that they are overriding.

As is so often the case in player autobiographies, Atherton's self-justification occasionally spills over into self-pity. Arguably, he dwells more on the wrongs he suffered as a result of his ball tampering than upon the wrongs of his ball tampering itself. He tells how the press hounded him around the country, two journalists even tracking him down to the Lake District where he had more or less gone into hiding. As one would expect from the England cricket captain, he lost them in his car with a 'James Bond-like manoeuvre up a country lane' (*Opening Up*, p. 112). Interestingly, he rejects what he sees as the implication of a *Times* editorial, that 'the England cricket captain has a greater obligation than the common man to uphold society's values' (p. 114).

More amusingly, Atherton tells how commentator and former Yorkshire and England opening batsman Geoffrey Boycott took it upon himself to phone him while he was lying low in the Lake District and offer the friendly advice that the affair would make his life a misery if he did not resign. 'Why's he so interested all of a sudden?' (*Opening Up*, p. 111).

As to the offending trousers that Atherton took along to Burge as evidence, England and Lancashire cricketer Neil Fairbrother left instructions with the dressing room at Old Trafford that the trousers were not to be washed as he wanted to 'auction them in his benefit year' (*Opening Up*, p. 112). I tweeted Fairbrother in an attempt to establish if he did indeed auction the famous trousers. Not surprisingly, he did not reply.

Another form of ball tampering is interfering with the seams: picking at the stitching of the primary seam or widening the quarter seams. This is a direct affront to the integrity of the ball that damages the ball structurally and changes its shape, an act of cricketing vandalism utterly without honour that, unlike illicitly polishing the ball with sugared saliva or unguents that have first been legitimately applied to a player's skin, dwells not in the fuzzy twilight zone of gamesmanship but always firmly in the clearly defined realms of cheating.

Having said all that, as will be seen shortly, attempts to illegitimately *roughen* the surface of the ball can also constitute the very worst kind of cheating, particularly if certain wider circumstances apply as they did in the deplorable ball tampering incident of 24 March 2018. Perhaps it would just be easier to say 'cheating is cheating' rather than attempt to erect a questionable theory about levels of cheating.

One of the worst cricket ball tampering controversies, one of the most rancorous incidents in the history of cricket, stemmed from a charge of quarter-seam interference levelled against Pakistan on 20 August 2006 during the fourth day of the fourth Test against England at the Kennington Oval.

A routine inspection of the ball, which was 56 overs old, led umpires Darrell Hair and Billy Doctrove to the conclusion that the leather along one of the quarter seams had been deliberately raised. Without consulting the Pakistan team the umpires awarded five penalty runs to England and allowed England batsman Paul Collingwood to choose a replacement ball that was then smashed around the park, not least by star batsman Kevin Pietersen, until an early tea was taken due to bad light.

Although Pakistan made no formal protest at the time of the incident or before tea, discussing it in the privacy of their dressing room caused their indignation to boil over. They were insulted and incensed by the fact that they had been effectively labelled as cheats by senior umpire Darrell Hair, who had not even bothered to consult with them. To top it all, the decision to penalize them had not been based upon an actual observation of ball tampering but only upon an inspection of the state of the ball itself. Arguably, as the evidence was forensic rather than eyewitness, it was feasible that the quarter seam could have been raised naturally.

Hair and the Pakistan team had been on a collision course for months following a series of incidents in earlier matches. Pakistan felt Hair was uncommunicative and inflexible, with a negative, even racist attitude towards them. Hair felt Pakistan were, to say the least, not always disposed towards the most sportsmanlike conduct. In the no-nonsense words of Geoffrey Boycott, on the evening after the incident, 'Somebody should have sorted this out because it's been building up like a volcano this has and it's been bound to erupt at some stage' (*Cricket on 5*, Channel 5, 20 August 2006).

After tea the Pakistan team protested by refusing to take the field. The umpires left the field, directed the Pakistan team to resume play, then returned to the field 15 minutes later. Two minutes after that, with Pakistan still not on the field, the umpires removed the bails and declared England the winners by forfeiture on the grounds that Pakistan had refused to play. To date, this is the only time in Test cricket history that a result has been decided in this way.

Interestingly, the ICC changed the result to 'match drawn – abandoned' in 2008, then back again to 'England win' the following year under pressure from the MCC, just one example of the extent to which the consequences of this incident rumbled on.

Pakistan finally took the field 55 minutes after the tea break had ended, only to be informed by the umpires that the bails had been removed and the result of the match declared.

A pragmatist will argue that with both teams willing and able to continue the match, a capacity crowd who had paid good money and wanted a show, and a fifth day's play and revenue at stake, the umpires should have reversed their decision. A purist will argue that removing the bails and declaring the result was a sacred act that simply could not be reversed without going against the time-honoured laws and traditions of the game.

Perhaps the umpires should have handled matters differently at the beginning. They could have at least consulted with Pakistan after they first judged the ball to have been tampered with. In ending the match the way they did, however, the umpires acted strictly in accordance with the letter of cricket law. Law 21.3(a): Umpires Awarding a Match, clearly states that 'A match shall be lost by a side which either (i) concedes defeat or (ii) in the opinion of the umpires refuses to play'.

The umpires also acted in accordance with Law 21.3(b) in that they made it clear to Pakistan that they considered them to be refusing to play and then gave them reasonable opportunity to desist from refusing to play. The application of Law 21.3(b) is, however, also an opportunity for diplomacy and the umpires could perhaps have been more tactful and diplomatic, politely explaining consequences and so forth, when they first informed Pakistan that they considered them to be refusing to play.

Former Pakistan captain turned politician Imran Khan once described Hair as an 'umpiring fundamentalist'. I am inclined to ask what other ethos an umpire should have? Then again, if all umpires were fundamentalists, bowlers would still be bowling underarm. On the other hand, there is a big difference between allowing innovative bowling techniques that are within the spirit of the game and allowing behaviour that brings the game into disrepute. The debate continues.

The incident had many other consequences besides the result of the match being changed then changed back again:

Forty per cent of the fourth-day ticket price and 100 per cent of the fifth-day ticket price had to be refunded to spectators. The Pakistan Cricket Board (PCB) were asked to pay the £800,000 cost of the refund. They refused to do so but later waived their fee for a Twenty20 match instead.

Pakistan captain Inzamam-ul-Haq was found guilty of bringing the game into disrepute but not guilty of changing the condition of the ball.

A long-running feud developed between the ICC and Hair. The ICC banned him from umpiring international games and he began legal proceedings against them and the PCB for racial discrimination. He later dropped the case. The ICC reinstated him as a top-flight umpire in March 2008 but he resigned a few months later. Hair was voted *The Wisden Cricketer* Umpire of the Season 2006.

All this as a result of an allegedly raised quarter seam. Where is that troublesome ball now?

A while back I was led to say that cheating is cheating, but if there is any sense to talk of *levels* of cheating then one of the worst, most flagrant examples of cheating ever to take place in a

Test match, via ball tampering or otherwise, took place on the 24 March 2018 on the third day of the third Test between South Africa and Australia at Newlands, Cape Town.

While fielding, Australia's opening batsman Cameron Bancroft was caught on camera appearing to rub and press one side of the ball with something he had concealed under his right hand. He then appeared to return whatever it was to his right trouser pocket. With his suspicious behaviour repeatedly replaying on the giant screen at the ground, as well as around the world, Bancroft was then caught on camera removing a yellow object from the same pocket and concealing it down the front of his trousers. When the umpires on the field, at the prompting of the third umpire, questioned Bancroft in the presence of Australian captain Steve Smith about what he had in his pockets, Bancroft showed them a black cloth bag he used for storing his sunglasses. At the time, the umpires appeared satisfied with his explanation and took no further action.

After close of play that day Bancroft and Smith gave a press conference at which it was claimed that the yellow object was a piece of adhesive tape that the team used for securing padding. Bancroft admitted using the tape, with grit stuck to the adhesive, as makeshift sandpaper to roughen one side of the ball. The precise details would emerge in due course but it was clearly a blatant attempt to change the condition of the ball, carried out with what Barney Ronay writing for the *Guardian* fittingly described as 'cinematic ineptitude' (*Guardian*, 26 March 2018).

All this was bad enough but the incident might still have been somewhat excused: A young player acting alone in the heat of the moment, stupidly not thinking that the dozens of powerful, HD TV cameras trained on the field of play were bound to catch him out. A silly fool panicking as he realized he had been rumbled, which then led him into the further folly of concealing the offending object in his trousers and misleading the umpires when they questioned him.

All this was bad enough but the real bombshell came when captain Smith admitted that 'the leadership group', which included himself of course, knew what was going on, had planned it during the lunch break and had even tasked their most junior player with carrying it out. Smith would not say who else he meant by 'the leadership group', but at the very least he meant vice-captain David Warner. He insisted that the coaches were not involved. Looking like a pair of pathetic, worried, contrite, near-tearful naughty schoolboys, Smith and Bancroft could simply not apologize enough as their awareness of the seriousness of the situation and their inability to draw a line under it sunk ever deeper into their tortured souls.

It was impossible for them or anyone else to imagine a more shameful incident in the long, largely proud history of Australian cricket, impossible to think of a more stark example of bringing the game into disrepute. The reputation of Australian cricket had been scarred for a generation. Smith, Bancroft and Warner had certainly ruined their own reputations if not their cricketing careers.

As Australian captain, a hugely prestigious role in that fiercely proud cricketing nation, Smith's integrity in particular was in tatters and he knew it. The only thing that saved him from utter ignominy was the fact that he had admitted his involvement and not left his most inexperienced player to take the rap alone – not that he would have been able to get away with doing so for long given the circumstances. Australian Prime Minister Malcolm Turnbull spoke for a stunned nation when he said, 'We all woke up this morning shocked and bitterly disappointed by the news from South Africa ... It beggars belief.'

More saddened than angry, cricket pundits and former players around the world, many of them Australians, some of them friends of Smith, expressed their deep disapproval of his actions before pointing out that he was not a bad bloke. Only naivety and rank stupidity could have led him down such a destructive path. What on earth was he thinking of? How could it ever have seemed like a good idea?

Apart from naivety and stupidity the only partial explanation that was offered was the particularly hard time that the South African media and fans had been giving the Australian players and their families during the increasingly ill-tempered tour. Only the day before the ball tampering incident took place, Cricket Australia had written a letter of complaint to Cricket South Africa about the 'disgraceful' verbal abuse aimed at players by sections of the Newlands crowd. Lost in some strange bubble of growing frustration, irritation and indignation, an element within the Australian team had somehow got to the point of feeling justified in attempting to beat South Africa by *any* means, temporarily forgetting that to win by cheating is always to be the biggest loser.

Actually, Australia did not go on to win that now forever infamous Test match by foul means or fair. With Smith and Warner obliged to stand down as captain and vice-captain for the remainder of the match, Australia collapsed in seeming shame in their second innings scoring only 107 runs, giving victory to South Africa by 322 runs. The match had become such that it would have been a further embarrassment to Australia had they won.

The ICC was swift to punish Smith and Bancroft in strict accordance with its rules on interfering with the ball, sanctions described on Twitter by former England captain Michael Vaughan as 'pathetic penalties'. Smith was fined 100 per cent of his match fee and banned for one Test match. Bancroft was fined 75 per cent of his match fee and given three demerit points – four demerit points within 24 months leads to a one Test-match ban.

As Cricket Australia despatched senior officials to South Africa to get to the bottom of it all, to establish how deep the rot went, Smith was obliged to stand down as captain of Indian Premier League side Rajasthan Royals, while Warner was soon obliged to stand down as captain of SunRisers Hyderabad. Meanwhile, the cricketing world buzzed with rumours, accusations and condemnations, not least because grainy but troubling footage emerged of Bancroft appearing to put sugar in his pocket during the 2017–18 Ashes series in Australia. The ICC quickly announced that they would not be investigating allegations of ball tampering during that series because under their rules such complaints had to be made within 18 hours of an alleged incident taking place.

With regard to what some were now calling 'Sandpaper Gate', everyone expected, indeed demanded, that the penalties imposed by Cricket Australia would be far harsher than those imposed by the ICC.

Cricket Australia reported its initial findings on 27 March 2018, three days after the incident. CEO of Cricket Australia James Sutherland confirmed that only Smith, Warner and Bancroft were involved in the ball-tampering incident and would be sent home in disgrace the following day. He added that 'significant sanctions' would be imposed upon these three players within the next 24 hours once due process had been followed. The broad consensus in the cricket media was that it seemed unlikely only these three batting specialists knew what was going on. Bowlers particularly are intimate with the state of the ball at all times during play and Australia's bowlers must surely have noticed that the ball was unusually roughened on one side.

It was also confirmed that head coach Darren Lehmann had no involvement in the plan or prior knowledge of it, and contrary to confident media expectations he kept his job. The widespread belief that he would be forced to resign was based on considerations of the clearly crooked culture he was presiding over and, arguably, ultimately responsible for. If he did not know what was going on then surely he should have done. Lehmann eventually announced that he would be stepping down from his role after the fourth and final Test of the series which started in Johannesburg on 30 March 2018.

Despite being repeatedly pressed by journalists, Sutherland, with a little help from one of his minders, narrowly managed to avoid using the C words 'cheat' and 'cheating'. He nevertheless acknowledged that what the three players had done was a clear breach of the Laws of Cricket as well as a breach of Article 2.3.5 of Cricket Australia's Code of Conduct.

When they finally came on 28 March 2018, the Cricket Australia sanctions against the tampering trio were as severe as the deep and widespread outrage at their foolish and deceitful actions demanded. Smith and Warner were banned from international cricket for one year and Bancroft for nine months. The oldest of the three, Warner, could never be considered for a leadership role in international cricket again, while Smith and Bancroft would have to wait 12 months after serving their bans before they could be considered for a leadership role, and even then this would be dependent upon the acceptability of the notion to fans and the public. All three were also required to undertake 100 hours each voluntary service in community cricket.

The punishments did not stop there. Having already stood down from their captaincy roles in the 2018 Indian Premier League, Smith and Warner were banned by the Board of Control for Cricket in India from playing in the IPL at all, meaning they would lose the hundreds of thousands of dollars for just a few weeks' work they were looking forward to earning during April and May 2018. Sponsors also began queuing up to withdraw lucrative advertising deals from the three. Warner, for example, was dropped like a ton of bricks by multinational electronics giant LG as the face of their TV advertising in Australia, while Smith was dumped as the 'Weet-Bix Kid'. More broadly, sponsors began placing various contracts with Cricket Australia under review.

Cricket Ball

It was all beginning to look excessively harsh amid increasing chatter that ICC rules on ball tampering were all rather muddled anyway. Certainly, the not too severe penalties handed down by the ICC somewhat reflected their view that ball tampering was not that uncommon or particularly serious. But really, it was not just the ball tampering itself but the level of deceit and premeditation, the mind-numbingly embarrassing ineptitude born of arrogance, the coercion of a junior player by senior players and, not least, the many enemies Smith's Australian team had made for itself as a result of its widely reported rudeness, self-importance and holier than thou attitude.

Compassion and mercy dried up even further when it emerged along with the sanctions that the yellow object Bancroft had hidden down his trousers was not grit encrusted adhesive tape after all but actual sandpaper. More evidence of extensive premeditation. It also showed that Smith and Bancroft, while they appeared to be making a full confession at the initial press conference on the 24 March 2018, were in fact still telling fibs. It was also revealed that Smith told Bancroft to hide the sandpaper down his trousers, or, as it says on the official Cricket Australia charge sheet under the name of Steve Smith: 'c) directing that evidence of attempted tampering be concealed on the field of play'.

The charge sheet also shows that Warner had not only instructed Bancroft to tamper with the ball 'using sandpaper', but had even demonstrated to him 'how it could be done'. This strongly suggests that Warner was experienced and adept at tampering with the ball using sandpaper.

It appeared that Warner, a superb batsman but a man with a reputation for bullying, was the real 'mastermind' behind it all, and to top it all the charge sheet found him guilty of 'g) failure to voluntarily report his knowledge of the plan after the match'. That is, guilty of at least an initial willingness to let other players take all the blame.

Amusingly, former Australian captain Greg Chappell, instigator of the infamous underhanded underarm delivery of 1981, said that he was relieved to no longer be first choice on Google as the arch villain of Australian cricket.

The new arch villain of Australian cricket apologized for his actions on social media and at the airport on returning to Australia but he did not give a press conference until the 31 March 2018. A tearful Warner took full responsibility for his actions and apologized unreservedly to everyone he could think of, saying he was going to take a long look at who he was as a man. When asked if others were involved besides those already named Warner avoided answering 'yes' or 'no', stressing instead that he was there to accept responsibility for *his* actions. When the question was repeated the journalist who asked it was sternly told by a minder that he had had his one question.

Having resisted using the C word on 27 March, the embattled Sutherland later called the whole sad circus what it undoubtedly was, cheating. I followed the sad circus closely as it unfolded and have to say that in the end I felt genuinely sorry for the three. Disapproval, punishment and abuse were heaped upon them. I myself have unavoidably contributed here to unsparingly recording their deeds for posterity. Smith particularly, as captain of the ship, was distraught with shame and regret, and I must say I became concerned for his welfare and mental health.

The three conspired to rub a ball with sandpaper, hardly crime of the century. When I tried to engage the interest of a non-cricketing acquaintance in the details of the affair he replied dismissively, 'But it's only a game, it isn't real, it doesn't matter'. But sport, especially if you follow it, is as real as anything else and, as ever in life, context is everything. The three betrayed the trust placed in them and the many honours bestowed upon them by their fans, their nation, their sponsors and their game, a game in which ethical conduct, playing in the right spirit, is so vital. But above all they let themselves and their exceptional talent down. They needlessly, wastefully, threw themselves from a very high pedestal.

I sincerely hope there is a way back for them in due course: summer seasons enough to write a new and noble chapter. If cricket is about gentlemanly conduct, as it damned well should be, then that also includes forgiveness and giving people a shot at redemption.

Let us move on from these controversial lows of the cricket ball in play to one of the great wonders of the cricket ball in play: fast bowling.

Fast bowling: pace is nothing without control

There are two main types of bowling in cricket: fast or pace bowling and spin bowling. Swing bowling, which we considered earlier when focusing on preservation and wear of the ball, is actually a form of fast bowling, not least because a reasonable amount of speed is required to get the ball to swing. Seam bowling is another name for fast bowling, referencing the fact that fast bowlers almost always bowl with the seam in line with the pitch, and pitch the ball on its seam, if they can, in order to get the line of the ball to deviate.

Contrary to popular belief, fast bowling is not all about the speed imparted to the ball by the bowler's long run-up, the rapid coiling of his arms and the flinging, trebuchet action of his delivery. There is generally a lot more to fast bowling than pure speed and what broadly counts as fast bowling can vary in speed from as low as 60 mph to over 100 mph.

Anything below 60 mph counts as slow bowling. Unless the ball is spinning, slow bowling is generally ineffective against a batsman with any level of skill and is highly likely to result in a run-fest. For this reason, slow bowling generally only occurs in informal games and the most friendly of formal games. It is not really a type of bowling in its own right, simply bowling that is just not fast enough and does not spin.

The official Guinness World Record for the fastest delivery of a cricket ball is currently 100.23 mph (161.3 km/h), set by the 'Rawalpindi Express', Shoaib Akhtar of Pakistan, on 22 February 2003 at Newlands, Cape Town, during a World Cup match against England. Mohammad Sami, also of Pakistan, may have bowled a couple of balls slightly faster since 2003 but the figures were declared unofficial due to concerns about the reliability of the radar speed guns used. The guns are not held to be particularly reliable by many cricket pundits. There may well have been a faster delivery than Akhtar's somewhere at some time but it is not officially recorded.

There are certainly many old-timers and romantics who feel that some of the legendary fast bowlers of the 1970s and 1980s, such as Jeff Thomson of Australia or Michael Holding of the West Indies, must have bowled faster. Indeed, every generation likes to make bold claims for the speed of its bowlers. Essex bowler Charles Kortright, whose first-class career spanned the years 1893–1907, had a reputation for being terrifyingly rapid. That reputation has clearly stuck because even to this day the ESPN Cricinfo website is prepared to describe him as 'probably the fastest bowler in the history of the game'.

Tailenders were known to throw their wicket away as soon as possible rather than face him. Following a famous confrontation between Kortright and W. G. Grace, described later in this book, Grace ordered last batsman Fred Roberts to stand his ground. Roberts asked what would become of his wife and family if he was killed.

> 'Oh, they'll be all right,' remarked W. G. 'Kortright may hit you but he can't kill you and if we win, there'll be an extra £1 for you. But if you get out, you'll never play for Gloucestershire again.'
>
> ROBERT LOW, *W. G.: A Life of W. G. Grace*, p. 261

Fortunately for Roberts, he survived and Gloucestershire won the match by one wicket, legendary batsman Gilbert Jessop hitting the winning runs.

It is important to note that 100.23 mph was the speed at which the ball left Akhtar's hand, its release or launch speed. This is always the moment at which a bowled cricket ball moves fastest. Akhtar's ball lost a certain amount of its initial speed of 100.23 mph due to air resistance between release and pitching, and a significant amount of its remaining speed on pitching.

So, release speed provides a way of comparing the *maximum* speed of different deliveries, it is not a measure of the speed of a delivery just before it pitches, just after it pitches, when it reaches the popping crease, the stumps and so on. It is possible to measure the speed of a ball at all these points, if it reaches all these points, and work out an average. As for the batsman facing, he must try to judge the speed at which the ball will reach him, or more to the point how soon it will reach him, long before it does so. How soon the ball reaches the batsman depends on:

a) Release speed.

b) How much air resistance the ball encounters during its flight. Air resistance varies according to atmospheric and ball-surface conditions. Moist air, surprisingly, is less dense than dry air, and a smooth ball with the seam aligned upright and along the pitch, such that the direction of the seam is constant, is subject to less drag than a rough ball with the seam scrambled.

c) Where the ball pitches. A full-pitched ball or yorker will travel further up the pitch before it loses a significant percentage of its remaining speed on pitching. Some estimates claim the ball loses 30–40 per cent of its remaining speed on pitching. A lot depends on the angle of incidence at which the ball pitches and the state of the pitch upon which it pitches. Is the wicket dry or sticky? So, other factors aside, a full-pitched delivery released at *x* speed will reach a batsman standing at his crease sooner than a short-pitched delivery released at the same speed.

d) How straight the trajectory of the ball is from the bowler's hand to the batsman. A straight line is the shortest distance between two points. A curved delivery has further to travel.

e) Where the batsman is. He might be at his crease, he might have stepped backwards to meet the ball later or he might have advanced down the pitch to meet it sooner.

f) Where the bat is. This point is so closely related to the previous one that it is, in a sense, already covered by it, but it is worth noting that some kinds of stroke make contact with the ball earlier than others. The batsman, of course, may not make contact with the ball, in which case it becomes more difficult to pin down exactly what is meant by the ball reaching the batsman and at precisely what moment this occurs.

So, who knows, when the 1970s and 1980s legends bowled a new ball dead straight and full pitched on the seam in moist air conditions they may well have sometimes got it up the track in less time – whatever that means precisely – than any bowler since, but there is no certainty that they did. After all, the new kids on the block also bowl the new ball straight and full in moist air conditions. Perhaps the 1970s and 1980s legends just seemed faster because they were more terrifying to batsmen wearing less protective gear, and less sophisticated protective gear, than is worn today.

There are other ways to intimidate batsmen besides sheer speed. Perhaps the great West Indies bowlers of the 1970s and 1980s seemed faster than they actually were to batsmen browbeaten by the deadly bouncers they loved to bowl. These bouncers were particularly terrifying and effective when delivered from a great height by a 6 feet 3½ inches Michael Holding or a 6 feet 8 inches Joel Garner. More on bouncers shortly.

The aggressive West Indian bowling of that era has been characterized, in the 2010 documentary film *Fire in Babylon*, for example, as an assertion of Black Power at a time of black emancipation. Many of the West Indian players of that era were certainly happy to see themselves as sticking it to bigoted white men everywhere, not least in revenge for the racial abuse they endured from some spectators, particularly in Australia.

Before the start of the first Test between England and West Indies at Trent Bridge in 1976, white South African England captain Tony Greig said he intended to 'make them grovel'. Greig was referring to the West Indies tendency – up to that point – to grovel around for runs and generally buckle when they were put under pressure, but his remark was tactless and insulting, particularly when it came from a white South African, and appeared to many people, black and white, to have racist overtones. Greig, who was not a racist, soon apologized for his comment but the red rag had been waved in no uncertain terms at the West Indian charging bull. Captain Clive Lloyd's legendary team went on to destroy England 3–0, making them grovel with a pace attack as withering and relentless as the long hot summer of that memorable year.

In a 2011 interview with *Empire* magazine about the film, Michael Holding denies that the West Indies team of the 1970s and 1980s were 'trying to show "black power"'. He insists that the team simply went out onto the field to win, whether they were playing England – 'who were a white team at the time' – or India. 'They ain't white!' He acknowledges, however, that the stunning achievements of the West Indies team of that era were hugely empowering to Afro-Caribbean people around the world. ('*Empire* Meets Michael Holding: The Cricketing Great on *Fire in Babylon*', *Empire*, 2011). The West Indies double 5–0 whitewashing of England in Test series in 1984 and 1985–6 is appropriately referred to as the 'blackwash' series. Between 1976 and 1994–5 the West Indies beat all-comers, losing only two Test series in nearly two decades.

The above reflections on fast bowling lead to the initially surprising conclusion that it is not really possible to make sense of the notion of 'the fastest bowler', unless you stick to the rather academic figure of release speed – always a much eroded figure by the time the ball reaches wherever the batsman is and difficult to measure accurately anyway.

Importantly, Akhtar's world-record ball, although obviously quick in the broad sense of the term, was by no means the fiercest, *fastest-looking* ball he ever bowled. England batsman Nick Knight simply nurdled it calmly for a single, totally unaware, until the release speed was displayed, that he had just faced a record-breaking ball.

What is not in doubt is that it is very difficult to launch a cricket ball ultra-fast, that is, at more than 100 mph. A fraction over 100 mph appears to present a ceiling that even the supreme athletes of the modern game, with all their sophisticated training, cannot break. Akhtar's record has, after all, stood for well over a decade, with several bowlers, most notably Sami and Australian ultra-quicks Shaun Tait and Brett Lee, coming within a whisker but never officially going beyond.

Once a bowler has good pace, the success of a fast delivery depends on so much more than release speed that straining for a fraction more release speed is rather pointless, unless he wants to break Akhtar's record. Not least, straining for release speed tends to compromise accuracy. To quote Pirelli tyres' famous advertising slogan, 'Power Is Nothing Without Control'. What matters every bit as much as good pace is *line* and *length*, and an intelligent fast bowler will significantly vary the release speed of his deliveries, as well as their line and length, in order to confound the batsman.

'Line and length, line and length' is a favourite mantra of bowling coaches everywhere. This strongly suggests that line and length are extremely important to bowling success. But what are they exactly? Let us reverse the mantra and consider length first.

Length

The length of a delivery is the distance between the point of release and the point where the ball pitches or, to put it more simply, the place along the pitch where the bowled ball bounces. The names of the different length deliveries are: short, good, full and yorker.

There is really no precise distance specified for these different length deliveries, although TV graphics find it useful to illustrate the 'yorker zone' as an area extending from the striker's wicket to 2 metres down the pitch, the 'full zone' as 2–6 metres down, the 'good zone' as 6–8 metres down and the 'short zone' as more than 8 metres down. In categorizing the length of a delivery in real life the height of the batsman is crucial.

A good-length delivery pitches up to the batsman at around waist height. From what place along the pitch the ball climbs to the height of a particular batsman's waist depends on the condition of the ball, how fast it is going when it pitches, the angle of incidence at which it pitches and the state of the pitch upon which it pitches – dry, damp, hard, soft, smooth, uneven, cracked and so on. In seeking to bowl a good-length delivery the bowler has to consider all these factors. A good-length delivery is called 'good' because in arriving at the batsman at waist height it is likely to make him uncertain whether to play a front-foot or a back-foot stroke, that is, whether to step forwards or backwards in his efforts to hit the ball.

In life generally, we say it is good to get an opponent on the back foot, acting defensively, backing away and so on, but cricket teaches us that it is best to render an opponent uncertain as to whether to come forward or to back off. Cricket is actually more complicated than life in that the batsman may act defensively in coming forward and attack the ball in going backwards. A good-length delivery is not always the best length to bowl. As with so much in cricket, what is good, what is best, depends on circumstances. For example, it is not good to bowl good-length deliveries to a batsman who is particularly good at playing good-length deliveries.

A delivery that pitches short of a good length is, not surprisingly, called a short-pitched delivery. After pitching it tends to climb well above the height of the batsman's waist often forcing him onto the back foot to play a stroke. A very short-pitched delivery, which by virtue of its very short length will hit the pitch at a steep angle, especially if the bowler is tall, is likely to bounce very high up the batsman's body or even over his head. This is the famous *bouncer*, so beloved of the West Indies bowlers of the 1970s and 1980s. A bouncer that goes over the head of a batsman standing more or less upright is likely to be called a wide by the umpire and is basically a wasted delivery that costs a run.

A good bouncer, from the point of view of the bowler, is one that reaches the batsman at shoulder or head height. One of the main aims of such a bouncer is to intimidate the batsman and cause him to lose his nerve, to tremble in fear at the very thought of the next delivery. Non-specialist batsmen, who bat further down the order, are likely to be more easily intimidated by bouncers than specialist batsmen.

A specialist batsman will not last long in top-level cricket, or indeed reach it in the first place, if he is particularly intimidated by bouncers. It is a matter of natural selection. Fast bowlers often consider a batsman's ability to deal with the bouncer to be a good indication of both his temperament and his general ability with the bat. As England fast bowler and poet John Snow is often quoted as saying, 'The bouncer is a short and emphatic examination paper that you put to the batsman'.

A good batsman will try to attack the bouncer, ideally use the speed and height the ball has when it reaches him to hook it for six, thus turning the tide of intimidation. If he mishits it though, mistimes it, fails to strike the ball cleanly with enough force, fails to give it enough height, as is easily done with a projectile racing towards the face, he is likely to be caught by virtue of the fact that he will be hitting the ball some distance through the air rather than along the ground. If he attacks the bouncer and misses it altogether then most likely he will be looking to his helmet to prevent serious injury or even death.

A common and sensible tactic with the bouncer is simply to duck out of the way, but in his haste to avoid serious injury, a batsman may still unintentionally leave his bat sticking up, perhaps because he started to play a shot then thought better of it as the instinct for self-preservation took over. The bouncer may well then strike his 'periscope' bat and be caught.

To prevent bowlers from resorting to entirely intimidatory tactics there are now limits to the number of bouncers that can be bowled in an over. Currently, two bouncers per over are allowed in ODI matches and one per over in Twenty20 and Test matches, with one- or two-run no-ball penalties for exceeding the quota. A bouncer is not to be confused with a beamer which is a delivery that reaches the batsman above waste height without pitching. A beamer is always a no-ball.

A short-pitched delivery that keeps low is called a long hop. Such a delivery tends to keep low because it is not particularly fast, but it may also keep low because it pitches on a patch of particularly soft ground. Usually, a batsman finds a long hop an easy ball to play because he has plenty of time to observe its speed and direction after it has pitched. In his sheer enthusiasm to smash the long hop, however, a batsman may fail to connect with it, in which case it is likely to plop onto his wicket for an embarrassingly easy dismissal. Also, a long hop that comes after a series of short-pitched, high-climbing deliveries can trick and wrong-foot a batsman if he steps back with his bat raised expecting the ball to climb high once more. The long hop is then likely to sneak under his bat and hit his legs or his wicket.

The age-old advice that is given to batsmen to avoid this kind of error is: expect nothing, play every ball on its own merits and do not commit yourself to any type of stroke too early. The heart of cricket, arguably, is the intimate battle of wits between bowler and batsman, the game within the game. The bowler striving to get the batsman to expect one type of delivery then bowling another, the batsman striving not to expect one type of delivery and being equally ready for any type of delivery.

The danger of trying to establish such neat little maxims when contemplating the complexities of bowler–batsman dialectics, however, is that there are almost always exceptions to any general cricketing principle. Some bowlers are so predictable that a batsman would be a fool not to ready himself for a certain type of delivery, for a certain type of run-scoring stroke.

Equally, some batsmen are so defensively weak that there is no point in the bowler 'mixing it up'. The bowler should just keep bowling the type of delivery he discerns the batsman is least able to defend against. To put it another way, a weak batsman should not be allowed to survive long enough for the bowler to need to 'mix it up' very much.

Recall Australia's eight slips and one gully cordon. Here, the bowler's very specific intention was crystal clear. Or was it? Bluff, double bluff, triple bluff. Perhaps he wanted to make the batsman so certain that he would bowl a particular type of delivery that the batsman would be totally unprepared when he bowled a very different type of delivery. Here, the bowler undoes the batsman, if the batsman takes the bait, not by making him uncertain, but rather by making him certain.

A delivery that pitches beyond a good length is called a full-length, full-pitched or overpitched delivery. The term 'overpitched' suggests it is not the best length to bowl and this is often the case. A full-pitched delivery, in bouncing closer to the batsman, does not have much time, much distance, in which to move or rise after pitching. With the ball arriving low down the batsman should be able to get over it to play a front-foot shot. A forward defensive stroke perhaps or, preferably, a run-scoring drive whereby the ball is driven back more or less the way it came, safely along the ground or lofted high over the heads of any fielders.

As is always the case in cricket, however, what is best depends on a complexity of specific circumstances. Just as a good length is not always the best length to bowl, so a full length is not always the worst length to bowl. If the ball has started swinging, a full-pitched delivery gives it longer to do so before it pitches. The batsman, invited to drive by the full length of the ball, may find himself misled by the swing into missing the ball altogether, chopping it on to his wicket or edging it for a catch. Much here, as elsewhere, depends on the *line* of the ball, which we shall consider shortly.

As was noted when we looked at swing bowling, a very full-length delivery that pitches on or near the batsman's toes when he is standing on or near the popping crease is called a yorker. A good yorker is a delivery that has a batsman expecting to play forward to a ball pitching a short distance in front of him, but then surprises him by staying in the air as far as his feet. The batsman will suddenly find himself having to shove his bat down to the ground by his feet in an attempt to 'dig out' the yorker. Simultaneously, he may well attempt to dance his feet backwards out of the way in order to avoid both an lbw trap and possible injury. As though tripped up by the yorker ball, less agile batsmen occasionally end up falling flat on their face.

The term 'yorker' is widely thought to derive from the eighteenth- and nineteenth-century phrase 'to pull Yorkshire', meaning to deceive or trick someone, or even from the Middle English 'yuerke' which means the same. Certainly, it is essential to the phenomenon of the yorker that it deceives the batsman. In conclusion, we might say that the yorker is the precise intimidatory opposite of the bouncer. Whereas the bouncer threatens to knock a batsman's block off, the yorker threatens to bite his ankles or stamp on his toes.

Line

Cricket's indispensable field furniture, the two sets of wickets, must, as Law 8.1 states, 'be pitched opposite and parallel to each other at a distance of 22 yards (20.12 metres) between the centres of the two middle stumps'. An imaginary straight line between the two middle stumps is the central line of the pitch. All mention of the line of a delivery is made with reference to this imaginary line. The line of a delivery is a measure of the extent to which the ball deviates to the left or right of this imaginary line as it travels up the pitch.

In discussing the pitch, however, the terms 'left' and 'right' are seldom used. For a right-handed batsman, the left side as you look up the pitch from the bowler's end, the side his bat is on, is the *off side*, while the right side, the side his legs are on, is the *leg side*. All is reversed for the left-handed batsman, quite simply because it would be impractical to continue referring to the right side of the pitch as the leg side when the batsman's legs are on the other side.

It is vital the entire fielding side know which way round the batsman is standing, as this has a huge bearing on where he will play his strokes and how he ought to be attacked and contained. The entire field, the positions of the fielders and the names of their positions, is always orientated around the batsman. As for the bowler, a ball aimed, for example, at the legs of a left-handed batsman will have to follow a very different line to a ball aimed at the legs of a right-handed batsman. Incidentally, it follows that having a left-handed and a right-handed batsman together on the field can be an advantage to the batting side as it can disorientate the fielding side.

A few batsmen are capable of occasionally switch-hitting: changing from a right-handed grip and stance to a left-handed grip and stance or vice versa just before the ball is delivered. One of the greatest exponents of the switch-hit is former England batsman Kevin Pietersen, who switch-hit New Zealand bowler Scott Styris for two sixes on his way to 110 not out during an ODI at the Riverside Ground, Chester-le-Street, Durham, on 15 June 2008.

Switch-hitting is controversial because a bowler is not allowed to change his bowling hand without informing the umpire, and the field is set according to the batsman's original stance. However, the MCC and the ICC have both declared switch-hitting to be legitimate. Any confusion created by switch-hitting over which is the off side and which the leg side, particularly with regard to adjudicating on wides and lbw, is dispelled by Law 36.3 which states that 'The off side of the striker's wicket shall be determined by the striker's stance at the moment the ball comes into play for that delivery'. That is, when the bowler starts his run-up.

In facing any delivery a batsman has two basic options. He can attempt to play the ball with his bat or he can attempt to leave it. A ball directed in a line that leads to the wicket must be played, otherwise it will go on to hit the wicket if it does not hit the batsman first. The advantages of bowling this line are pretty obvious. If the batsman must offer a stroke he runs the risk of being caught, if he misses the ball he will be out lbw or bowled. Bowlers often sum up the virtues of this 'route one' delivery with the phrase, 'They miss, you hit'.

One major disadvantage to the bowler of a delivery that is obviously going on to hit the wicket is that the batsman knows he must attempt to get his bat to it. That is, he is not placed in a state of uncertainty with regard to playing or leaving the ball. Also, if the line is straight, a reasonably skilled batsman who is competent at reading length should not have too much trouble defending his wicket.

It must be said, however, that a bowler who very consistently bowls the kind of perfect line and length that restricts the batsman to nothing but defending will pretty soon frustrate the batsman whose task, usually, is to score runs as well as to occupy the crease. As soon as the frustrated batsman attempts to play a run-scoring shot against perfect line and length he is in grave danger of dismissal.

The best example of a line and length bowler is Australia's Glenn McGrath. His capacity to bowl the perfect line and length with metronomic consistency, the worst line and length from the point of view of the batsman, has made him the world's leading fast bowler to date in terms of Test wickets taken. McGrath, who was central to Australia's almost total domination of world cricket during the years in which he played (1993–2007), was only fast-medium pace (81–88 mph on average) but devastatingly accurate, able to 'land the ball on a sixpence' time and time again.

That McGrath often frustrated batsmen into losing their wicket is evidenced by the fact that his 563 Test wickets cost only 21.64 runs each. He also bowled more maidens (runless overs) than any other fast bowler in Test history.

No decent bowler aims exclusively at the stumps. Depending on a host of circumstances, there may well be lines of delivery more likely to claim a wicket. Circumstances include: the state of the ball and its current behavioural tendencies, the batsman facing, the weather, the time of day and above all the state of the pitch. 'The state of the turf is the clue to every cricket match,' says Cardus. 'No other game comes as much under the influence of material circumstances; the elements are cricket's presiding geniuses' (*English Cricket*, p. 12). Cardus tells a tale of two players pressing expert fingers into the turf at Headingley, discussing what time the pitch will become a 'sticky wicket'. 'Four o'clock,' says one. 'No,' corrects the other, 'half-past' (p. 12).

Bowlers often pursue a line on the off side just outside off stump. This line is aptly named 'the corridor of uncertainty' because a ball travelling along it renders the batsman unsure of what to do. He does not really want to hit the ball because the line is such that if he fails to hit it cleanly with the middle of his bat he is highly likely to outside edge it behind for a catch or inside edge it on to his wicket. On the other hand, he does not really want to leave the ball because he is not sure it will go on to miss his wicket.

More often than not, the need to make sure his wicket is protected wins out and the batsman plays the ball in the hope that he can do so safely. Sometimes the batsman leaves the ball and it sails past or over his wicket, in which case he is praised for his good judgement. The closer the unplayed ball sails to his wicket the more his judgement is called into question. Sometimes the batsman leaves the ball and it hits his wicket, in which case his judgement is deemed poor because the line of the ball was not outside his off stump after all.

But the point is, of course, the line of the ball *looked* to the batsman like it was going to be outside his off stump, the reason why he left the ball alone. The bowler has deceived the batsman with regard to the line of a ball that, for reasons relating to pitch and swing, did not move away from the wicket as the batsman believed it would, but instead unexpectedly 'nipped back' towards the wicket. Bowling success so often lies in getting the batsman to think one thing is happening when, actually, another thing is happening. Bowling is about location, location, location, but it is also about deception, deception, deception.

Just about the first piece of advice that is given to all trainee batsmen is that they should strive to hit through the line of the ball rather than across it. That is, they should meet the ball with a bat that swings through the line along which the ball appears to be proceeding. This greatly increases the batsman's chances of hitting the ball cleanly by greatly increasing the time frame in which it is possible for bat and ball to connect. The ball is allowed a certain amount of time to come on to the bat, which gives the batsman time to fine tune the position of the bat for a well controlled stroke.

Hitting across the line of the ball, moving the bat in a direction that is lateral to that of the ball, slogging, allows only a fraction of time in which it is possible for the bat to connect with the ball, let alone connect cleanly. Clearly, the chances of edging the ball to a fielder or missing it altogether are greatly increased by hitting across the line of the ball.

Line is often used in conjunction with a particular field setting to restrict run scoring. For example, a bowler might place most of his fielders on the leg side then consistently bowl a leg-side line that makes it difficult for the batsman to play the ball to the off side. This is particularly useful in limited overs cricket when the batting side are chasing a certain total and the fielding side know they can win the match simply by restricting the run rate rather than taking wickets.

The line of the ball was at the heart of what remains perhaps the biggest controversy in cricket history apart from the various match-fixing and spot-fixing scandals that have troubled the game in recent years. Actually, in some respects, match-fixing is less controversial because there is no dispute about its unacceptability.

Bodyline

The England team of the early 1930s were at a loss as to how to deal with Australian batsman Donald Bradman, probably the best batsman in the history of cricket. In the five-match Ashes Test series of 1930, played in England, 'The Don' scored 974 runs with a batting average of 139.14. His overall Test average stands at a remarkable 99.94 in 80 innings, 38.07 higher than the next batsman on the roll of honour, Australia's Adam Voges. Incredible though Bradman's

Test average is, most people respond to hearing about it with the unappreciative comment that it is a pity he was *unable* to achieve an average of 100! One more boundary would have done it.

By the time of the next Ashes Test series, played in Australia in 1932–3, England, under the captaincy of Douglas Jardine, had developed a method of bowling that they insisted on calling fast leg theory, but which is referred to in the annals of cricketing infamy as *bodyline*. As the name more than suggests, bodyline involved bowling at the batsman's body; delivering short-pitched balls in line with leg stump that reared up at the batsman.

The tactic, executed mainly by England fast bowlers Harold Larwood and Bill Voce, was clearly intimidatory, its main objective being to limit scoring opportunities by maximizing the batsman's defensiveness. It also aimed at creating leg-side deflections that could be caught by a cordon of close-in leg-side fielders, most of who were positioned behind square leg, that is, behind the popping crease.

Bodyline was devastatingly effective. It limited the ability of Bradman and the rest of the Australian team to score runs and England eventually won the series 4–1. In an age before helmets and sophisticated padding, each individual innings was a near-death experience for every Australian batsman. Each fought with skill and courage against the Larwood–Voce peppering, sustaining terrible bruises before succumbing to the onslaught. Miraculously, no serious injuries were sustained. A ball bowled by Larwood fractured Bert Oldfield's skull but ironically this was not from a bodyline delivery, emphasizing that cricket does not need bodyline to make it dangerous.

Australia's captain, Bill Woodruff, viewed bowling bodyline as ungentlemanly conduct and resisted calls to retaliate in like manner. Australia's indignation reached the level of a diplomatic crisis when the Australian Board of Control for Cricket sent the following cable to the MCC on 18 January 1933:

Body line bowling assumed such proportions as to menace best interests of game, making protection of body by batsmen the main consideration. Causing intensely bitter feeling between players as well as injury. In our opinion is unsportsmanlike. Unless stopped at once likely to upset friendly relations existing between Australia and England.

'Bodyline: The Letters', Lord's website: www.lords.org

The England team, the MCC and the British public were outraged by such a strongly worded reaction to what was a perfectly lawful and, in their view, mostly harmless tactic. They particularly objected to the term 'unsportsmanlike' and Jardine threatened to withdraw from the remaining Tests if the slur was not retracted.

Just two days before the next Test the Australian Board backed down, but only after Australian Prime Minister Joseph Lyons met with them to express concerns regarding the economic impact of a British boycott of Australian goods. The Australian economy was saved but there is no doubt that bodyline seriously soured relations between England and Australia throughout the 1930s until the Second World War intervened and, it has to be said, put things into perspective.

In the spring of 1933 the Australian Board banned bodyline in Australia. At first the MCC declared this unilateral move impractical, but a growing consensus that bodyline constituted a direct physical attack upon the batsman, and was therefore against the spirit of the game, eventually led them to change the law.

In 1934, in an effort to repair relations with Australia, the MCC sought to express their commitment not to use bodyline in the next Ashes Test series. Rather pathetically, they asked Larwood to sign a statement apologizing for his bowling during the 1932–3 tour. Larwood, the MCC insisted, would never play for England again if he refused. Understandably indignant, not least because he was proud of his bowling achievements, Larwood rejected the MCCs ridiculous request outright, arguing that he had only been following his captain's orders. No apology of any kind was requested from Jardine. Larwood never played for England again.

Much has been made of this injustice since, and certainly it seems to smack of the snobbery and class distinction that was rife in the English game at the time and is still there today to some extent. For many years the distinction that developed between amateur Gentlemen and professional Players functioned as a class apartheid within the game with the two groups often having different entrances to the field of play and so on. The system echoed the military distinction between officers and men and their various differing rights and privileges. What Fred Trueman described as a 'ludicrous business' (*Ball of Fire*, p. 57) was not abolished until the end of the 1962 season.

So, the working-class Larwood, a former Nottinghamshire miner, was commanded to kowtow to the MCC and the

Australian Board, while the upper-class Jardine, a former student of Winchester College and Oxford, received no such insult. Although true as far as it goes, this is not quite the whole story.

Jardine had ruled himself out of the next Ashes Test series, whereas Larwood was expected to play. Larwood had also been badmouthing the Australians in the press. He claimed that Bradman was unable to deal with fast leg theory because he was scared. He insisted the Australian crowds were an 'unsportsmanlike gang' (*Sunday Express*, 7 May 1933) who knew nothing about cricket and were only interested in watching Bradman stack up runs.

Larwood may have had a point – although perhaps he was being a snob himself about the Australian spectators – but it was precisely this lack of diplomacy that the MCC wanted to show disapproval of. Then, as now, England's cricket authorities were quite prepared to sacrifice a star player for what they saw as the higher interests of the game.

Larwood emigrated to Australia in 1950 where, ironically, he was warmly welcomed by the nation he had roughed up and insulted. In 1993, in belated recognition of his achievements as a cricketer, he was awarded an MBE by cricket-loving British Prime Minister John Major. Larwood died in Sydney in 1995 aged 90. Jardine had died of cancer back in 1958 aged only 57.

Much has been written about bodyline, even by the verbose standards of cricket writing, far more than I can go into here. So, I invite you to conduct your own further research into the fascinating subject of bodyline, if you want to, and to make up your own mind about the rights and wrongs of it. All that remains to be done here is to consider the changes to cricket law that the bodyline storm left in its wake.

Law 41.5 states that 'At the instant of the bowler's delivery there shall not be more than two fielders, other than the wicket-keeper, behind the popping crease on the on side [leg side]'. Infringement of this law results in a no-ball. This law prevents the setting of the aforementioned cordon of leg-side fielders, most of who need to be behind the popping crease for bodyline to be fully effective.

If law 41.5 renders bodyline far less effective, law 42.6, which deals with Dangerous and Unfair Bowling, rules it out altogether, certainly as a sustained tactic. Law 42.6(a)(i) states:

> The bowling of fast short pitched balls is dangerous and unfair if the umpire at the bowler's end considers that by their repetition and taking into account their length, height and direction they are likely to inflict physical injury on the striker, irrespective of the protective equipment he may be wearing.

If the batsman places his body in the line of a legal delivery, however, that is his problem.

Spin bowling: the art of confusion

We come at last to the other main type of bowling in cricket: spin bowling. If fast bowling is a sort of aggressive, technical science, then spin bowling is a gentle, mystical art intended to mesmerize the batsman by imparting the devious spinning of the ball to his very thoughts.

Fast bowler Glenn McGrath, considered earlier, is currently the fourth most successful Test bowler of all-time in terms of wickets taken. The three bowlers currently above him in that prestigious ranking are all spinners, which perhaps tells you all you need to know about the overall effectiveness of spin bowling. In fairness, however, it must be said that fast bowlers are often deployed as strike bowlers to achieve a breakthrough against top-order batsmen in the first phase of an innings. As a rule, top-order wickets are harder to come by, whereas spinners often get to clean up the easier wickets of the tailenders on a deteriorating pitch. Spin bowling is also less strenuous than fast bowling enabling spinners to bowl more overs.

In reverse order, the three most successful spin bowlers of all-time in terms of Test wickets taken are: India's Anil Kumble (619 Test wickets), Australia's Shane Warne (708 Test wickets) and, king of them all, Sri Lanka's Muttiah Muralitharan (800 Test wickets).

Basically, spin bowling involves imparting rotation to the ball as it is delivered such that its line and length are rendered unpredictable to the batsman and therefore likely to deceive him. However, as with all things cricket, there is far more to the art of spin bowling than meets the eye of the casual observer or, indeed, the mind of the superficial thinker.

Recall what was said earlier in this book about a new cricket ball not necessarily being the perfect cricket ball. Spin bowlers are seldom if ever given a new ball to bowl with. The new, hard, shiny pill is a far more effective weapon in the hands of fast bowlers. The spin bowler definitely prefers an older ball with a worn surface that affords him better grip as he imparts rotation to the ball. This worn, rotating surface bites the ground as the ball pitches, causing it to deviate.

The spin bowler also prefers an older, drier pitch with rough patches of cracked and crumbling earth. Hence, the spin bowler tends to come into his own later on in a match when the pitch has started to visibly deteriorate. Pitching the spinning ball on the rough patches of a deteriorating pitch causes it to deviate far more and with far greater unpredictability than pitching it on a fresh, smooth pitch.

The amount of deviation achieved by the greatest deliveries of the greatest spinners is one of the outstanding visual spectacles of cricket. When you see such deliveries it is hard to believe the spinner's capacity to further influence the ball ended when it left his hand many yards back. It is as though he were still manipulating the trajectory of the ball via telekinesis or remote control. More about the very greatest of these spin deliveries in my sixth delivery: 'Cricket Ball Fame'.

Spin bowling is generally much slower than fast bowling. Whereas the slowest fast delivery is 60 mph, a typical spin delivery is 45–55 mph. In most cases, too much forward speed is counter-productive, as the forces of rapid forward motion overwhelm the less powerful rotational forces and what the spin bowler hopes to achieve with them. There are, however, some spin bowlers who have developed a particularly rapid style, with a few releasing the occasional spin delivery at over 80 mph, equivalent to fast-medium pace in fast bowling terms.

As there is far less emphasis on speed, the spin bowler does not require much of a run-up. Such run-up as most spin bowlers have, a short jog to the crease or even a walk of a few paces, is largely a trigger movement aimed at establishing the right pattern of bodily motion for the delivery, something that a stand and deliver approach would not achieve.

There are many types of spin delivery deriving from subtle variations of the basic spin techniques. To begin to understand the basic spin techniques you have to ask two key questions: Is the spinner right-handed or left-handed? Is the spinner imparting spin to the ball primarily with his fingers or with his wrist? It is also useful to keep in mind that spin-bowling terminology, for supposed ease of explanation, tends to assume a right-handed batsman, such that from the bowler's point of view *off* is on the left side of middle stump and *leg* on the right side.

Now, if we take our two key questions together, there are four possible answers. Each answer gives us one of the four basic spin techniques. Let us list them before we examine what actually happens in each case: To bowl right-handed with finger spin is to bowl an *off-break* delivery, often called an off-spin delivery or off spinner. To bowl right-handed with wrist spin is to bowl a *leg-break* delivery, often called a leg-spin delivery or leg spinner. To bowl left-handed with finger spin is to bowl a *left-arm orthodox spin* delivery. To bowl left-handed with wrist spin is to bowl a *left-arm unorthodox spin* delivery, sometimes called a Chinaman after Ellis 'Puss' Achong, a 1930s West Indian player of Chinese origin who bowled it to great effect.

Rather than examine all four techniques it will serve our purpose of understanding the basics of spin bowling to examine the first two. Suffice to say that left-arm orthodox spin resembles an off break in terms of bowler's action and a leg break in terms of line, while left-arm unorthodox spin resembles a leg break in terms of bowler's action and an off break in terms of line. Confused? Well, there is nothing in cricket more likely to make your head spin than examining spin bowling. The writings of the great philosophers are mere notes to the milkman by comparison. Hang in there though because with a little thought and re-reading it will become clear.

The most popular type of spin delivery is the off break. This is because finger spin is easier to master than wrist spin and because approximately 90 per cent of the general population are right-handed, a statistic that is roughly reflected in the bowling population. Let us examine the off break.

For an off-break delivery the ball is held with the seam running underneath and across the fingers. This contrasts with fast bowling where the fingers, certainly the index finger and the middle finger, are always in line with the seam. The ball may be gripped with the top knuckles of the index finger and middle finger, that is, pinched between them, or it may be gripped with the middle finger over the top of the ball while the index finger grips the ball to one side and the ring finger grips it to the other. The first grip is traditional or two-finger spin, the second is middle or three-finger spin.

Just before release, as the arm arrives at the top of the delivery arc and the seam is upright, the fingers gripping the ball are rapidly rotated in a clockwise direction as viewed from the back of the hand. The hand is also flicked sideways at the wrist, that is, forwards in terms of the direction in which the ball is going. Finally, as the ball is being released, the index finger is 'ripped' back along the seam as the ball rolls over and off it. Together, these hand and finger movements impart maximum forward spin to the ball as the arm propels it towards the batsman. Ideally, the ball should 'fizz' with rapid spin. The faster the ball is spinning the more likely it is to turn, to deviate, when it pitches.

An off break is so called because when it pitches its spin causes it to break away from the off side towards the leg side. In other words, the ball turns in towards the batsman on pitching. In order to get his bat in line with the ball the batsman needs to read its length and its degree of turn, which will vary somewhat with each delivery as a result of natural variation if not the bowler's intention. The great spin bowler Shane Warne argues that natural variation is the spinner's best weapon.

The batsman's task may be made even harder due to the spin of the ball causing it to drift sideways in the air before it pitches. The spin may also help the ball to dip to the pitch earlier than expected or to bounce higher than expected after pitching. Finally, to further add to the mischief, the ball can be given more flight, a little more height than usual, so that it spends a little longer in the air, allowing it more time to drift and to deceive the batsman as to its speed.

All these factors, which the good spin bowler will try to utilize to the maximum, make it difficult for the batsman to time his shot. The great danger of the off break is that a ball turning in towards the batsman is likely to hit his legs if he fails to hit it with his bat. If it hits his legs he will be dismissed lbw, unless, of course, the spinning ball has turned so much that it would, in the judgement of the umpire and/or computerized ball-tracking technology such as Hawk-Eye, have gone on to miss leg stump.

Turning now to the leg break, the master of leg spin Shane Warne always demonstrates the leg-break grip by holding his right hand out, palm up, index finger and middle finger down and spread, ring finger and little finger up ('Shane Warne: King of Spin – Leg Spin Tutorial', YouTube). He then slots the ball onto the first two fingers with the seam running across them. The ring finger touches the seam to the side. The grip of the three fingers on the ball should be comfortable; not too loose, not too tight.

As the ball is delivered, the wrist is rotated from right to left with the back of the hand facing the bowler while the ring finger straightens and flicks the ball to give it anticlockwise spin as viewed from the back of the hand, forward spin up the pitch. Partly because of the difficulty of perfecting the all-important ring finger flick, the leg break is harder to bowl effectively, with sufficient turn and so on, than the off break.

A successful leg break will break away from the leg side towards the off side when it pitches. In other words, the ball moves away from the batsman's body. The batsman has to turn to get to the line of a ball that is approaching him almost from behind as he stands sideways at the crease. With the ball turning to the off side, if the batsman fails to read its line correctly he is likely to outside edge it for a catch to the wicket-keeper or the slips.

A leg break that pitches outside of leg stump and turns sharply can even go behind the batsman and hit his wicket. This is known as being bowled around the legs and is one of the great spectacles of leg spin; one of the great embarrassments if you happen to be the batsman. Like the great off spinner, the great leg spinner will also utilize variations of line, length, flight, drift, dip and bounce to bemuse and bewilder the batsman.

Expert spinners have a whole range of 'variation' deliveries that they hope the batsman will mistake for a standard off break or leg break. The trick is to bowl mostly standard spin deliveries in order to create a sense of expectation in the batsman and then to unexpectedly bowl something different. A competent batsman will expect something different every ball but he may still find it hard to suddenly adjust his body movements to a new situation if he has been locked into dealing with a given situation for several balls. Not least, the expectation of something very different every ball is, in itself, disconcerting to most batsmen. The expert spinner employs psychological warfare against the batsman across several deliveries. He toys with the batsman like a cat with a mouse, the mouse never knowing when the cat will pounce.

One very effective off-spin variation is the arm ball. The initial finger grip is similar but at the point of delivery the fingers and the thumb rotate the ball backwards so that it is released with backspin. Instead of breaking away from the off side the arm ball carries on in a straight line, in the same direction as the delivery arm. A batsman expecting an off break, a ball that turns in towards him, is likely to get his bat too far inside the line of the arm ball to strike it cleanly. He is likely to outside edge it behind for a slip catch or deflect it more or less at a right angle into the hands of silly point. An arm ball might even swing out somewhat on pitching, in the opposite direction to the off break.

Perhaps the most devious ball in the off spinner's armoury is a delivery pioneered by Pakistani spin magician Saqlain Mushtaq called the doosra, a word meaning 'second one' or 'other one' in Urdu. Muralitharan became a master of the doosra and the ball certainly played a significant role in making him the current leading wicket taker in Test history. The doosra finger action is the same as for an off break but at the point of delivery the wrist is cocked so far that the back of the hand faces the batsman. The doosra is delivered from the back of the hand with a lot of topspin.

Many top-level pundits and coaches have argued that the doosra requires such contortions of hand, wrist and arm that it cannot be delivered with a legal arm action. In short, it is always a throw. Muralitharan's doosra was judged by the ICC to be just within the 15 degrees of elbow extension allowed since 2005, but other spinners have been banned from delivering the doosra because they cannot do so without throwing it.

Although the doosra looks like an off break to all but the most observant batsman, it will break away from the leg side on pitching. Should it, therefore, really be called a leg break? Well, it is generally described as a leg break bowled with an apparent off-break action. The doosra is the off spinner's equivalent of the leg spinner's googly: an off break bowled with an apparent leg-break action.

These days, the googly, bosie or bosey, after its inventor, early twentieth-century English cricketer Bernard Bosanquet, is often called the wrong'un. Warne's grip on the ball for the wrong'un is the same as for a leg break, except that he spreads his index finger and middle finger a little wider. Warne delivers the wrong'un with the back of his hand facing fine leg. Like the doosra, the wrong'un is delivered from the back of the hand. In terms of line, the wrong'un goes the 'wrong' way compared to a leg break, very much the right way for the spinner who claims a wicket with it.

I believe you are now enough of an expert on spin bowling to work out for yourself the various dangers presented to a batsman by an apparent off break that actually turns to the off side or an apparent leg break that actually turns to the leg side.

Other leg-spin variations bowled by masters of the art of leg spin are the top-spinner, the flipper and the slider.

The top-spinner or over-spinner is bowled with the back of the hand towards the batsman. No spin is imparted with the ring finger but rolling the ball out of the back of the hand gives it plenty of topspin. Importantly, it goes straight on after pitching, thus deceiving the batsman who has picked it as a leg break.

Even Shane Warne describes the flipper as quite a tough delivery to bowl. Instead of being delivered from the back of the hand the ball is squeezed out under the hand by a finger and thumb clicking action. The flipper backspins with a flat trajectory and skids on low after pitching. It is a great delivery to a batsman expecting more bounce. It is likely to get under his bat for an lbw or a bowled.

The slider or zooter is delivered with the same finger action as a leg break but with the palm of the hand facing the batsman so that the ball travels towards him with an upright though usually wobbling seam that is perpendicular to the length of the pitch. The slider is a fuller delivery that after pitching keeps surprisingly low and slides straight on, ideally achieving an lbw or a bowled against the batsman expecting a bouncier leg break or even a bouncier wrong'un.

There are images of Warne bowling deliveries with the seam in the same position as the slider but with a lot of anticlockwise seam rotation as viewed from the bowler's end. This ball turns sharply towards the off side as the seam bites the ground.

England off spinner Graeme Swann liked to bowl the occasional flat-spinner, seam horizontal, spinning like a top. The ball tends to go straight on. He called the delivery his 'flying saucer ball'.

Then there is the teesra, Urdu for 'the third one'. Saqlain Mushtaq, doubtless trying to psych out Pakistan's opponents, spun the media a yarn that the teesra or jalebi is a supernatural level beyond the doosra in terms of sheer contortive difficulty and utter deviousness, but most pundits say it is simply an orthodox, finger-spun back-spinner. Its effectiveness seems to lie largely in the fact that the teesra bowling action gives the impression that the ball will turn a lot but then, like the wrist spinner's slider, it deceives the batsman by going straight on.

In the end, the sheer variety of spin deliveries begins to defy categorization. Techniques vary somewhat between spinners, even for the better-known deliveries, and sometimes they bowl deliveries that are clearly a combination of different techniques. Sometimes a textbook spin delivery is punished by the batsman, while a delivery that comes out 'all wrong' achieves the perfect result. As Warne says, natural variation is a spinner's best weapon.

Warne advises young spinners to invent their own mystery ball once they have learnt the basics, and always to create a sense of big theatre when bowling. Eyeball the batsman, make him wait, reposition fielders necessarily and unnecessarily; do anything within the rules to unsettle the batsman and cause him to worry about what is coming next; anything to make his head spin before the ball is even spun to him. The Strauss Ball, considered in my sixth delivery, reveals Warne at his theatrical best.

Really, it is only spin jargon that gets complicated as it struggles to keep pace with the huge variety of spin deliveries that are possible. Spin itself is just a matter of spinning the ball in some clever way or other so that its movement deceives the batsman. As long as the ball is legally bowled, as long as it is not thrown and so on, there are no laws governing how it must be spun from the naked hand. Basically, it can be spun in any way that the spinner is able to spin it, any kind of seam position, finger grip, finger rotation, wrist rotation, rip, twist or flick, and over the years the professors of spin, the spin doctors and the fizz kids have been very successful at inventing new and mysterious ways to weave their magic.

Sometimes, despite zoom lenses and super slowmo, the pundits do not quite know what is being spun, and the master spinners, like all master craftsmen and weapons makers, are reluctant to give away all their trade secrets. Cricket, after all, is a perpetual arms race.

So ends our long journey through the labyrinth of spin. Perhaps you found it difficult, perhaps even tortuous. All those subtle movements are certainly not easy to comprehend, and even harder to write about. Hopefully, you feel the journey was worth it, now that you can bore people at parties explaining the difference between a doosra and a googly. What was the difference again?

Fielding: the art of attentiveness

We have largely focused on the bowler and the batsman so far, but what about the ball after it hits or misses the bat, when, in its endless round, it enters into the spacious realm of the fielder?

The aim of fielding is to stop the ball as soon as possible, and ideally to catch it; that is, to gather it in one hand or both directly from the bat before it touches the ground. A catch is the fielder's sweetest moment, just as dismissing the batsman is the bowler's sweetest moment and hitting the ball safely for runs is the batsman's sweetest moment. So, each main function – bowling, batting, fielding – has its sweetest moment in relation to the ball, its own sweet spot, a moment where what is done with the ball brings elation, and of course desolation to the opposition.

Bowler and batsman know without doubt that they are always involved in the action of the ball. The fielder does not know. The ball may come to him, it may not. The art of fielding, apart from being able to stop, retrieve, catch and throw the ball with skill and confidence, is the art of remaining focused for long periods of time while standing on a field that may well be bathed in blazing sunshine and withering heat. Most coaching manuals for fielding list attentiveness as the number one fielding skill because without it all the other fielding skills are undermined beforehand. Always being *ready* to catch or stop the ball is part and parcel of what it is to be good at catching and stopping balls.

Sustained concentration is particularly difficult for the outfielder. The infielder is closer to the action, more likely to get a sniff of the ball on any occasion; he has other fielders close by to hold him to his task and the threat of the ball hitting him somewhere painful if he does not pay close attention to it. But the outfielder is out in the deep all on his own and may get nothing of the ball for several overs. Yet, after doing little else for a good while, except walk in a few steps with the bowler's run-up – fielders are made to walk in, not least to keep them on their toes – the outfielder suddenly becomes the centre of the action as the ball hurtles in his direction.

The waiting game is over in an instant. Such intense concentration is required to judge the precise height and direction of the ball that the outfielder already needs to have been concentrating thoroughly beforehand for his reading of the situation and his response to it to be sufficiently rapid. His various dilemmas in that instant are: Is a catch possible or will the ball come to ground long before it reaches me? Am I already in the best position to catch or stop the ball or do I need to move backwards, forwards or sideways? Do I need to sprint after the ball to intercept it before it reaches the boundary? If so, can I stop the ball with my foot or is a dive required? Has the ball completely beaten me already and is it therefore pointless and a waste of energy to do anything except retrieve it from beyond the boundary in due course with minimum effort? Can I get in front of the ball before it reaches the boundary and allow it to roll along the ground into my cupped hands, shielded from behind by a 'long barrier'? As every schoolboy cricketer knows, in receiving the ball along the ground the hands should not dangle hopefully between open legs but should be cupped and shielded from behind by a 'long barrier' formed from a kneeling lower leg and the other foot.

Obviously, the fielder does not actually think all this. Such a thoughtful, deliberating, philosophical fielder would lack the required spontaneity. The ball would be over the boundary before he ceased his cogitations and made his move. Rather, he acts with the situation, unselfconsciously using his experience and muscle memory to do what is required. Nonetheless, what is required may indeed be a little patience.

This is particularly true with regard to a ball that has been mishit high into the air and looks more or less certain to come down inside the boundary. Clearly, the fielder needs to make sure he is in the general area of the ball's descent as soon as possible. However, he also needs to wait and see precisely where it is going to come down before he commits himself to a precise position, otherwise he may find he has gone too far in the wrong direction to get back to where he needs to be. In other words, he needs to time his movements on the field with the descent of the ball so that the two come together successfully.

One of the main difficulties of catching such a lofted ball is the relatively vast length of time the fielder has to watch and wait for a possibly swirling ball to fall down to him. There is certainly enough time for him to become self-conscious, to think about all the eyes focused on him in those moments, possibly millions of them, their good or bad will towards him, the hopes of the team resting upon him, his expectations of glory, his fear of failure and humiliation. On the subject of the lonely fielder in the deep, Cardus writes:

> The team's destiny in a match might rest on somebody who all day has passed unobserved at deep long-on. So far he has had no opportunity to show that he is taking part in the match at all, except as a constituent of the colour scheme of greens and whites and yellows. Suddenly a huge hit soars aloft; the ball endomes the heavens. Deep long-on is now exposed and rendered notable. Where is the team-spirit now and its blessed brotherly influence and aid in this crisis?

> *English Cricket*, p. 7

Cricket is a thinking game, but at times it does not pay for a fielder to be too contemplative. Certainly, in the catching situation, the fielder needs to keep his mind clear and just catch the bloody thing according to his training. Eyes firmly on the ball, an awareness of his position on the field rather than his broader situation, an awareness of the position of other fielders so as to avoid collision, cupped hands ready to receive the ball, soft hands as the ball descends into them.

Soft hands are relaxed hands that follow through in the direction of the ball, hands that draw the ball to a stop as they gently but firmly enfold it rather than abruptly halt it. The ball is likely to bounce out of hard hands or even to injure them. Hard hands are weak and vulnerable hands when confronted with an unyieldingly hard cricket ball travelling like a tracer bullet from the bat or falling like a stone from the heavens.

For a game that is in some respects leisurely, or often described as such, cricket frequently requires lightning responses. All top cricketers have pretty good reflexes, otherwise they would not have made it to the top. Good reflexes are an essential part of the basic skill set of any good cricketer. To some extent, good reflexes are a natural gift, an instinct, but almost anyone's reflexes can be improved with training and practice, especially when they are young.

My respectful nickname for former Australian captain Ricky Ponting was 'the human fly' because his reflexes, both as a batsman and a fielder, were so incredibly fast. I once saw Ponting dive full stretch for a slip catch then somehow pull out of the dive in mid-air as he realized that the ball was better left to the slip fielder next to him, who incidentally caught the ball. All this in the blink of an eye. If Ponting had not been quite so reactive he might have left the ball alone, but it was nonetheless a remarkable demonstration of reflex action, rapid rethinking of a situation, coordination and sheer agility.

Fielders with the best reflexes, like Ponting, make the best infielders. They field close to the batsman where they must react immediately to the ball racing in their direction if they want to catch it. There is no time for thinking, only time for an automatic response to kick in, one that has been deeply trained into every muscle of their body through practice, practice, practice.

Lightning-quick fielders, usually little guys because small tends to mean nimble, may field very close to the batsman at one of several fielding positions prefixed with the term 'silly': silly point, silly mid on, silly mid off. As you may have already guessed, these positions are called 'silly' because in terms of personal safety they are a very silly place to stand, even if tactically they are a very clever place to stand. The use of the word 'silly', a mild rebuke for foolishness or having or showing a lack of common sense, is a classic piece of upper-class English politeness and understatement because fielding at silly point or silly mid on is not just silly, it is totally insane.

It has been suggested that instead of silly mid on we should have suicide mid on and so on, as it appears to be little short of suicidal to stand as close as two metres away from a full-grown warrior with a great, thick bat, who is eager to smash a hard, unforgiving ball for all he is worth. And make no mistake, he is perfectly entitled within the rules to smash the ball into the face of the silly, annoying fielders standing virtually on top of him. If a fielder cops one on his noggin or in his private parts then it is entirely his fault for standing there, or perhaps his captain for ordering him to do so. These days, very close-in fielders invariably wear a helmet and a box to avoid anything worse than severe bruising or the occasional cracked rib.

Allow me to end this all too brief section on fielding with an anecdote that would fit equally well into either of the two following deliveries: 'Cricket Ball Pain' and 'Cricket Ball Fame'. In his classic book *The Art of Captaincy: What Sport Teaches Us about Leadership* – a must-read for captains of industry as well as captains of cricket teams – former England captain turned psychoanalyst Mike Brearley OBE tells a tale of another legendary England captain, Brian Close, whose long Test career spanned the years 1949 to 1976.

True to his name, Close's idea of leading from the front was to field very close to the bat, and in those days fielders never wore anything so sissy as a helmet. After all, they had a skull to protect their brain. 'Fielding incredibly close in at short square-leg, the great dome of his head thrust belligerently forward, he was regularly struck by the ball' (*The Art of Captaincy*, p. 38). Short square leg, or square short leg, does not have the 'silly' prefix, but I assure you, it is a very silly place to stand.

On one occasion, while playing for Yorkshire, the ball rebounded off Close's dome towards second slip. Instead of collapsing in agony or unconsciousness, Close ordered second slip to 'Catch it!', which he did. In the catch celebrations that followed, interspersed with concerned commiserations, Close assured the team he was alright. '"But what if it had hit you an inch lower?" one asked. "He'd have been caught in t' gully," Close replied' (*The Art of Captaincy*, p. 38).

Transcendental ball

As we have seen, the cricket ball in play is the same yet not the same as the cricket ball surveyed and made. The philosophy of phenomenological ontology – existentialism – sheds light on why this is.

During any close examination of the cricket ball in play, the ball itself, the object itself, largely vanishes, replaced by a collection of possibilities and potentials for achieving desired outcomes. In action, the ball itself 'disappears' behind its own activity. It is no longer primarily a ball but rather the very locus and focus of match activity moment by moment. As a phenomenon, the ball is transcended by its activity, it is no longer an object but the means of delivering intentions and achieving goals, goals in cricket being runs and wickets. It is a bundle of intentions rather than a thing, a collection of meanings rather than an object. As the existentialist philosopher Jean-Paul Sartre would argue, while in action the cricket ball is not a ball but a to-be-bowled, a to-be-hit, a to-be-caught and so on.

In his major work *Being and Nothingness*, Sartre talks about how a naked person can conceal their nakedness, their being as an object, if their bodily movements are sufficiently graceful. Consider, for example, a naked dancer who is so graceful in their movements that there is nothing obscene about their flesh, a dancer who is so graceful that as they move they cease to be mere naked flesh and become instead a precision instrument.

> Facticity [objectness] then is clothed and disguised by grace; the nudity of the flesh is wholly present, but it can not be seen. Therefore the supreme coquetry and the supreme challenge of grace is to exhibit the body unveiled with no clothing, with no veil except grace itself. The most graceful body is the naked

body whose acts enclose it with an invisible visible garment while entirely disrobing its flesh, while the flesh is totally present to the eyes of the spectators.

Being and Nothingness, p. 422

In the same way, the naked leather flesh of the cricket ball in action is wholly present, but is not really seen, unless one stops the graceful ball in one's mind or on the TV screen and specifically dwells upon it as an object. In action, in motion, the ball as object is transcended by the ball as instrument, is veiled and obscured by the ball as instrument.

During a cricket match we always see the ball yet in a way we seldom see the ball, and I do not simply mean that we seldom see the ball close up. I mean that the ball is usually so far lost in the heart of the game, with all its motions and machinations, that it is hardly noticed as a ball. It is right there in front of our eyes, of course, but we see it as a vehicle for all the action that is taking place, as that which constantly animates play, rather than as a mere ball.

Another existentialist philosopher, Martin Heidegger, would argue that while in use the cricket ball itself is an overlooked and forgotten tool surpassed towards the fulfilment of the various tasks for which it is being employed. So long as the tool is functioning correctly in the skilful hands of the players who are using it, the ball kind of goes missing as an object to become one with the purposes, hopes and dreams of a team of people striving together in the world to achieve an objective.

The ball-in-action is what Heidegger, in his major work *Being and Time*, describes as *ready-to-hand* (*zuhanden*). That is, the way of being or mode of existence of an *instrument* when it becomes an extension of the body of a person who is acting to achieve a goal. Any object is potentially an instrument.

Heidegger contrasts the state of being ready-to-hand with the state of being *present-at-hand* (*vorhanden*). That is, the way of being or mode of existence of an instrument that is not in use or cannot be used due to malfunction or lack of skill. Tools, instruments, cricket balls, cricket bats, assert their independence from a person and remind him of their existence as objects, as mere stuff, when they cannot be utilized. That is, when they cease to be instruments that are ready-to-hand in the service of his purposes and become instead obstacles that are merely present-at-hand.

It might be argued that while the cricket ball is certainly an instrument for the bowler, it is only an object for the batsman because he strikes it with an instrument, namely his bat. That is, he does not act *with* the ball as the bowler does, but *upon* the ball. For both parties, however, the ball is a *means* to an end. If it makes sense to say the bowler employs the ball to achieve his ends, then surely it makes sense to say the batsman employs bat *and* ball to achieve his ends. The ball is *instrumental* in both cases, for bowler and batsman.

It is time now to consider specific instances of the cricket ball in play, those occasions when the cricket ball has delivered great fame and admiration, and those occasions when it has delivered great pain or even death.

Fifth Delivery

Cricket Ball Pain

As this book is largely a celebration of the cricket ball I will consider cricket ball pain first in order to get the bad news out of the way before moving onward and upward to the good news of cricket ball fame. Having said that, cricket ball pain and cricket ball fame are not entirely separable, as it is a sad truth that a number of cricketing names have been immortalized precisely by the pain or even death that the cricket ball inflicted upon them.

Comedy and tragedy

Cricket ball pain is both comedy and tragedy. We laugh at the Brian Close anecdote, partly in admiration of his Yorkshire grit, but what if the ball really had hit him 'an inch lower'? He might well have been killed. But he was not, so it is funny and not tragic.

In the 2015 Ashes Test series, the then England captain, Alastair Cook, received a tracer bullet of a ball smack in his private parts while fielding at some silly close-in position or other. Even as his team-mates commiserated with him and called for medical back-up, some of them sniggered behind their hands.

As any man knows who has ever been struck below deck, and what cricketer has not, it is a slow-burning, debilitating agony and absolutely not funny, except for everyone else. Such is the nature of black comedy. As Gideon Haigh says in *Silent Revolutions: Writings on Cricket History*:

> No cricket injury, of course, is quite so visibly incapacitating, yet causes such mirth and companionable feeling, as the blow to the box. The twin sensations among witnesses to mishaps, of identification and relief, are never more pronounced.

p. 96

Sometimes, cricket ball pain really is not funny. Cricketers have been stretchered from the field of play and hospitalized, usually after being hit by a cricket ball on the head or in the face. In a few cases men have died on the spot or expired several days later after fighting for their young lives. In these cases, cricket goes beyond a game, even beyond the political and nationalistic, to the highly personal. Nobody should die playing cricket, although there is always a risk, a risk the backroom boys are continually striving to reduce by constantly improving the protective gear worn by close-in fielders and, above all, by batsmen.

The batsman, of course, is always the figure most in the line of fire, it goes with the territory, and not surprisingly it is mainly batsmen who are seriously injured and killed. The exacting nature of cricket means that no player escapes the line of fire.

Sooner or later, over a period of several matches, every player is required to bat, required to stride to the middle of the arena to be roughed up. For all its real and apparent air of civilization, cricket is a brutal gladiatorial contest, the cause of constant hurt, sting, soreness and injury. The pitiless author of most of this suffering, the wicked cricket ball itself, is nothing less than a serial killer.

Nobody should die playing cricket, but given that death will eventually dismiss us all one way or another from life's brief innings, there are surely worse ways to go than playing the noble game of cricket: out there in the middle with your boots on, among comrades, taking the fight to the opposition, burning out rather than fading away. Cricket is nothing if not meticulous in recording its past and nostalgic in recalling it, so any person who dies playing cricket will certainly be forever remembered with honour and respect. What more, in the end, can we realistically hope for than to be esteemed after we die?

Unlike the hall of cricketing fame, the hall of cricketing pain is not an exclusive club. Anyone, man or woman, who has ever played cricket with any degree of seriousness, that is, with a proper cricket ball, is inevitably a fully paid-up member, such is the cricket ball's hard-hearted propensity to bruise skin, draw blood and fracture bone. Even umpires, spectators and animals who happened to be in the wrong place at the wrong time have not escaped the agony the cricket ball loves to deal out.

Barty-King tells how in August 1825 at Ticehurst in Sussex a struck cricket ball was involuntarily 'caught on the point of a knife which a woman named Stapley, who was running a ginger beer stall on the ground, happened to be holding in her hand at the time' (*Quilt Winders and Pod Shavers*, p. 56). The press reported that Stapley's hand was severely cut and that it took considerable force to draw the blade from the ball. Admittedly, the blade not the ball sliced Stapley's hand but it was the ball that instigated the injury.

Far more recently, in March 2016, and this time *on* the field of play, Pakistan's superstar all-rounder Javeria Khan collapsed and was stretchered off during a world Twenty20 match against the West Indies at Chennai after a bouncer she tried to pull away struck her on the thumb and then on the jaw below her ear. A CT scan revealed that there was fortunately no serious injury to her head, but it was soon discovered that her thumb was broken meaning that she was unable to take part in the remainder of the tournament.

Also in 2016, Deandra Dottin and Laura Harris suffered a sickening head collision while chasing the ball over the boundary during a Women's Big Bash League match between Brisbane Heat and Melbourne Stars at Allan Border Field, Brisbane. The collision can be seen on YouTube and, I'm pretty sure, heard as well, which emphasizes the force of the impact as the two women 'collect each other'. Dottin was taken to hospital with suspected concussion where she was found to have fractured her cheekbone while Harris received treatment at the ground.

I stand to be corrected but I can find no record of a woman dying while playing cricket, and if that is so may it remain an inequality with men.

According to Cardus and others, although the story may be apocryphal because far too good a yarn to be true, super-fast underarm bowler Brown of Brighton, around the year 1818, killed a dog on the boundary with a particularly vicious delivery. The canine fatality occurred, so legend has it, despite long stop holding out a coat to protect the unwitting beast (*English Cricket*, p. 14). What is more certain is that one of Brown's long stops was in the habit of tying a sack of straw to his chest for protection.

Long stop, incidentally, is a fielding position now seldom seen. Politely referred to as 'very fine leg', a long stop is a sort of back-up wicket-keeper used when the wicket-keeper himself is incompetent.

Pitches, padding and cane-handle bats

The hall of cricketing pain began to fill from the earliest days of the game. Make no mistake, even though the founding fathers bowled underarm then roundarm, and the first All-England Eleven found it fitting to play in top hats, the early game was incredibly dangerous. This was largely due to a combination of little or no protective gear and very uneven pitches.

Cricket itself has been one of the engines of turf perfection, but good, flat, firm turf was not easy to come by in an age before sophisticated weed killers, lawn conditioners and powered mowers. It was illegal to sweep or roll a pitch between innings until 1849 and even then the rollers were far lighter than the mechanized heavy rollers used in formal cricket today. Cardus tells how in the mid-nineteenth century, Fuller Pilch, one of the few batsmen to truly achieve mastery over the roundarm cannonade, found the turf 'so rudely close to nature that at the beginning of one match he felt obliged to borrow a scythe and mow the grass a little smoother' (*English Cricket*, p. 15).

The main danger of a very uneven pitch, apart perhaps from tripping over, is uneven and unpredictable bounce. As Cardus writes:

> The perils faced by batsmen on the crude turf of the older times against fast bowling – and it *was* fast – could not be anticipated; they came without warning; the best length ball might at any moment fly upward and knock a man out.
>
> *English Cricket*, p. 16

Even the hallowed turf at Lord's was not well laid. Describing the condition of the Lord's pitch the first time the great W. G. Grace played on it a few days after his sixteenth birthday in 1864, Robert Low writes:

> The pitch, uncared for, full of holes and covered with small pebbles, was lethal; that very summer Sussex refused to play there because of it. Surrey had done the same in 1859. The creases were not marked with chalk but with inch-deep trenches which deteriorated rapidly. W. G. himself recounted that an over might contain three 'shooters' but also balls that hit the stones and reared up at the batsman.
>
> *W. G.: A Life of W. G. Grace*, p. 44

The Lord's pitch was still in a poor state as late as 1870. It certainly played a major part in the demise of Nottinghamshire batsman George Summers, who was hit on the cheek by a rising delivery from MCC fast bowler John Platts. Although Summers retired hurt and had to be carried off, he recovered enough to take a train back to Nottingham. Unfortunately, he died three days later of what was diagnosed as concussion of the brain.

The MCC made considerable efforts to improve the quality of the Lord's pitch as a consequence, although famously the field still slopes down by 8 feet 2 inches (2.5 metres) from its north-west side to its south-east side. This now time-honoured geographical feature offers a complex variety of dangers and opportunities to both batting and fielding sides.

The next batsman in after Summers, Richard Daft, came to the crease wearing a towel around his head in protest at the dangerous bowling, just about the nearest the game came to protective headgear for another century.

It is an old joke in cricket circles that cricketers have always been more interested in protecting their crown jewels than their brain. Certainly, the cricket helmet did not enter common use until the 1970s, whereas the box, the abdominal protector, was in general use at least 120 years earlier and probably long before. A helmet is always going to be a reasonably sophisticated piece of kit, but it does not take much ingenuity to stuff something suitable down the front of the trousers to cushion the blow. In *And God Created Cricket: An Irreverent History of the Greatest Game on Earth*, Simon Hughes acknowledges the ancient practice of packing a handkerchief around the genitals, adding that the first public reference to a professionally manufactured protector appeared in the 1850s:

Not until the 1850s was such an accessory mentioned, described as 'a cross-bar India rubber guard' and superseded eventually by 'Palmer's Patent Groin Protector', a sort of padded codpiece. Later still, in the 1930s, you could get a tin version, and if, as sometimes happens, the batsman was hit 'amidships', he often removed it and knocked the dints out with his bat handle.

p. 57

If the ball failed to fly upward it would often 'shoot', skid on much lower than expected after pitching then crunch into the batman's unprotected shins. Star player Alfred Mynn, 'the Lion of Kent', a gargantuan man said to have hands the size of a leg of mutton and himself a demon roundarm bowler, was eventually stretchered off at Leicester in 1836 after his unpadded leg was repeatedly struck by fast deliveries during a long innings in which he made his only century. His leg splinted, Mynn made an agonizing journey to London on the roof of a stage coach. Unable to continue to Kent, he was visited by surgeons at the Angel Tavern who discussed amputating his leg from the hip. Fortunately, they decided not to operate and sent him instead to Bart's Hospital. It was two long years before Mynn was able to return, padded, to the field of combat.

It appears that some batsmen had for a long time sewn or somehow wedged various kinds of makeshift padding inside their trouser legs. The practice, however, was frowned upon. When the malevolent and bad-tempered Lord Frederick Beauclerk became president of the MCC in 1826 he 'decreed that "leggings" must not be worn' (*And God Created Cricket*,

p. 56). Beauclerk was a clergyman without an ounce of Christian charity, a devious man who bet on roundarm bowlers while seeking to ban them and a person so universally unpopular that when he died in 1850 *The Times* denied him an obituary.

Attitudes towards 'leggings' began to soften after the Mynn affair, however, and by the 1840s professionally manufactured cork leg guards were available. In 1845, master cricket ball maker Robert Dark – the pupil of Small and the teacher of Twort – boldly advertised as follows on the front page of *Bell's Life in London & Sporting Chronicle*:

> CRICKET, under PATRONGE of the MARYLBONE CLUB. – ROBERT DARK, sole inventor and manufacturer of the Tubular India Rubber Gloves and the Improved Leg Guards, respectfully informs the lovers of the game of Cricket that he has a large supply of these essential articles, in addition to his celebrated Cricket Balls (no others are used in the great Matches on Lord's Ground).

Pads and gloves for batsmen, and pretty soon wicket-keepers too, became 'a necessary fashion' (*English Cricket*, p. 16) that greatly reduced the risk of lower-limb maiming and amputation. Cardus describes the pads and gloves even of the 1860s as 'almost apologetically frail' (*English Cricket*, p. 16) but they were far better than nothing and protective gear continued to improve steadily for the next 150 years. Indeed, protective gear remains subject to constant innovation as lighter, stronger materials are invented and the Machiavellian orb exposes dangerous or even fatal chinks in the existing armour.

Even if the batsman of old hit the ball with his bat, rather than the ball hit his person, the bat itself, handle and blade carved from a single piece of wood, could still be a source of 'much physical pain and nervous shock' (*English Cricket*, p. 16). Driving the ball with a one-piece bat, a wafer-thin implement compared with the chunky bats of today, with no gloves or frail gloves at best, was a particularly bone-jarring experience. An agonizing jolt like a heavy electric shock would send vibrations buzzing and jangling through the batsman's hands, up the marrow of his forearms and on into his entire skeleton, leaving a deep arm ache in its slowly dissipating wake. Not surprisingly, driving the ball was little practised in those far off times, with nurdling and scoring behind the wicket being the preferred options.

The solution to the worst of the jarring was the introduction of the cane-handle bat around 1836, the cane handle spliced into the blade and secured with glue. 'Dark bats of 1836–40 may have been spliced, and the first Duke bats of 1848 would certainly have been' (*Quilt Winders and Pod Shavers*, p. 98).

The introduction of the tapered splice in the 1880s ensured a more gradual transfer of load from blade to handle than was possible with a non-tapered splice. As well as further facilitating comfortable striking of the ball, this innovation greatly reduced the incidence of blades breaking off on contact with the ball. Blade throw still presents an occasional danger to players in the form of a flying lump of willow and attendant splinters. See various YouTube clips of bats snapping and detached blades flying through the air as far as the popping crease at the bowler's end.

Another important innovation was the introduction of three rubber laminations within the length of the cane handle. These laminations, along with the replaceable rubber handle grip, greatly increased shock absorption. Some modern cricket bat handles incorporate a carbon fibre shaft, reducing overall weight while further increasing shock absorption, bat strength and striking power.

In 2008, to maintain the all-important 'equal balance between bat and ball' the MCC legislated against excessive innovation in bat-handle technology, ruling that '90% of the volume of bat handles should be made of cane, wood and/or twine' ('High-Tech Bats To Be Made Illegal', BBC Sport: Cricket Website, 8 May 2008).

As cricket developed into the twentieth century some batsmen adopted every protective innovation available while others scorned all but the bare minimum. The bare minimum meant leg guards, the familiar vertical ribbed batting pads with a foot slot and a knee roll that are strapped to the front of the lower legs. In the 1930s, long before the advent of the cricket helmet, England batsman Patsy Hendren wore a homemade protective rubber hat with three peaks, two of which came down each side of his head.

Meanwhile, other players refused even to wear a box, declaring them to be too uncomfortable. On the subject of Eric Rowan, who played Test cricket for South Africa from 1935 to 1951, Haigh writes: 'Springbok opener Eric Rowan admitted in a documentary history of South African cricket a few years ago that he went bare into battles with Lindwall and Miller [Australian fast bowlers] because it "made me concentrate". As it would' (*Silent Revolutions*, p. 96)

As the cricket helmet finally came into use in the 1970s, largely as a response to the bowling of deadly bouncers, particularly by the West Indies, there were those who wondered if the wearing of helmets actually encouraged dangerous bowling. England captain turned commentator Tony Greig shared this concern, even though he was himself a helmet pioneer. Other early helmet pioneers were England captain Mike Brearley, England batsman Dennis Amiss and Australian batsman Graham Yallop.

Yallop was the first player to wear a helmet in Test cricket. On 17 March 1978 at Bridgetown, Barbados, he wore a sort of modified scooter helmet with a Perspex visor to protect his skull from the withering pace attack of Andy Roberts, Colin Croft and Joel Garner. He was loudly booed by the merciless, bloodthirsty West Indian crowd for his 'cowardice' but the sense of it was undeniable and the cricket helmet was here to stay.

Yallop's helmet has been praised for its good visibility – most modern purpose-built cricket helmets have a grille to guard the face – though the Perspex visor must surely have steamed up. It was also heavy and very hot to wear while running up and down in blazing sunshine. Even state of the art cricket helmets, with their lightweight construction and air holes, are not exactly cool to wear and players can be seen pouring the sweat out of them during a long innings.

The wearing of an array of protective gear in modern cricket can hardly be described as 'health and safety gone mad'. Cricket balls are as hard and merciless as a 1970s West Indian crowd, especially when delivered at high speed or smashed off the meat of the bat, and almost all players now accept that it is plain common sense to take every reasonable precaution to avoid career-threatening or even life-threatening injuries.

Resistance to protective gear in the past was not only the result of 'back in the day' bravado. The gear was made from heavy, rigid materials with leather straps, metal buckles and so on. It was uncomfortable to wear and difficult to move around in. Today we have Lycra, Velcro, Kevlar, Neoprene, carbon fibre, PVC, PU, TPU, HDF and so on. These space-age materials are utilized to make a wide range of flexible, lightweight protective gear that provides players with a high level of safety, comfort and freedom of movement.

From top to toe the modern batsman is able to wear the following body armour:

A carbon fibre and Kevlar helmet with face grille, generously padded inside with shock-absorbing sponge. Some helmets even incorporate an inflatable element within, providing further protection and ensuring a snug fit.

A large chest protector pad that is positioned under the left arm of the right-handed batsman and held in place with straps around the upper body and over the right shoulder.

An elbow guard, a forearm guard and batting gloves with thick sausages or slabs of padding to protect the back of the hands and the back of the fingers. Inner cotton gloves are also worn that provide further protection and support, although their main purpose is to absorb sweat, thus assisting the batsman's grip on his first line of defence.

Cricket boxer shorts with a front pouch for the all-important box, about which much has been said already.

A thigh pad and inner thigh pad. These are often worn as one piece of kit that straps around the waist and both thighs. The larger thigh pad protects the outer left thigh of the right-handed batsman while the smaller inner thigh pad protects his inner right thigh.

Leg guards made of reinforced cane rods encased in PVC. These have HDF side wings, vertical bolsters, knee locators and generous low-density padding made from various space-age materials at the back. They are held in place by non-chafing, fully adjustable Velcro straps.

Finally, lightweight, spiked cricket shoes with toughened uppers and reinforced toes.

Close-in fielders and wicket-keepers also wear some of the above kit. Fielding helmets have a specialized fielding grille that protects the throat as well as the face. Wicket-keeping pads are shorter and lighter than batting pads, while wicket-keeping gloves have a padded palm and webbing between thumb and index finger. Unlike batting gloves, which are designed to protect the back of the hands from the ball, wicket-keeping gloves are, of course, designed for safe catching of the ball. The wicket-keeper is the only fielder allowed to wear external leg guards and gloves, and is also advised to wear protective glasses and a helmet, especially when 'standing up' close to the wicket.

The career of South African wicket-keeper Mark Boucher, who holds the current record for most wicket-keeping dismissals in Test matches (555), ended abruptly on 9 July 2012 at the Somerset ground, Taunton, when his left eye was seriously damaged by a bail sent flying by a spin delivery. Believing he was safe against slow bowling, Boucher was wearing neither helmet nor glasses. The career of England and Middlesex wicket-keeper Paul Downton was also abruptly ended when a flying bail hit him in the left eye in 1990.

I once heard of a local wicket-keeper who had his front teeth knocked out by the ball in a village match. As a result of the incident, the captain, a friend of mine, banned the crate of beer the team had been regularly consuming before entering the field of play.

Death toll

In 1946 Cardus wrote, 'The danger of severe physical hurt has almost passed from first-class cricket' (*English Cricket*, p. 16). If there is any truth in this remark – Cardus takes as his evidence the fact that nobody was killed during the Bodyline series of 1932–3 – then the cricket of the older times must have been carnage, because severe physical injury is still relatively common in the game. For sure, with all the protective gear now available, cricket is safer than it has ever been – even the boundary rope is padded these days – but not every injury or even death in cricket can be prevented by protective gear.

In April 2015, a young, highly promising Bengal player, Ankit Keshri, collided with his team-mate, Sourabh Mondal, during a match in Kolkata while attempting to catch a ball hit towards cover. Fielders are supposed to call to prevent such a collision from happening, but sometimes in their enthusiasm even professional cricketers make schoolboy errors.

According to ESPN Cricinfo, 'Mondal's knee crashed into Keshri's head and neck region. As Mondal went down, wincing in pain, Keshri was lying flat and not breathing' (ESPN Cricinfo, 20 April 2015). Attempts to resuscitate Keshri were successful and he was rushed to hospital where he appeared to improve. Sadly, like George Summers in 1870, Keshri died of his injuries three days later. The official cause of death was given as cardiac arrest. Keshri was just 20 years old.

Wicket-keepers blinded by bails, fielders suffering fatal collisions. In these cases it was not the ball that did the damage directly, but as with Stapley's cut hand way back in 1825, it was, in a sense, the little devil that instigated it. Only in a sense, of course, because whatever extravagant animistic narrative it is possible to concoct, the cricket ball does not, after all, have a will of its own, let alone malign intentions. It is subject in part to the will of the players, in part to a multitude of physical conditions. It is enslaved within chains of cause and effect reaching back to the beginning of time itself, to the big bang or God Almighty; to whatever was the uncaused cause of the universe.

As we have seen, the batsman is by far the best-protected player on the field – he needs to be – yet despite all that armour a top-level batsman died as a direct result of being struck by a cricket ball as recently as November 2014.

In 2009, at the age of just 20, Australian batsman, Phillip Hughes, became the youngest player in history to score a century in both innings of a Test match. In 2013 he became the first Australian batsman to score an ODI century on debut. On 25 November 2014, while playing for South Australia at Sydney Cricket Ground, Hughes faced a bouncer from New South Wales fast bowler Sean Abbott. Choosing to attack the bouncer with a hook shot, he mistimed his stroke.

Although Hughes was wearing a helmet, the ball struck him below his left ear at the top of his neck and the base of his skull. A left-handed batsman, Hughes staggered away from the wicket towards the off side before collapsing flat on his face and ceasing to breath. Players and staff ran to his aid and he received mouth-to-mouth resuscitation before being rushed to St Vincent's Hospital, Sydney, where he was placed in an induced coma after undergoing emergency surgery.

The ball had struck his left vertebral artery which carries blood to the brain. The impact caused a rare vertebral artery dissection, a split or tear in the artery wall. This is turn led to a subarachnoid haemorrhage (SAH), bleeding between the lower meninges membranes that enclose and cushion the brain. SAH is a form of stroke caused by interruption of blood supply to the brain and the pressure of internal bleeding upon it. Fifty per cent of SAH cases are fatal, 10–15 per cent of them rapidly so, and survival often involves severe physical and cognitive impairment.

Tragically, Phillip Hughes failed to regain consciousness and died on 27 November 2014, three days short of his 26th birthday. Tributes poured in from fellow cricketers and fans around the world, including those from the then Australian captain and close personal friend Michael Clarke. Hughes's funeral was attended by Australian Prime Minister Tony Abbott, and his ODI shirt, number 64, was retired in remembrance.

With the popularity of Twenty20 cricket encouraging batsmen to attempt riskier shots, the focus of cricket helmet improvement had been on protecting the face. Hughes's fatal accident revealed that the back of the neck had been neglected and that there was no cricket helmet available that would have prevented his injury.

Within a few weeks of the accident, leading cricket helmet manufacturer Hampshire-based Masuri were laboratory testing the 'stemguard'. The device, made of military-specification, high-density foam and shock-absorbing honeycomb plastic, clips onto the back of any Masuri Vision Series helmet, thus shielding the top of the neck behind each ear.

Interviewed by the BBC, Masuri design consultant Alan Meeks said, 'Even though it moves around and will touch the player when the ball hits them, it will absorb a significant amount of energy' ('Phillip Hughes: Cricket Helmets Redesigned After Batsman's Death', BBC Sport: Cricket Website, 11 February 2015).

Stemguards were much in evidence during the 2015 Ashes Test series with several batsmen on both teams choosing to attach one to their helmet. The item could be purchased from reputable cricket retailers as early as August 2015, only nine months after Hughes's death. Hughes suffered a freak and universally unforeseen accident, but hopefully it is now one that can never happen again, at least to a suitably protected batsman.

The deaths of Ankit Keshri and Phillip Hughes are two of the most recent in a series of cricket ball-related fatalities stretching back hundreds of years. We have considered the demise of poor George Summers back in 1870, but the earliest recorded cricket ball-related death was nearly 250 years before that. To be precise, it was actually a cricket bat-related death, but a cricket ball was closely involved, so it is worthy of mention.

A coroner's court of 1624 recorded a verdict of misadventure in relation to the death of fielder Jasper Vinall, who was hit on the forehead with a bat wielded by Edward Tye while attempting a catch during a match at Horsted Keynes, West Sussex. Vinall died of his injury an unlucky 13 days after the incident. The verdict implies that Tye did not deliberately attack Vinall; rather he was simply trying to hit the ball a second time to avoid being caught. At the time, there was no law against the ludicrously dangerous practice of fielder and batsman – fielder and bat – competing for control of an already struck cricket ball.

It was a fatal accident waiting to happen, and sure enough it happened again only 23 years later in 1647, this time at Selsey in West Sussex, when fielder Henry Brand was struck on the head by the bat of Thomas Latter.

Hitting the ball twice was outlawed in 1744 in the earliest known Laws of Cricket. Today, Law 34 severely restricts the circumstances under which a batsman can legally hit the ball twice. Also, a batsman who seeks to prevent a catch by attempting to hit the ball twice is, under Law 37, guilty of wilfully obstructing the field. 'Hit the ball twice' and 'Obstructing the field' are, with certain limited exceptions, both 'methods of dismissal'. To date, no Test batsman has been dismissed 'Hit the ball twice'.

Several cricketers have died of a heart attack suffered on the field of play, and at least two have died on the rest day of first-class matches they were playing in for reasons not related to the match itself. As these are not cricket ball-related fatalities they do not concern us; suffice to say that the two documented deaths that occurred on the rest day of first-class matches constitute perhaps the strangest coincidence in the history of cricket. I cannot now resist telling the story.

In 1934, Worcestershire player Maurice Nichol was found dead in his hotel bed the morning after the rest day of a match against Essex at Chelmsford. Five years later in 1939, Worcestershire player Charles Bull died in a car crash on the rest day of the same Chelmsford fixture. To top it all, another Worcestershire player, Syd Buller, who was injured in the same car crash, died of a heart attack in 1970 during a rain break while umpiring at Edgbaston. Make of that what you will.

No one knows exactly how many cricket ball-related deaths have occurred around the world throughout the long history of the game, but the best-known ones, besides those we have already considered, are probably these:

Karachi batsman Abdul Aziz, was struck over the heart in 1959 by a not particularly fast off break that appears to have aggravated a previously undiagnosed heart condition. Still only a teenager, Aziz collapsed unconscious before the next delivery and died before reaching hospital.

Lancashire left-arm bowler Ian Folley was destined to play for England before the so-called yips and an injury to his bowling arm forced him out of top-class cricket in the early 1990s. The yips is the loss of the fine motor skills required to release the ball at the right moment during delivery. It is cricket's most obvious and crushing self-fulfilling prophecy because its main cause seems to be a bowler's anxiety that he will suffer the yips. It appears to afflict left-arm bowlers like Folley more than right-arm bowlers and has ended several top-class careers.

Folley's run of bad luck continued in 1993 when, aged 30, he was hit by the ball under the eye while batting as the club professional for Cumbrian side Whitehaven. He died under anaesthetic at Cumberland Infirmary in Carlisle during a minor operation to repair his perforated eyeball. The hospital finally admitted negligence and liability in a televised apology five and a half years after the tragic incident.

Former Indian cricketer 38-year-old Raman Lamba was struck on the temple by the ball in 1998 while fielding at forward short leg for Bangladeshi club Abahani Krira Chakra. Lamba had declined to wear a helmet. The ball struck his head so hard that it rebounded beyond the wicket-keeper who had to backpedal to catch it. Lamba was able to walk from the field of play but was in a coma by the time he reached hospital. Surgery to remove a blood clot from the left side of his brain was ineffective and a specialist flown in from Delhi diagnosed his condition as terminal. Three days after he was struck his family agreed to switch off his life-support system.

On the 27 October 2013, while batting in a match between Old Selbornians and Fore Hare University at Alice in South Africa's Eastern Cape province, Border cricket team wicket-keeper Darryn Randall collapsed after being struck on the head by the ball while attempting a pull shot. Medical staff at nearby Alice Hospital fought to save the life of the 32-year-old but to no avail.

Princes, umpires and pigeons

No respecter of rank in cricket or society, the cricket ball may even have claimed the life of Frederick Louis, Prince of Wales, son of George II and father of George III. An enthusiastic player and patron of the game, as well as president of the aforementioned London Cricket Club, Frederick died in 1751 of a burst abscess in his lung which some accounts claim was caused by a cricket ball striking him in the side. Then again, the abscess may have been caused by a real tennis ball or no ball at all. The Scottish poet, novelist and historian Tobias Smollett has it that Frederick simply died aged 44 of a 'pleuritic disorder' suffered 'in consequence of a cold caught in his garden at Kew' (quoted in Barty-King, *Quilt Winders and Pod Shavers*, p. 56).

Batsmen and fielders are not the only people on the field of play, and certainly umpires have not escaped the ravages of the cricket ball. The bowler's end umpire is forever in the line of fire of the straightest of straight drives and therefore must always be ready to duck his helmetless head out of the way of the ball or simply step aside.

Evasive tactics, however, proved ineffective in the case of 55-year-old umpire Hillel Awaskar, who was struck on the neck by a driven ball that ricocheted off the bowler's-end stumps during a match at Ashdod, Israel, in 2014. Awaskar, former captain of Israel, suffered a heart attack after being struck by the ball and died later in hospital. Bizarrely, the tragic incident occurred on 29 November 2014, only two days after the death of Phillip Hughes.

In 2009, 72-year-old Alcwyn Jenkins died after being hit by the ball on the right side of his head while umpiring a match between Swansea and Llangennech. The ball was thrown by fielder Stephen Davies, who was attempting a run-out. Davies retrieved and returned the ball in one motion, throwing it at the stumps before he had time to realize that Jenkins was in the way and had his back to him as he manoeuvred into position to make his judgement. Warnings were shouted but Jenkins either did not hear them, did not have time to react to them or did not want to take his experienced umpire's eyes of the wicket and the popping crease. Jenkins died in the line of duty centrally involved in the game he loved. A good death as deaths go.

With all due respect to those who have paid cricket's ultimate price, I would like to end this gruesome chapter on a slightly lighter note; lighter unless you happen to be a certain Yorkshire pigeon. The canine death by cricket ball of c. 1818 may be apocryphal, but the pigeon death by cricket ball of 2009 is certainly not. The irrefutable evidence, Sky Sports 1 footage, is there on YouTube for all the world to see.

While fielding for Yorkshire against Lancashire in a Twenty20 match at Headingley, South Africa's Jacques Rudolph accidentally hit a pigeon in flight as he threw a white ball in from the deep. The freak, one-in-a-million airstrike killed the bird instantly as ball and bird collided head on. A Sky Sports commentator wittily described the throw as having 'about as much accuracy as a patriot missile'.

Acknowledging the cheers of the crowd, Rudolph calmly walked in, picked the pigeon up by its legs and deposited it over the boundary before returning to his fielding position in the deep to await the next ball and its potential dangers.

Thine are these orbs of light and shade;
Thou madest Life in man and brute;
Thou madest Death; and lo, thy foot
Is on the skull which thou hast made.

ALFRED LORD TENNYSON, *In Memoriam A. H. H.*

Sixth Delivery

Cricket Ball Fame

The cricket ball, as was noted at the start of this book, is like fire: a good servant and a bad master. The previous chapter shows the extent to which it is a cruel and unforgiving master. This chapter shows how great mastery *with* the ball for bowlers, and great mastery *over* the ball for batsmen and fielders, has led to lasting fame and glory for individual players and entire teams.

As the cricket ball has happily produced far more fame and glory over the centuries than it has produced serious injury and death, this chapter can only offer a flavour of cricket ball fame; can only consider some of the outstanding cricketers, cricket performances and cricket moments worthy of mention. I can only apologize in advance if your own personal favourite is not included in this overview, although I am sure that any cricket lover will find more than enough to marvel at in all the cricketing wonders that are included.

Although there are, of course, outstanding players and achievements in all formats and at all levels of the game, this chapter is restricted largely to a consideration of Test-match players and achievements. This restriction is partly for the sake of brevity, but the main reason is that Test matches usually showcase the world's finest players at any one time, put mercilessly to the test against one another in the most comprehensively demanding of cricket arenas.

Sadly, except for Ashes series, Test-match crowd numbers are currently falling as busy people increasingly favour shorter forms of the game. This has led some pundits to express concerns for the long-term future of Test matches. But surely what the philosopher Voltaire said about God is also true of Test matches: if they did not exist it would be necessary to invent them. Without Test matches cricket would be only a partially formed game, a game that restricted its own infinite possibilities and prevented the fullest realization of the talents of its best players.

If pink ball, day–night Test matches and other commercially driven initiatives, such as the excellent but currently shelved plans for a World Test Championship, fail to make the supreme format more lucrative, then it must continue to be subsidized by shorter forms of the game. Twenty20 cricket, tasty snack though it is, is mere junk food in comparison with the fine cuisine of Test-match cricket and can serve no higher purpose than helping to fund Test-match cricket. This may sound like snobbery and elitism, but it is really no more than the reasonable expectation that a mere limb of the body protect the head and brain of the body from decapitation.

Well done to the excellent county players and the big hitters of boisterous, knockabout, razzmatazz Twenty20 tournaments, national and international, but what every cricket connoisseur and purist wants to know about a player doing well in these lesser professional formats is: how would this player fare in a Test match, or in a whole series of Test matches? How good is he over a prolonged period of time against the toughest opposition a nation can muster, and what is the true extent of his skill set, defensively as well as offensively? Does he have the stamina to match his strength, the brains to match his brawn, the character to match his bravado, the patience to match his enthusiasm? Only Test matches can establish the true worth of a professional cricketer. Only Test matches can discover and reveal the state of the art of the cricket art form.

Geoffrey Boycott, whose mastery over the cricket ball led him to 22 Test centuries, made the very valid point recently on BBC *Test Match Special* that 'County cricket is not Test cricket'. Many good players at the county or even ODI level simply do not transfer successfully to the Test-match arena.

To be called up to the Test side a player must be a very good player and at the height of his form so far, but to survive in the Test side a player must be, or must rapidly become, a great player. Once the Test format emerged in the latter half of the nineteenth century – the first Test match was played between Australia and England at Melbourne in March 1877 – surviving and thriving in a Test side over a period of years soon became the only way in which a player could hope to take his place among the greatest players in the history of the game. Genius is as genius does.

Great players, stats and performances

The names of several of the greatest cricketers of all time have already found their way into these pages, from early pioneers such as John Small and Alfred Mynn, through twentieth-century legends such as Donald Bradman and Michael Holding, to twenty-first-century greats such as James Anderson and Alastair Cook who, as I write, are busy re-writing the record books.

James Anderson became England's leading Test wicket taker in April 2015 when he overtook the previous record of 383 Test wickets set by Ian Botham in February 1992. England bowler Stuart Broad also overtook Botham's record in August 2017. On 8 September 2017, during the third Test between England and West Indies at Lords, Anderson became only the sixth bowler in history to achieve 500 Test wickets. Taking nine wickets in the match he rapidly moved on to 506 Test wickets as he closed in on the career tally of 519 Test wickets set in April 2001 by renowned West Indies fast bowler Courtney Walsh. Anderson overtook Walsh during the 2017–18 five-match Ashes Test series in Australia, one of few golden moments for England in a series where Australia hammered them 4–0.

If and when Anderson reaches 564 Test wickets he will become the most successful fast bowler of all time in terms of Test wickets taken, exceeding the awesome tally of 563 Test wickets set in January 2007 by Australia's Glenn McGrath. Anderson will still, however, be a long way short of spinners Muttiah Muralitharan and Shane Warne, with their 800 and 708 Test wickets apiece.

Anderson took his place among the top ten Test wicket takers of all time on 13 October 2015 in the first test between Pakistan and England at Abu Dhabi, the same day that Alastair Cook became England's leading Test catcher (non-wicket-keeper). Meanwhile, Younis Khan broke Javed Miandad's 22-year-old record of 8,832 Test runs to become Pakistan's leading Test run-scorer. Khan exceeded 10,000 Test runs in April 2017, just prior to retiring from Test cricket a few weeks later.

In the same Abu Dhabi Test, on the following days, Cook achieved a first innings score of 263 runs, completing the third longest innings by time in Test history, the longest to date by an English batsman. Test statistics march ever on and each Test and each Test player is forever intimately linked by the stats to every other Test and every other Test player. Test cricket is on ongoing, ever growing epic.

Apart from being a stats-fest, the 2015 Abu Dhabi Test nearly became a desert classic, or at least nearly produced a remarkable result given the context established during the first four days. After the following big first innings totals – Pakistan 523–8 declared, England 598–9 declared – Pakistan's second innings collapsed on the final day. England were set a target of just 99 runs in the third and final session. They chased it to within 25 runs, Twenty20 style, before the match became a classic case for pink ball advocates by ending in a draw due to bad light. Cook was awarded Man of the Match.

Cook has now accumulated far more Test runs than any other English batsman. On 30 May 2016, on the fourth day of the second Test between England and Sri Lanka at Chester-le-Street,

Durham, Cook became the first English batsman to exceed 10,000 Test runs. By January 2018 he had exceeded 12,000 Test runs, although a string of poor performances following his reaching of that milestone meant that by May 2018 he had only moved on to 12,099 Test runs. Graham Gooch, who retired from Test cricket in 1995, is currently England's second highest scoring batsman with 8,900 Test runs. Cook has also hit more Test centuries than any other English batsman, 32 as of January 2018. One other remarkable figure that is forever enshrined in the annals of cricketing excellence is Cook's phenomenal 766 runs in 7 innings in 2010–11 to secure England's first Ashes series win in Australia in 24 years.

Cook is still, however, a long way short of India's legendary Sachin Tendulkar, who retired in 2013 having accumulated an awesome 15,921 runs and 51 centuries in his Test career; far more runs and six more centuries than any other player in the history of Test cricket. His online batting tutorials, *Padding Up with Sachin*, are like taking lessons from Leonardo da Vinci on how to wield a paint brush. His teaching style is as elegant as the strokes he demonstrates.

Tendulkar's record is likely to stand for a long time if not forever, with the closest figures to his being those of former Australian captain Ricky Ponting, who ended his Test career the year before Tendulkar on 13,378 runs. A massive achievement in itself, quite apart from his 41 Test centuries, but nonetheless 2,543 runs short of Tendulkar's monumental record. In third place, South Africa's Jacques Kallis, who retired in 2013, scored 13,289 Test runs, but managed to include four more centuries than Ponting. Having said all this, Cook could conceivably take Tendulkar's record. The Indian press, doubtless steeling itself for the worst well ahead of time, acknowledged as much after Cook scored 243 runs during the first Test between England and the West Indies at Edgbaston in August 2017.

All I can say, in the absence of a crystal ball, is that Test records are being matched and broken all the time. On 25 August 2017, in the second test between England and West Indies at Headingley, young England captain Joe Root achieved half-centuries in 12 consecutive Tests, matching the record previously set by South African superstar AB de Villiers. Currently only 27, Root is already a great player, and certainly a candidate to become an all-time great player.

As to fielding, the current record for the most number of catches in a Test career goes to aforementioned, bail-blinded wicket-keeper Mark Boucher, who caught 532 of his 555 dismissals, the other 23 dismissals being, of course, stumpings.

As wicket-keepers are at a distinct advantage when it comes to taking catches, the statisticians list the most non-wicket-keeper catches separately. Between 1996 and 2012, India's Rahul Dravid took a record-breaking 210 Test catches. A batsman by trade, Dravid also has the fourth highest number of Test runs: 13,288 – just one run behind Kallis.

In the history of Test matches, only three non-wicket-keepers have taken 200 or more catches, including Sri Lanka's wonderfully named Denagamage Proboth Mahela de Silva Jayawardene, with 205, and that man again, Kallis, with 200. Ponting retired needing just four more catches to join the exclusive 200 club. These figures are a testament to the awesome patience of fielders as they carry out their essential but largely thankless task. Even 210 Test catches does not seem that many for all those long days standing in the field ... waiting. Then again, to put Dravid's achievement into perspective, it can be said that he dismissed the equivalent of 21 Test batting sides with catches alone. As a bowler he took only one Test wicket.

Very good career figures tend to require regular selection and longevity of top-class career, and certainly regular selection and longevity of top-class career are indicators of a player's greatness. Overall career figures do not lie. They are certainly not, however, the whole story. In assessing greatness we have also to consider the opposition a player was up against. When a player scored a double century not out or took eight wickets in an innings, was he up against a legendary Australian or West Indies side, or was he, with all due respect, taking advantage of a relatively novice Bangladeshi side with newly acquired Test status? For the record, Bangladesh became the tenth Test playing nation only quite recently, in November 2000, beating England in a Test match for the first time in October 2016.

Not surprisingly, all the players with the very best Test career figures have produced outstanding performances on occasion, in an innings, a match or a series. That is, they were not merely boringly consistent over a long period of time, although there is, of course, much to be said for consistency.

A Test team would, for example, give anything for a batsman who scored 60 runs every innings. Such consistency would in fact be a form of greatness – it would give him the current seventh highest Test batting average of all time – but it would, nonetheless, be frustrating to him and to everyone else that he never scored a century, and he would be widely viewed as an underachiever. We might also accuse him of failing to fully entertain. Cricket is, after all, showbiz, and great cricketers tend to be great crowd pleasers.

The point is, a great performance or two against the toughest opposition, especially when his team are 'up against it', will establish a player's fame in the game as much if not more than great career figures. Some players are legends of the game on the basis of one or two outstanding performances.

Consider Jim Laker, for example. In terms of number of Test wickets taken, he is somewhat down the list of English bowlers, and way down the list of all bowlers. However, by taking 19 wickets for 90 runs in the fourth Test against Australia at Old Trafford in 1956 – 9/37 in the first innings and 10/53 in the second – Laker immediately became immortal within the game and established himself as one of its enduring legends. As John Woodcock says in *The Times One Hundred Greatest Cricketers*, where he places Laker at number 70:

> If cricket is played for another thousand years Jim Laker's nineteen wickets for ninety runs for England against Australia at Old Trafford in 1956 will surely remain the most remarkable Test bowling analysis ever recorded. It made him, overnight, one of the legends of the game.
>
> *The Times One Hundred Greatest Cricketers*, #70

Very incidentally, the one wicket that Laker did not take was taken by Tony Lock, who had to be content with match figures of 1/106. To give him his due, Lock is currently ranked a very respectable number 19 on the list of England's leading Test wicket takers.

The only other 10-wicket haul in a Test innings was achieved by India's almost unplayable leg spinner Anil Kumble against Pakistan at Delhi in 1999. Kumble's remarkable second innings figures of 10/74 were only a little more expensive than Laker's second innings figures, but in the first innings Kumble could only muster a respectable 4/75, a mere 14 wickets in total. With respect to Kumble, there are 18 bowlers who have achieved better Test match figures than his best, including, of course, Laker.

There are actually 19 performances on the list above Kumble, but remarkably two of them are by the same bowler. Legendary England bowler Sydney Barnes achieved figures of 17/159 in 1913 against South Africa at Johannesburg – the second best Test-match bowling figures of all time – and in 1914, just a couple of Test matches later in the same series, figures of 14/144 at Durban. Woodcock places Barnes number six on his list of all-time greatest cricketers.

A moody Midlander who earned good money in Saturday league matches, Barnes was often passed over for Test selection because of his antagonistic character. Woodcock sums him up well when he says that to the South African batsmen of 1913–14 his 'unfailingly accurate' fast-medium bowling was 'a living nightmare' (*The Times One Hundred Greatest Cricketers*, #6).

The highest scoring individual batting performance in the history of Test cricket is Brian Lara's 400 not out for the West Indies against England in the fourth Test at Antigua in 2004.

There are images of Lara kissing the pitch after breaking the previous record of 380 runs set only the previous year by Australia's Matthew Hayden against Zimbabwe at Perth.

Although impressive, Lara's 400 not out is certainly not the single most remarkable batting performance in the history of Test cricket. Significantly, unlike Hayden's performance, it did not win his team the match. Although England, who batted second, were forced to follow on after they achieved only 285 runs in reply to West Indies 751–5 declared, the match ended in a draw with England on 422–5 in their second innings. The fact that three other players also made centuries in the match, two of them not-out centuries, suggests that it was, to say the least, a good batting strip.

The match was also a dead rubber with England having already won the previous three games in the four-match series. Even with the best will in the world, England's bowlers were not exactly fired up, which gave Lara the ideal opportunity to showcase his prestigious talent and to break Hayden's recently set record.

The greatest batting performances are achieved on difficult, sticky wickets against the sternest, fired up opposition, when the fact that both teams still have everything to play for ensures maximum pressure. Perhaps the greatest batting performance is that of an opening batsman who carries his bat throughout an innings on a difficult wicket against hostile bowling as the rest of his team collapse around him, especially if his performance snatches victory from the jaws of defeat. Perhaps it is not an individual performance at all but a partnership, a couple of tailenders wagging the tail for 100 decisive runs when the top and middle order have been skittled out for next to nothing.

The point is that context is everything. Truly great performances with bat or ball are forged in adversity. What figures and statistics do not always show is how difficult it was, under the circumstances, to score that century or take those five wickets, or even to score those 15 runs or take that one wicket.

In his excellent foreword to John Woodcock's *The Times One Hundred Greatest Cricketers*, Mike Brearley says:

> The cricketer we call 'great' may earn this term because of his ability to master conditions in which ordinary, first-class players can only struggle, desperately trying to survive. I think of Hobbs, who on good pitches would often give his wicket to the most deserving of the professional bowlers so as to give others a chance, but on difficult pitches, against the better bowlers, knew 'that was the time you had to knuckle down and make a century if you could . . . that was the time you had to earn your living. After all, Surrey paid me to make runs; not just runs when we didn't need them, but runs when we did need them.' Or I think of Compton, whose genius evoked awe in his team-mates: Titmus and Bennett used to say of Compton's innings of 150 against Sussex on a drying pitch at Lord's, out of a total of around 200, that he played shots that you would have said were impossible on such a pitch.

> *The Times One Hundred Greatest Cricketers*, p. vi

A word or two now on great players, stats and performances in women's cricket. Women's cricket has exploded in popularity in recent years but it is by no means a new phenomenon. The first recorded women's cricket match took place way back in 1745 between, in the words of *The Reading Mercury* of 26 July of that year, 'eleven maids of Bramley and eleven maids of Hambledon, all dressed in white'. The first women's Test match took place at Brisbane in 1934, with England beating Australia by nine wickets.

As audiences keen to watch women play shorter formats of the game have rapidly increased, so the playing of women's Test cricket has actually declined. Women have always played far less Test cricket than men, and very rarely outside of England, Australia and New Zealand. As a consequence, women's Test career figures are simply not comparable to those of men, and indeed should not be compared. As cricket journalist and former Indian cricketer Snehal Pradhan says, 'Women's cricket is pushing the envelope of its own existence. It is on the upward curve, it is a better sport than ever before if you would bother to put it up on its own pedestal, not side by side with the men' (*Firstpost*, 24 June 2017).

Pradhan wrote these remarks in response to men, some of them sadly professional cricket pundits, who repeatedly ask her who is the fastest woman bowler, then proceed to sneer at the answer because the fastest female bowler is significantly slower than the fastest male bowlers. For the record, Cathryn Fitzpatrick of Australia, who retired from international cricket in 2006, is recognized as the fastest woman bowler. She bowled at up to 77.67 mph (125 km/h).

Like other traditionally male-dominated sports, cricket is, I believe, rapidly cleansing itself of sexism, but it still has a long way to go before it is as free of sexism as, say, athletics. Do we ever, except when specifically contemplating differences in physiology, compare the world's fastest female sprinters with the world's fastest male sprinters? The answer is 'No', because we put women's running up on its own pedestal.

Betty Wilson, who played Test cricket for Australia in 1947–8 and 1957–8, became the first Test cricketer, man or woman (comparison!), to score a century and take ten wickets in the same Test match. This match, which took place in Melbourne in February 1958, actually saw Wilson take 11 English wickets, with remarkable bowling figures of 7/7 in the first innings and 4/9 in the second. ESPN Cricinfo describes Wilson as 'one of women cricket's greatest players, and her tag as the female Bradman is not untoward'. There goes the comparison with men again but this is surely another good one.

The best single-innings bowling figures in women's Test cricket belong to Neetu David of India who took 8/53 against England at Jamshedpur in November 1995. As for batting, the highest number of individual runs in an innings in a women's Test match is 242, scored by Pakistan's peerless Kiran Baluch against West Indies at Karachi in March 2004. In the same match, Pakistan captain Shaiza Khan took a record 13 wickets, including a hat-trick.

The women's record for the most runs in a Test career currently belongs to England's Janette Brittin, who made 1,935 runs, including an unrivalled five Test centuries, in the 27 Tests in which she played between 1979 and 1998. This achievement will almost certainly not be beaten unless the current decline in the amount of women's Test cricket played is reversed. There is no woman currently playing cricket who is anywhere near rivalling Brittin's Test career run total. Brittin also played in four more Tests than any other woman, with England's Charlotte Edwards achieving a total of 23 Tests and England's most famous woman cricketer, Rachael Heyhoe Flint, achieving a total of 22 Tests.

For several years Brittin also held the highest tally of women's ODI runs, 2,121, until she was finally surpassed by Charlotte Edwards in 2003. Brittin died of cancer in 2017 aged only 58. Writing Brittin's obituary in the *Guardian* on 19 September 2017, Peter Mason noted that Edwards, who idolized Brittin, belonged to the modern generation of 'trousers and Twenty20', while Brittin and Heyhoe Flint were among the greats of 'the be-skirted days' of women's cricket.

Baroness Rachael Heyhoe Flint OBE, who died aged 77 on 18 January 2017, played cricket for England from 1960 to 1982 and captained England from 1966 to 1978. She led England to victory in 1973 in the first ever Women's Cricket World Cup. She was also the first woman to hit a six in a Test match, but perhaps her most remarkable achievement in cricket came in 2004 when she became the first woman to be elected onto the MCC Committee.

It was only in 1999, after over 200 years of resistance, that the MCC finally abandoned seeing itself as a men's club as well as a cricket club, and welcomed its first women members into the hallowed Long Room at Lord's. As a player, and later as a House of Lords politician, Heyhoe Flint worked tirelessly to promote the cause of women's cricket. She did more than anyone else to break through various glass ceilings of sexual discrimination within the game of cricket as a whole and contributed hugely towards making women's cricket the exciting, dynamic, alluring, rapidly growing phenomenon it is today. To make a further *good* comparison with the men's game, Heyhoe Flint's pioneering achievements have led to her being widely described as the W. G. Grace of women's cricket. High praise indeed. More on W. G. Grace shortly.

A cricketer is arguably less reliant on pure physical power than, say, a footballer or a rugby player, and cricket is certainly a game where skill, technique, agility, reflex, quick wittedness, cunning, deception, tactics and strategy can make *all* the difference. It is therefore the ideal field game for women and girls, of whatever physical build, to take up and excel at, and many are doing so, attracting in their wake an ever increasing number of spectators of all sexes and an ever increasing amount of coverage and sponsorship.

When England beat New Zealand to win the 1993 Women's World Cup Final at Lord's, the crowd numbered just 4,500. When England beat India to win the 2017 Women's World Cup Final at Lord's, the ground, with its capacity of 30,000, was completely sold-out, with millions more around the world watching on TV or listening on the radio. On that day, 23 July 2017, amid scenes of high drama, England's Anya Shrubsole MBE snatched victory from India by nine runs when she took five wickets in 22 balls and played a crucial role in the run-out of Shikha Pandey. Shrubsole was awarded Player of the Match for her priceless overall contribution. She did not bat but her final bowling figures were 6/46 off 9.4 overs.

The perfect showcase of just how exhilarating and cool women's cricket can be, this thrilling match has already been widely hailed as a watershed moment, significantly raising the profile of the women's game and the celebrity status of its star players. England's women cricketers went on to win the BBC Sports Personality Team of the Year Award 2017, at the same time as their male counterparts where being humiliated in the 2017–18 Ashes Test series in Australia. To top it all, to the sound of another cricket glass ceiling breaking, Shrubsole, in April 2018, became the first woman in its 155-year history to feature on the famous primrose yellow front cover of *Wisden Cricketers' Almanack*. This achievement is likely to be repeated, given the amount of awesome young female cricketing talent that is emerging around the world.

In saying earlier that cricket is much deeper than 'a mere visual spectacle' I did not mean to suggest that the visual spectacle is unimportant – far from it. One only has to see Lord's in all its splendour on the first day of the first Test of the season – the bright blue sky with a few high cumulus clouds, the glossy, crowded stands, the pristine, green chequered field, the athletic, suntanned players in their gleaming whites arranged so carefully upon its wide expanse, the blood-red, gold-flecked ball at the heart of the panorama – to realize that cricket is pure aesthetics, a landscape painting in motion, an HD, Technicolor movie showing a sublime regularity of graceful movement punctuated with captivating, all-action unpredictability. The movement, of course, belongs to the players; the movement *is* the players. Bat and ball are an extension of their will. And all this movement is deeply pleasing to the eye, to the soul, to primal instincts that value agility as an essential human survival mechanism.

Only the most sad and sedentary sofa spud would not delight in the sight of a great, diving catch, a hook for six or a bowler beating the bat to send the smooth stumps flying. I have watched all day willing the wicket of Ricky Ponting, Graeme Smith or some other opposition batting genius to fall, while at the same time finding myself thoroughly entertained and gratified by their pure artistry with the bat, the recurrent, highly refined movements of their entire body and the sporting genius with which they repeatedly master the ball and the will of 11 hostile men.

C. L. R. James is quite right to argue that the greatness of most of the greatest cricketers is based, not least, on the grace and elegance of their physical performance as they push the limits of the physically possible. In writing this book I watched certain great cricket deliveries, shots, stops and catches again and again, in order to get the description of them right, and again and again the sheer physical brilliance of them made me laugh with delight.

I cannot, for example, think of Alastair Cook, most famous as a batsman, without thinking of him against Australia in 2015, diving full stretch backwards, horizontal in mid-air, catching a ball in one far outstretched hand, a ball he has just parried up with his finger tips in order to slow it down. This is artistry as great as that of the greatest musicians and painters. Like a great painting or a great piece of music, such feats etch themselves in the memory, and these days, if the memory fades a little, there is always the replay. Cricket and the super-slow-motion replay were made for each other.

Some players who do not feature at the very top of the all-time rankings, who may not even be famous for a decisive performance, are nonetheless famous for the general elegance of their play; the *style* with which they played. For example, pundits still become dewy-eyed when recalling the relaxed technical brilliance, lazy elegance and effortless poise of the subtle strokeplay of England batsman David Gower.

For his part, and for complex reasons, Mark Ramprakash underperformed for England in statistical terms, but his batting, at its confident best, is fondly remembered by all cricket lovers as being poetry in motion; a display of master craftsmanship far more significant than the mere result of a match. It is not surprising that in 2006 Ramprakash had the strength, control, coordination and rhythm to win the BBC dance competition *Strictly Come Dancing*. England bowler Darren Gough won the same dance competition the year before.

Back in the nineteenth century, manager and captain of the All-England Eleven William Clarke extolled the virtues of his star batsman Joe Guy with the famous words, 'All ease and elegance, fit to play before the Queen in her majesty's parlour' (quoted in Gideon Haigh, 'The Gold Standard', ESPN Cricinfo, 29 November 2010).

Great cricket writers such as John Arlott, Simon Hughes and Neville Cardus have waxed even more lyrical than Clarke in seeking to convey the allure, romanticism and aesthetic power of cricket and cricketers.

In his *Book of Cricketers*, Arlott writes at length about the bowling of England's Maurice Tate. Through a detailed analysis of the technical features of Tate's bowling, Arlott manages to transcend sport science to convey a sense of the awe-inspiring, almost God-given loveliness of Tate's bowling action.

> You would hardly have called Maurice Tate's physique graceful, yet his bowling action remains – and not only for me – as lovely a piece of movement as even cricket has ever produced.... All these things the textbook will tell you to do: yet no one has ever achieved so perfectly a co-ordination and exploitation of wrist, shoulders, waist, legs and feet as Maurice Tate did. It was as if bowling had been implanted in him at birth, and came out – as the great arts come out – after due digestion, at that peak of greatness which is not created – but only confirmed – by instruction.
>
> *Book of Cricketers*, p. 12

In developing his detailed philosophical thesis that cricket is an art form, and a high one at that, C. L. R. James analyses at length Arlott's analysis of Tate's bowling. He is led to the telling conclusion that, 'There have been many bowlers whose method of delivery has seemed to spectators the perfection of form, irrespective of the fate which befell the balls bowled' (*Beyond a Boundary*, p. 273).

In an excellent article in *The Times*, Simon Hughes likens a successful Alastair Cook innings to a sculptor crafting a masterpiece. A Cook century or double century is a thing of beauty because of the masterful control, concentration and care with which he purposefully and relentlessly chips away hour after hour at the block of marble that confronts him. It is as though the century is already there to be had if it can only be carved out of perpetual adversity by supreme artistry.

> He never gets deflected from playing his game. He adheres rigidly to his scoring areas, principally the clip to leg and the cut, he never gets delusions of grandeur and attempts to explore a new avenue. He is a sculptor employing the same implement to chip away relentlessly at the marble – with subtle changes of emphasis, slightly more rotation of the wrist here and there – to create his masterpiece.
>
> *The Times*, 19 October 2015

More than any other writer, Cardus seeks to convey the aesthetic appeal of cricket, constantly comparing the mesmerizing motions of the game to the classical music he knew so well. He was both cricket correspondent and music critic of the *Manchester Guardian* from 1927 to 1940. As is so often the case when contemplating any aspect of cricket, Cardus deserves the last word. Here he is, eulogizing England amateur batsman Reginald Spooner, whose supreme artistry, for Cardus, encapsulated the sublimity, romance and poetry of the most beautiful and refined of games.

> He was the most lyrical of cricketers, and for that reason he had no need to play a long inning to tell us his secret. The only difference between 30 by Spooner and 150 by Spooner was a matter of external and unessential form or duration; the spirit moved him from the very beginning. A rondo by Mozart is just as complete as a symphony by him … and a single stroke by Spooner was likewise a quality absolute, beyond the means

of mensuration or any mathematical means of valuation whatever.... And Spooner's cricket in spirit was kin with sweet music, and the wind that makes long grasses wave, and the singing of Elisabeth Schumann in Johann Strauss, and the poetry of Herrick. Why do we deny the art of a cricketer, and rank it lower than a vocalist's or a fiddler's? If anybody tells me that R. H. Spooner did not compel a pleasure as any compelled by the most celebrated Italian tenor I will write him down a purist and an ass.

Good Days, pp. 74–6

Botham rises from the ashes

One of the most memorable and heroic achievements with bat and ball, forged in the most extreme adversity, is the succession of brilliant performances by England all-rounder Ian Botham in the Ashes Test series of 1981. This series has come to be known as Botham's Ashes, although the huge contribution of England fast bowler Bob Willis should not be overlooked when assessing what was achieved.

England lost the first Test of the series at Trent Bridge and drew the second Test at Lord's, where star player Botham was dismissed for a pair of spectacles (0–0). Jumping before he was pushed, Botham resigned from a short-lived, troubled captaincy in which England had done badly and he had lost form. With Mike Brearley reinstated as captain, England arrived at Headingley for the third Test amid controversy, bad feeling and – with the exception of Botham himself perhaps – universally low expectations.

Free of the burden of captaincy and undoubtedly burning with an odd mixture of devil-may-care abandon, wounded pride and measured fury directed at himself and everyone else, Botham took 6/95 after Australia won the toss and elected to bat. It was not enough to halt Australia's apparently relentless march towards victory, however, and when they declared after tea on the second day they had accumulated a seemingly unassailable 401 runs.

Botham top scored with 50 runs in England's otherwise dismal reply, an innings devastated by the pace of Dennis Lillee and the gnawing accuracy of Terry Alderman. The next highest score was 34 extras and the total a meagre 174. Not surprisingly, Australia enforced the follow-on and put the Champagne on ice. The bookies offered odds of 500–1 on an England win.

Boycott dug in for a tenacious 46 runs off 141 balls after the mighty Graham Gooch went for a duck. England collapsed around Boycott until at a desperate 105–5 Botham entered the fray. So far, Australia had encountered only Botham's slow-burning fuse, but they were about to take the full force of the high explosive.

Boycott's dismissal lbw made it 133–6, then wicket-keeper Bob Taylor came and went with only two more runs added to the total, one of which he scored himself. It was as though Botham was waiting for the older, more conservative batsmen to leave the stage. When young, blond-bombshell Graham Dilley reached the middle, Botham reportedly said to him, 'Right then, let's have a bit of fun'. The comment is the stuff of legend, but then so is everything else about this remarkable match.

Bearded, helmetless, a Spartan warrior at the battle of Thermopylae claiming the glory due to him, Botham rode his luck and played his magnificent, blistering strokes through the remainder of the afternoon and on towards evening. Australia were powerless to stop the ball again and again finding the meat of Beefy's bat and then the boundary.

Young Dilley, Botham's bright, eager lieutenant, supported him superbly until finally he succumbed to Alderman, bowled for an invaluable 56. Chris Old added a useful 29, but more importantly held up his end, until he was bowled by Geoff Lawson. Meanwhile, Botham batted on, seeing it big, entirely in the zone, a man calmly possessed or lucidly high, absolute self-belief backing calm, steely determination. By the close of play he was on 145 not out, having hit 26 fours and one six. He seemed poised to do it all again the next day. There was only one problem. He was running out of partners.

Botham hit one more four on the morning of the final day before Willis was caught by Allan Border off the bowling of Alderman. Botham, the colossus, emerged undefeated on 149 not out. England had scored 356 in their second innings, setting Australia a target of just 130 to win. As Paul Fitzpatrick wrote in the *Guardian* on 23 July 1981, in his famous article 'England Evoke a Golden Age', 'That blistering, sustained attack on the Australian bowling turned the match upside down on Monday afternoon, but in spite of its magnificence it seemed at best a heroic gesture'. But Botham had inspired England, the team and the nation, and another giant of an Englishman was not about to let the cauldron into which Botham had pitched the Aussies go off the boil.

Bob Willis, England's 6 feet 6 inches, fast-bowling, slightly ageing, injury-cursed warhorse was dropped for the Headingley

Test due to concerns over his fitness, but managed to persuade the selectors to reinstate him. Like Botham, he had reason to be indignant and something to prove, although he proved nothing during Australia's first innings, bowling 30 wicketless overs.

Early in Australia's second innings, Willis told Brearley that he was too old now to be bowling uphill into the wind. The great captain duly gave him the downhill slope from the Kirkstall Lane end and everything clicked into place. Assisted by gravity and a decent tailwind, the big man with the big hair thundered in on his exceptionally long run-up to deliver fast, shortish, straight, no-nonsense balls onto a deteriorating pitch.

Botham had dismissed Graeme Wood when Australia were on just 13, but at 56–2 the Aussies looked to be safely on course for victory. With only two more runs added to the score, however, Willis had Australian captain Kim Hughes caught at third slip for a duck by none other than Botham. Only with the benefit of hindsight could the fall of the Australian captain to the Willis–Botham double act be seen as an omen. Hughes was only Willis's second scalp of the match and Australia still had plenty of firepower waiting in the pavilion.

It was when Willis took out Yallop for a duck, third ball he faced, with the score stuck on 58, that the spectre of terminal collapse began to haunt the Australian dressing room, the iced Champagne began to look a little premature and the bookies began to look a little foolish. There was something portentous in the wind that blew the tall poplar trees at the Kirkstall Lane end, an airborne fever that had ignited Botham yesterday and had spread to Willis and the rest of the team today.

Just seven runs later Old bowled Border for nought, bringing legendary Australian wicket-keeper Rodney Marsh to the crease. Australian opener John Dyson had been slightly holding up proceedings for far too long, so Willis had him caught behind. The score was 68–6. Australia crawled through their 70s for the price of two more Willis wickets, the wicket of Marsh falling to a brilliant Dilley pressure catch out at long leg. Catches win matches – I had to utter this great truth at least once – and England's catching was superb that day.

Lower-order batsmen often feel the pressure and anxiety induced by a collapse far less, it being the fault of higher-order batsmen who should have done better that they find themselves in the thick of the action so soon. Tailenders Ray Bright and Dennis Lillee – Woodcock's number 19 greatest cricketer of all time – began to steady the ship. With great intelligence, skill and daring, Lillee repeatedly upper cut Willis's short-pitched deliveries over the slips to the short boundary. Willis finally responded by pitching one up, causing Lillee to miscue into the hands of Mike Gatting at mid on. The score was now 110–9 and the mere 20 runs standing between Australia and victory appeared mountainous.

Most fittingly in this *Boy's Own Annual* tale of derring-do, Australia managed just one more run before Willis secured one of the most remarkable victories in Test history by uprooting Bright's middle stump. Only once before, in 1894, had a side following on won a Test match.

Although Willis ended with career best figures of 8/43, it is a testament to the greatness of the match that he nonetheless failed to claim Man of the Match. That, of course, went to I. T. Botham for his 50, 149 not out, seven wickets, two catches and priceless contribution of Homerically proportioned inspiration.

In the final analysis, this glorious match reveals the extent to which cricket, despite the laurels it grants to talented individuals, is essentially a team game. The match perfectly showcased individual batting and bowling brilliance under great pressure and in the face of huge adversity, but in terms of victory all that individual brilliance would have probably come to nought if any catch that was held had been dropped or the footnote performance of any also-ran player had not occurred. Certainly, without the triumph of the *team*, the awesome performances of Botham and Willis would be far less well remembered than they are and would exist in an entirely different context. Indeed, had anything at all been different from what it was, those awesome performances would have been different from what they were and might never have occurred at all.

> The personal achievement may be of the utmost competence or brilliance. Its ultimate value is whether it assists the side to victory or staves off defeat. This has nothing to do with morals. It is the organizational structure on which the whole spectacle is built.
>
> *Beyond a Boundary*, p. 259

Credit too to the Australians, because a famous victory is only possible through the defeat of famously good opposition – the reason why England's 1981 and 2005 Ashes series wins were so special, while their recent 2015 Ashes series win, despite its entertainment value, was not so special. In 2015, Australia were just not very good. On a final note, before we move on from Headingley 1981, England had to negotiate with Australia to buy that iced Champagne.

With the series squared at 1–1 the circus rolled on to Edgbaston where England again got themselves into trouble. Batting last, Australia slumped to 105–5 but still looked likely to chase down the mere 151 runs they needed for victory. That was until a reluctant Botham was thrown the ball. Exactly why he was reluctant to bowl is unclear. He had had a subdued match up to that point and, despite his achievements at Headingley, perhaps felt that he was not fully back on form. Bob Taylor tells how Brearley had to order Botham during the interval to return to the field in his bowling boots rather than his tennis shoes. He proceeded to rip Australia to shreds in 28 balls taking five wickets for only one run, giving England victory by 29 runs.

At Old Trafford, Botham went for a duck in the first innings only to return in the second to smash a decisive 118 runs, including six sixes, in just over two hours. Australia fought hard to reach the target of 506 runs that Botham had more than helped to set, but they fell short by 104 runs giving England victory by 103 runs and an unassailable lead in the series.

Botham took six wickets in the first innings and four in the second innings of the sixth and final Test of the series at the Kennington Oval which ended in a draw. England won the series 3–1 and Botham, not surprisingly, was declared Man of the Series. His knighthood in 2007 confirmed his status as a national icon. John Woodcock places Botham a very respectable number nine in his list of the one hundred greatest cricketers of all time.

There are more amazing performances, matches and series in the history of cricket than could possibly be considered even in a book that was ten times longer than this one, but the series of Tests known as Botham's Ashes stands out as perfectly representative of the magic that great mastery with and over the cricket ball can produce, particularly in the face of great adversity when victory must be strenuously snatched by undaunted heroes from the jaws of near-certain defeat.

Each great cricket event really deserves a whole book to itself, and indeed whole books have been written about single extraordinary matches or even single extraordinary overs; for example, *500–1: The Miracle of Headingley '81* by Rob Steen and Alastair McLellan. Grahame Lloyd wrote *Six of the Best: Cricket's Most Famous Over*, a book about a single legendary over bowled during a match between Glamorgan and Nottinghamshire at Swansea on 31 August 1968 in which Garry Sobers hit six sixes off the bowling of Malcolm Nash. Lloyd then wrote another book called *Howzat? The Six Sixes Ball Mystery* about the intriguing controversy surrounding which ball was used and which was not. So, if you think the main theme of this book is as specific as it gets, then think again. I will return to the six sixes ball mystery in due course.

Easeful Atlas

John Woodcock was cricket correspondent for *The Times* from 1954 to 1988 and covered over 400 Test matches for the paper – there had only been 1,112 Test matches in all by the end of 1988. He was well placed, therefore, to write *The Times One Hundred Greatest Cricketers*. The selection and ranking is, nonetheless, only his opinion. As Mike Brearley points out, 'Woodcock has laid himself open to differences of opinion with followers of every age and in every region of the world' (*The Times One Hundred Greatest Cricketers*, p. viii). The list has certainly stimulated a great deal of interesting debate and proved invaluable to those who love to pick their all-time best 11 and then argue for it.

As Woodcock himself readily acknowledges, there is in reality no definitive list of greatest cricketers. 'The order in which they are placed, as if on some scholarship roll, is inevitably invidious and essentially provocative. It is essential to the exercise, I am afraid, that all such lists are flawed by sins of omission and commission' (*The Times One Hundred Greatest Cricketers*, p. ix). How, for example, does one compare the greatness of a batsman with the greatness of a bowler, or either specialist with an outstanding all-rounder, or a cricketer of the olden days with a cricketer of the modern era? Nonetheless, many of his choices are surely irrefutable: Victor Trumper, Viv Richards, Garry Sobers, Jack Hobbs, Denis Compton, Walter Hammond, Leonard Hutton, Imran Khan, Kapil Dev, Richard Hadlee, Allan Border.

His ranking is perhaps more debatable. Cricket marches ever on and the list, published in *The Times* in 1997 and in book form in 1998, surely needs to be somewhat updated. Muralitharan, for example, came to prominence too recently to be included, and Tendulkar surely needs to be pushed up the order from a nonetheless respectable number 25. The big question is who gets pushed out as new bright stars dazzle their way in?

The inevitable inclusion in any revised list of Muralitharan, McGrath, Ponting, Kallis, Kumble, Anderson, and one or two other great players of recent times you might care to argue for, would certainly force those at the bottom of the current list out of the picture. Former New Zealand captain John Richard Reid has the distinction of being number 100 on the current list, so would certainly be ousted from any revised list. Even if Reid was demoted by 10 places, however, it would still be an immense achievement to be considered the number 110 greatest cricketer of all time.

The number one greatest cricketer of all time, in Woodcock's considered opinion, is W. G. Grace. Some people, particularly many Australians, thought Woodcock should have chosen Donald Bradman, who is awarded the silver medal spot. W. G. Grace is given top billing not only for his figures and his famous performances, but for the remarkable longevity of his career and his enormous contribution to the development of cricket in general and the art of batting in particular. Woodcock follows Cardus in his high opinion of the great champion. In 1946 Cardus wrote:

> To this day, when his records have been surpassed by the Hammonds and Bradmans and Ponsfords, he still dwarfs them; he is a happy easeful Atlas holding up in his hand, but as though it were a cricket ball, the world in which they enjoy their brief statistical day; for 'W. G.' invented them, so to say;

he created the conditions under which they came into existence at all.

English Cricket, p. 22

William Gilbert Grace was born in 1848 into a cricket-obsessed family. His parents, Henry and Martha, his brothers, his sisters and even the family dogs all had a great enthusiasm for the game. The family would all rise each day at dawn to practise on the excellent pitch Henry had prepared in their Gloucestershire orchard.

Martha, in particular, knew a great deal about cricket. At West Gloucestershire, which the Graces ran almost as a private club, batsmen had to pay their respects to her after they were dismissed so that she could explain to them exactly where they had gone wrong. My own mother was up to playing this role herself. Had Martha lived in the following century she may well have been a professional player, achieving great things with ball and bat alongside the likes of Heyhoe Flint and Brittin.

Martha played a decisive role, alongside her husband and her brother, Alfred Pocock, in expertly coaching W. G. and her other sons. E. M., seven years older than W. G., and Fred, two years younger, both played for Gloucestershire and England. From 6 to 8 September 1880 they played alongside W. G. against Australia at the Kennington Oval in the first ever English Test match.

Like all geniuses, W. G. was the product of a perfect combination of maximum natural gifts, maximum opportunity to develop them almost from birth and maximum encouragement to do so. Before he compelled it to respond to him, Grace was skilful far beyond the standards of his era. In addition, he was supremely athletic, utterly tenacious, tactically brilliant, deviously cunning and fiercely competitive.

He made his career debut for West Gloucestershire on 19 July 1857, the day after his ninth birthday. It was a few years before the boy acquired the strength and reach to have much impact on matches but all the while he gained valuable skills playing with men far above him in age and experience.

He demonstrated such exceptional potential that a month before his 16th birthday in June 1864 he was invited to play for the All-England Eleven against Lansdown. He made a careful 15 in half an hour, batting in partnership with the great John Lillywhite, co-founder of the famous sports department store. The Lillywhites and the Graces were the two great cricketing dynasties of the Victorian era.

In 1865 he made his first appearance for the amateur Gentlemen against the professional Players, 'the fixture that embodied the yawning social gulf that divided the game' (*W. G.: A Life of W. G. Grace*, p. 46). The renowned Gentlemen versus Players fixture, played twice a season at Lord's and the Kennington Oval, had been won by the Players 19 times consecutively since 1854. Grace transformed the fortunes of the Gentlemen who, with him on board, went on to lose only four times between 1865 and 1906.

> He was to dominate the fixture as no one else before or since, scoring 6,008 runs and taking 276 wickets. He made fifteen centuries, more than any other batsman, and frequently carried his team to success on his own shoulders.
>
> *W. G.: A Life of W. G. Grace*, p. 46

By 1865 his rapidly improving all-round performances meant that he was in high demand. 'Everybody wanted the extraordinary youth from Gloucestershire in their team' (*W. G.: A Life of W. G. Grace*, p. 45). The public were no less enthusiastic and clamoured to see the boy wonder in action. Until his retirement in April 1908, aged almost 60, W. G. would remain cricket's major draw. The span of his first-class career is generally given as 1865–1908, an incredible 44 years. He died in 1915 at the age of 67.

W. G. was already 28 when the first Test match was played between Australia and England at Melbourne in March 1877 – he did not take part – and there were far fewer Test matches back then, so his Test figures do not appear high in the overall rankings. He played in 22 Tests altogether – the same number as that other Grace-like pioneer, Rachael Heyhoe Flint – and captained England several times between 1888 and 1899. His first-class figures, however, speak for themselves: 1,478 innings, 54,211 runs, 39.45 batting average, 2,809 wickets, 18.14 bowling average (W. G. Grace, ESPN Cricinfo). In May 1895, aged nearly 47, he reached his hundredth century and accumulated over 1,000 runs during that month alone.

Beyond his figures, beyond even his longevity, was Grace's unsurpassable contribution to the advancement of cricket. 'He was the arch over which the game advanced out of a dim legendary past into authentic and contemporary history' (*English Cricket*, p. 26).

K. S. Ranjitsinhji, an Indian prince and pioneering master batsman who played for England from 1896 to 1902 and alongside Grace, points out, in his *Jubilee Book of Cricket*, that before W. G. Grace batsmen played either a forward game or a back game. Batsmen specialized almost exclusively in their own favourite stroke, defending everything else including the straight ball, which it was considered bad cricket to hit. Recall that before the introduction of the cane-handle bat, only a few decades before Grace began his career, driving the straight ball back the way it had come was to self-inflict bone-jarring agony. Certain shots, such as pulling a slow long hop, were even considered immoral.

Grace changed all this. He turned the leisurely art of batting into a science, deploying every stroke of every batsman that had gone before him. His style did not aim at elegance and beauty, but it was elegant and beautiful in its variety, effectiveness and sheer run-scoring utility. Grace did not invent the wheel but he did, so to speak, invent the full orthodox cricket shots wagon wheel, the spokes of which, listed clockwise for the right-handed batsman, are: leg glance, hook, pull, on drive, straight drive, off drive, cover drive, square drive, square cut, cut, late cut.

What W. G. did was unite in his mighty self all the good points of all the good players, and to make utility the criterion of style. He founded the modern theory of batting by making forward- and back-play of equal importance, relying neither on the one nor on the other, but on both. Any cricketer who thinks for a moment can see the enormous change W. G. introduced into the game. I hold him to be, not only the finest player born or unborn, but the maker of modern batting. He turned the old one-stringed instrument into a many-chorded lyre. And, in addition, he made his execution equal his invention.

The Jubilee Book of Cricket, p. 460

The Jubilee Book of Cricket, with its many drawings and photographs, was compiled for the Diamond Jubilee of Queen Victoria in 1897. Much of this beautiful book, including, probably, the above passage, was written by Ranjitsinhji's friend C. B. Fry. Fry represented England at both cricket and football. He captained the England Cricket Team in 1912. Meanwhile, he established himself as one of the great cricket writers. He was an all-round sporting and academic genius; an athlete, politician, diplomat, editor and publisher who once equalled the world long-jump record and is even reputed to have been offered the throne of Albania.

'The history of cricket is one long battle of wits between batsman and bowler, the groundsman holding the ring' (*English Cricket*, p. 28). Cardus recognizes that Grace's huge success as a batsman was based partly on bowlers having no real answer to his abilities until bowling itself underwent its own revolution. Different bowlers possessed different elements of what was needed in terms of line, length, pace, spin and so on, but the game required an individual who could combine all these elements together, and in so doing apply real pressure to Grace and those who were emulating his style.

That individual was Frederick Spofforth, 'the first authentic modern bowler' (*English Cricket*, p. 28). Spofforth, the next phase in cricket's perpetual and glorious arms race, sailed in from

Australia in 1878 to spearhead an attack that ripped Grace's hitherto invincible MCC to shreds at Lord's in a single day, bowling them out for 33 runs in their first innings and 19 in their second. W. G. Grace was not God after all. God, it had been revealed, was not even an Englishman.

Four years later, in 1882, at the Kennington Oval, Grace opened the batting for an English side that went on to be beaten by Australia by seven runs. It was Australia's first Test victory on English soil. Spofforth took 14 wickets for 90 runs and was chaired from the field. Soon after, the *Sporting Times* published an obituary, 'In Affectionate Remembrance of English Cricket ...' The obituary concluded with a famous line, the origin of the term 'the Ashes': 'The body will be cremated and the ashes taken to Australia.' The real truth of 1878 and 1882, however, was that the English game was far from dead. Instead, it had finally blossomed into a truly international sport, and Grace, in many ways, had been the light source and catalyst for that blossoming.

Grace's success and personal charisma made him a national institution long before the end of his vast career. He still stands with the most eminent of eminent Victorians, a maker of that golden age as much as Charles Dickens, Florence Nightingale or the Queen herself. His appearances drew huge crowds and his great stamina allowed him to be generous to a fault in attending exhibition and benefit matches across the country. In the words of C. L. R. James:

> He was strong with the strength of men who are filling a social need. Every new achievement made a clearing in the forest,

drew new layers of the population, wiped off debts, built pavilions. How warmly the county secretaries and treasurers must have met him at the gates.

Beyond a Boundary, p. 241

Grace has something of a reputation for unsportsmanlike conduct. This reputation was largely forged in those exhibition matches where, for fear of disappointing enormous, expectant crowds paying hard-earned money for that new pavilion or that old player's retirement, some umpires were as reluctant to give him out as he was reluctant to be given out. Hence, the famous, 'Play on. They came to see me bat, not you umpire' (quoted in Steve James, *The Art of Centuries*, p. 127).

Also, as the prototype of the modern batsman, Grace seldom if ever 'walked'. He was too fiercely competitive, too cunning, too steeped in the arts of gamesmanship not to wait to be dismissed on appeal according to the letter of the law. And doubtless his confidence and ability often led him to genuinely believe that he was not out, that he could not possibly have nicked it; that if his stumps went flying it must be because the bowler had overstepped the mark.

A few umpires were undoubtedly intimidated by his reputation and therefore erred too much on the side of caution in responding to appeals for his wicket – perhaps they too believed that W. G. could not really be out – but there is no evidence of him directly overruling an umpire in a non-exhibition match where showcasing his talent was not the main event. Even W. G. did not have the power to do that.

Robert Low tells the story of how Grace once queried a caught and bowled decision because he firmly believed – we have no reason to doubt – that it was a bump ball. He roared the question 'What, George?' at the umpire, who had given the decision in response to an appeal. The umpire, George Burton, who could and perhaps should have stood his ground, immediately changed his mind. Intimidated, Burton then declined an appeal for plumb lbw and an appeal for caught behind. Finally, Essex super-fast bowler Charles Kortright, fired up with indignation, uprooted two of Grace's stumps. 'As he slowly turned to leave the crease, the triumphant Kortright approached and remarked: "Surely you're not going, Doctor – there's still one stump standing"' (*W. G.: A Life of W. G. Grace*, p. 261).

I see here a weak umpire, a Grace whose gamesmanship apparently extended to intimidating weak umpires and a Grace who, like many batsmen, was not in the habit of walking. I see no actual cheating here because if indeed the umpire thought Grace was out then he could have made him go, first, second or third time, and Grace would have had no choice but to have gone. I realize that we have now arrived at the cusp of that most thorny of cricket's perennial ethical debates: 'Is *not walking* cheating?'

I do not think not walking is cheating because it is the umpire's responsibility to dismiss the batsman or not in response to an appeal by the fielding side. It is not the batsman's responsibility to dismiss himself. Some batsmen choose to walk, occasionally under the *misapprehension* that they are out, while others choose not to. It is a matter of personal choice, not a matter of moral obligation.

Given that there is now enough review technology available, at least in top-class cricket, for amicable dismissal decisions to be reached on almost every occasion by those responsible for making them, perhaps there should even be a law that prevents a batsman from walking, a law that spares him from ever feeling obliged to decide for himself. I cannot, however, see how such a law could be enforced because I cannot see what reasonable penalty there could be for breaking it.

Perhaps the Laws of Cricket should state that the batsman is under no obligation to walk and that he can, with a clean conscience, await the decision of the umpire. This, however, would not be a law but a mere recommendation. Arguably, the Laws of Cricket effectively imply that the batsman is under no obligation to walk by not insisting that he is under an obligation to walk. Law 27.1 merely states that a batsman is not debarred from leaving his wicket, which seems to bring us back to walking being a matter of personal choice.

It is part of the infinitely intriguing nature of cricket that it can throw up an issue that so pointedly sets personal choice and pragmatism against what some people view as a matter of moral obligation. As several articles on ESPN Cricinfo and elsewhere suggest, cricket lovers and cricket anoraks, being au fait with the practical and philosophical minutiae of the game, tend to see walking as entirely a matter of personal choice, whereas the popular media, always looking to stir up the kind of moral outrage that sells newspapers, tend to see walking as a moral obligation.

Finally, a word on Grace's bowling. He liked to bowl high-tossed, leg breaks, some of which did not in fact break but fooled the batsman by going straight on. Grace, no doubt, was the forerunner of Shane Warne, a lethal combination of skill, shrewdness and bravado. His formidable reputation preceded him and he had all the same showmanship in creating a sense of foreboding in the batsman's mind, a sense that what was coming next would be bewildering and unplayable. Either that or he would appeal to the batsman's greed, enticing him beyond the limits of his restraint into a stroke as big as it was rash.

> He would run to the wicket, elbows out, huge yellow cap on his head, whiskers blowing in the wind, and he would turn his wrist and emit a grunt indicative of a terrible spin; and the ball would go straight through the air, inviting a mighty hit to leg – where 'W. G.' always had a man ready near the boundary. He 'diddled' hundreds of victims out that way.
>
> *English Cricket*, p. 24

Once, a prudent young man, seeing through Grace's game, refused to be tempted. Rather than slog the Old Man's slow balls through the air and down the throat of a fielder planted in the deep, he tapped them safely along the ground for ones and twos. According to Cardus, after a few overs of the Old Man grunting and twisting, the kid nurdling and tapping, the Old Man lost patience and marched up the pitch, exclaiming: 'Looky here, young feller, if you keep on doing that I'll take myself off I will, I'll take myself off' (*English Cricket*, p. 24). Grace's gamesmanship included a short fuse when it suited him and not liking it at all when others refused to play *his* game.

The Gatting Ball

In contemplating cricket fame we can consider long, glorious careers, the outstanding achievements of a series, remarkable performances within a match, great overs for bowler or batsman or single deliveries of such mind-boggling brilliance that they have become the stuff of legend. These single, legendary deliveries belong to the TV and internet age, where they are bowled ad infinitum in replays, each repeat adding to the cult of that tiny moment in time. The most famous and celebrated of these single deliveries has come to be known as the Gatting Ball, the Ball of the Century, the Ball from Hell or, simply, That Ball.

The Gatting Ball was bowled by Australian leg spinner Shane Warne to England batsman Mike Gatting on 4 June 1993, the second day of the first Ashes Test at Old Trafford. It immediately established Warne as a world-class player; the central force of a devastatingly powerful Australian team that would go on to dominate world cricket for years to come. It also saw the revival of the ancient, near-forgotten art of leg spin after two decades in which Test-match bowling had been almost entirely monopolized by pace.

True to that emphasis, Australia arrived in England in 1993 with a three-pronged pace attack. The lone spinner, Warne, was intended to play very much a supporting role. The 23-year-old Warne had played in 11 Tests up to that point but with only moderate success. His bowling average was then over 30.

Having said this, Australia clearly had some faith in the young man's potential, otherwise selectors would not have included him in the Ashes side when they had so many other talented players waiting in the wings. Australia's wicket-keeper during the 1993 series, Ian Healy, recounts that during the 1992–3 Test series against New Zealand, Warne was getting so much turn that they had to move his line well outside leg stump so that the ball would not miss the bat by 6 inches on the off side. The Gatting Ball reveals that by the English summer of 1993 Warne's line was perfected beyond even the highest hopes of the Australian selectors.

Batting second, England were ticking over nicely against Australia's pace attack, with Gooch and Atherton putting on 71 before Atherton was caught by Healy off the bowling of Merv Hughes, a player famous for his imposing delivery action and for having perhaps the largest moustache in the history of the game. Gatting came to the crease and soon hit a boundary. In response, Australian captain Allan Border called upon Warne to turn his arm and his wrist for the very first time in a Test match against England.

Most onlookers expected the grizzly old warhorse Gatting to give the fresh-faced Warne, with his peroxide-blond hair, bling and sissy sunblock, applied liberally to lips and nose tip, a good spanking for the very insolence of his demeanour. Those more in the know were interested to see if Warne had further developed his technique since the winter and what amount of turn he would achieve with his first Test ball on an English pitch.

Warne's run-up was a stroll of a few paces. It meant a lot to him, he said later, to bowl his first ball against England and he was a bit nervous. His intention was simply to calm his nerves, to find a bit of rhythm and momentum and to get himself into the feel of the game. He certainly did not mean to bowl anything spectacular. That he did bowl something spectacular reveals that he had far more talent than even he realized at the time.

There was also undoubtedly an element of luck in the way the ball turned out; in the way the ball turned. Recall what Warne said in the section on spin bowling, about natural variation being a spinner's best weapon. Whatever its exact ingredients, the ball changed Warne's life in an instant by boosting his confidence and self-belief sky-high for the rest of his illustrious career. He ceased to be 'that blond bloke' and became, instead, the all-time daddy of leg spin.

He says the delivery, bowled right-handed over the wicket, felt pretty good out of his hand. A slowish, reasonably well-flighted ball, it went straight on for at least half the length of the pitch before drifting a good way to the leg side then suddenly dipping. Not enough credit is given to this sudden dip, but in the expert analysis of Tony Greig, it was the dip that began the process to the inevitable by wrong-footing Gatting in terms of the ball's length. Gatting was stranded too far back to even begin to hope to deal with the now mythical rip and turn of the ball.

I say mythical because its degree of turn seems to grow with the years like the size of the fish in the proverbial fisherman's tale. Warne himself has joked that when he is an old man telling the story in the pub the ball will have turned the width of his fully outstretched arms. At the time, level-headed Richie Benaud, who was commentating on the match for the BBC, dismissed as exaggerated claims that the ball drifted 2 feet to the leg side then spun 2 feet back. His own conservative estimate was 9 inches each way. The BBC Cricket website now estimates the turn of the ball to have been 'about 18 inches from where it had pitched', placing the amount of turn, if not the drift, closer to the exaggerated claims that Benaud dismissed than to his own conservative estimate.

Whatever the exact parameters of the trajectory, the ball certainly pitched well outside the line of leg stump, and somewhat outside the line of Gatting himself, who was standing some way to the leg side in readiness for the leg break. It then turned all the way across to the far-distant region of the top of off stump. That the ball ended up striking the wicket in that far-off upper corner also says a lot for how much it climbed again after drifting, dipping and turning.

It was undoubtedly the perfect leg-spin delivery on the perfect occasion, a dream of a ball, an unplayable delivery really, certainly once its dip deceived Gatting as to its length and marooned him so far back. Part of the perfection of the Gatting Ball is that it was bowled *to Gatting*, one of the top 30 highest-scoring English Test batsmen of all time with a formidable reputation for forcing captains to take their spinners off. As Matthew Engel writes on ESPN Cricinfo, 'Gatt murdered spinners'. Had the delivery been bowled to a tailender, with no such reputation, it would not be half so famous.

Gatting's stance was textbook correctness for facing the leg spinner: bat in line with leg stump, a squat, muscular figure with soft hands upon the bat handle, ready to smother to death the spin of the ball as it broke away from the leg side. It is a sort of defence of Gatting to say that despite all this correctness of stance and grip, a certain nonchalance was part of his undoing. He was too fully anticipating a run-of-the-mill leg break, if not a loosener, from the very first delivery of the new kid in town. As Irish pop band and cricket poets The Duckworth Lewis Method joke in their highly amusing ditty 'Jiggery Pokery', Gatting felt he had little reason to fear Australia's new leg spinner and was more interested in contemplating what he would soon be having for lunch.

Gatting liked his food, and like many great batsmen took full advantage of the good centre of gravity afforded by a little rotundity. Batting at the other end, captain Graham Gooch – not exactly Slimmer of the Year himself by that time – later joked that Gatting 'looked as though someone had just nicked his lunch'. Drawing on this wisecrack, Martin Johnson of the *Independent* quipped, perhaps even more wittily, 'How anyone can spin a ball the width of Gatting boggles the mind'.

Gatting had no idea what had hit him, or rather what he had not hit and what had removed his off-side bail. There is an excellent photograph of Gatting looking down at his broken wicket for answers as the Australians celebrate in the background. Healy said later that Gatting seemed to think that 'something suspicious had happened', that he (Healy) had perhaps removed the off-side bail with his gloves.

As Gatting set off towards the pavilion he asked square-leg umpire Ken Palmer for confirmation, which Palmer gave with a raised eyebrow and a little nod. Benaud captured the mood of Gatting's departure perfectly when he said, 'Gatting has absolutely no idea what has happened to it. He still doesn't know.' Much has been made of Gatting looking stunned and so on, but really as he left the now famous scene he simply looked world-wearily resigned to some fate he did not as yet fully understand, rather than profoundly bewildered.

It is better to have bowled the Gatting Ball than to be the guy who received it and gave it its name, but as Oscar Wilde stresses, 'There is only one thing in the world worse than being talked about, and that is not being talked about' (*The Picture of Dorian Gray*, p. 6). Magnanimously, Gatting later made it clear that he felt it was good to be a part of cricket history and to have been beaten so thoroughly by 'probably the best leg spinner of all time' rather than by some obscure, also-ran bowler. In the chorus of 'Jiggery Pokery', The Duckworth Lewis Method portray a far less magnanimous Gatting, a batsman willing to accuse the Aussies not only of jiggery-pokery, but also of skulduggery, robbery and muggery. The song concludes with Gatting loudly declaring that he hates Shane Warne.

Another feature of the Gatting Ball was that England never really recovered from it, in that first match or for the rest of the 1993 Ashes series. Warne had Robin Smith caught at slip a few balls later with a very similar delivery, equally good in fact but hardly remembered now. By the end of his first Test-match bowling spell in England, Warne had figures of 3/14 off nine overs. By the close of play that day, England had lost eight wickets for a mere 122 runs. 'What a Shane!' exclaimed the *Daily Express* the following morning.

That summer, Warne went on to take 34 wickets at a cost of 25.79 runs apiece and was made Man of the Series. Australia won the series 4–1.

The Strauss Ball

Just about the only other *delivery* in cricket famous enough to have its own name is the Strauss Ball, not to be confused with an evening of waltzing to the music of Johann Strauss. The Strauss Ball was bowled by that man again, Shane Warne, to England opener and later captain Andrew Strauss on day two of the second Ashes Test at Edgbaston on 5 August 2005. The delivery was the extraordinary centrepiece of an epic struggle between two highly talented, motivated and evenly matched sides.

England had lost the previous eight Ashes Test series against Australia, their last series win having taken place nearly two decades earlier during their 1986–7 tour Down Under. England had, however, won their previous five non-Ashes Test series, so expectations were higher than they had been for years. These high hopes were soon dashed when Australia won the first Test at Lord's by 239 runs.

In unexpectedly winning the Edgbaston battle royal that followed less than two weeks later, by just two runs, England turned the tide, not only of the series but of the previous two decades. The remarkable five-match series ended 2–1 to England. The fact that England managed to overcome a team that had a bowler such as Shane Warne in it, a man that could perform the wizardry of the Strauss Ball, is a measure of the size of their achievement.

Every winning team needs a little initial luck. England's came in the form of Australia's other star bowler, Glenn McGrath, tripping on a cricket ball during warm-up and being ruled out of the match with a twisted ankle. Australian captain Ricky Ponting won the toss and put England into bat. In choosing to bowl first, Ponting was allowing himself to be influenced by the outcome of the vast majority of Tests at Edgbaston since 1991. For his part, England captain Michael Vaughan knew the actual pitch was not the historical one and could scarcely conceal his delight at Ponting's decision. England were all out before the close of play on the first day but had scored 407 runs, the highest first-day score against Australia since 1938.

In reply, Australia were all out for 308 runs after tea on the second day, giving England a useful but not decisive lead of 99. The first two innings had lasted 155.2 overs, during which there had been 715 runs, 20 wickets, 94 fours, 10 sixes and a run rate of 4.60.

The shadows were beginning to lengthen across Edgbaston as England commenced their second innings with just seven overs to face. Trescothick and Strauss started well, hitting Australia's pace men for 25 runs, including five boundaries, in six overs. Cometh the hour, cometh the man; cometh the moment, cometh the ball.

With one over to go before close of play on the second day, Ponting finally threw the ball to Warne. His first delivery around the wicket to the left-handed Strauss broke nicely from the off side and was gathered on the leg side by wicket-keeper Adam Gilchrist, without Strauss making contact with it. Warne liked the look of it. Thoughtful, he stuck his tongue out a little way in concentration before mouthing 'phew' to his team-mates as he walked back towards his marker.

As the evening breeze ruffled his spiky, bleach-blond hair, the great showman and ringmaster, the guru of the Gatting Ball and many other wonder balls besides, proceeded to make a big show of directing traffic. Shouting, gesticulating, he enthusiastically discussed tactics with his captain and together they repositioned fielders necessarily and unnecessarily. It was all calculated psychological warfare that exploited to the full Warne's fearsome reputation. Keep the batsman waiting, give him time to fret, raise the level of anticipation in and around him and throughout the entire ground to fever pitch.

The mark of a truly great champion is to raise hopes and expectations to an absurd height, to put himself on the spot, to risk looking foolish before a vast crowd, and then to deliver on those hopes and expectations with a calm, skilful, decisive genius of which he alone is capable.

With five balls to go until close of play, Warne finally finished setting his scene, fielders crowding the batsman. A run-up of a few paces bought him in around the wicket to deliver the ball from his right hand a long way to the off side. The ball drifted in somewhat as it travelled up the pitch then dipped sooner than Strauss expected. It was still, however, a long way to the off side as it finished dipping. It was this dip that initially wrong-footed Strauss but, as with the Gatting Ball, the dip was a harbinger of doom eclipsed for fame by the remarkable turn that followed it.

As it travelled forwards, the seam of the ball was almost perfectly perpendicular to the length of the pitch and spinning rapidly in an anticlockwise direction. On pitching, this perpendicular, anticlockwise spinning seam bit into the ground, launching the ball massively towards the leg side. From the point of view of the camera behind the bowler, the ball looked as though it had turned almost 90 degrees. This was, however, only a foreshortening effect produced by the zoom lens. In pitching fairly short, the ball still needed to travel a considerable way forwards in order to make contact with the stumps.

Strauss stepped a good distance to the off side and seemingly attempted to kick or pad the ball away. Certainly, seeking to avoid the ball spinning off the face of his bat for a catch, he kept his bat up and back and well out of contact. Meanwhile, the ball stubbornly refused to conform to any of his reasonable expectations regarding it or even to be remotely where he thought it should be. Turning prodigiously across and behind him, the ball clipped his middle stump and bashed into the top of his leg stump.

In analysing the delivery for Channel 4 the following day, Simon Hughes used the ball-tracking technology of Hawk-Eye to compare the Strauss Ball with a virtual ball that went straight on after pitching. At the batsman or popping crease the difference or turn was 24.2 inches, while at the stumps it was 35.1 inches. In short, the Strauss Ball turned nearly 3 feet from the off side to break the wicket on the leg side.

Strauss's wicket was broken behind his back. By the time he turned around to look there was nothing to see but an aftermath of splayed, un-bailed stumps. Bewildered, impressed, he headed for the pavilion like so many before him, Warne's hundredth Test victim in England. Warne had become the first bowler in history to take 100 Test wickets in a country outside his own.

To a right-handed batsman the Strauss Ball would have been a leg break, except that Strauss being left-handed made it an off break. In a sense, therefore, it was a googly – an off break bowled with an apparent leg-break action – except that the leg-break action was not apparent but real. Then again, it did not have a forward seam and forward spin like a conventional leg break, but a perpendicular, anticlockwise spinning seam.

It seems safest to say that it was an off break delivered with a broadly leg-break action that incorporated a perfect mixture of Warne variation and natural variation. Really, the Strauss Ball was in a category of its own, which is why we are making such a fuss about it; an absolute ripper of a ball whatever the hell it should be called in technical terms.

England narrowly survived Warne's four remaining balls, ending the day with nine wickets in hand and a lead of 124. The Strauss Ball seemed to hang over England's second innings like a curse, however, and they never really recovered from it. Warne took five more wickets to add to the Strauss dismissal and the four he had taken in the first innings. England were reduced to 182 all out with only Andrew Flintoff showing any real resistance.

Flintoff struck a magnificent and invaluable 73 runs, including four sixes, before Warne bowled him. Such was Flintoff's firepower during one phase of his innings that Ponting had nine men back on the boundary. Flintoff simply went over the top of them. More Champagne moments of that glorious contest.

Set a target of 282, Australia struggled, despite some heroic performances, and by the close of play had slumped to 175–8. With what proved to be the last ball of the day, the fourth of the over, Steve Harmison foxed Australia's last recognized batsman, Michael Clarke, with a ball slower than his usual fast-medium pace that splayed Clarke's stumps. Mark Nicholas, commentating for Channel 4, captured the significance of the delivery when he said, 'One of the great balls. Given the moment, given the batsman and given the match, that is a staggering gamble that's paid off for Harmison.' If Clarke had survived the scheduled over to be there the following morning then the history of Test cricket might well have been very different.

There are pundits who argue that, given the context, given how vital it was to England's chances of victory to see the back of Clarke – currently the twenty-first most successful Test batsman of all time in terms of runs scored – this ball was an even greater ball than the Strauss Ball. It certainly deserves to be known as the Harmison Ball and that is what I am now christening it.

A total of 17 wickets had fallen that third day. Needing only two lower-order wickets, England had the whip hand, but the Australian tailenders, including Warne, fought doggedly the following morning.

It was intense, nail-biting, almost unbearable cricket, the most excruciating and enthralling sport anyone could ever watch. Certainly, the only thing that kept millions of TV viewers from a nervous breakdown was the calm, collected, authoritative commentary of Tony Greig, Richie Benaud and the rest of the Channel 4 team.

In the intensity of those moments the result seemed somehow more important than life itself, as though life, for an Englishman, would be unbearable shame and sorrow if England somehow lost this match against the old enemy after everything that had happened; after victory seemed to be so clearly theirs for the taking at the start of that fourth day.

With the score on 220 Australia lost Warne, out hit wicket off the bowling of Flintoff, but the final pair of Brett Lee and Michael Kasprowicz soldiered on, edging closer and closer to success, transforming English anxious expectation into agony. The blasted Baggy Greens were going to get the better of England once again. Was there no way on earth to lift the curse?

Lee struck out for the boundary to get the four runs Australia needed for victory but the ball was successfully fielded at cover. Lee should have stood his ground but instead he and Michael Kasprowicz crossed for a single, placing the weaker number 11 batsman on strike.

With Australia needing just three runs to win, Kasprowicz gloved a short ball from Harmison to wicket-keeper Geraint Jones and it was all over. England had clinched a historic victory from the jaws of defeat – the cliché is entirely pertinent – in an epic encounter where the pendulum of fortune had swung backwards and forwards relentlessly.

In a final twist, replays revealed that when the ball struck Kasprowicz's glove, the glove was not in fact in contact with the handle of his bat, meaning that he should not have been given out. The result, however, had been declared. How might things have turned out had Kasprowicz been able to question the verdict under the Umpire Decision Review System introduced a few years later? Then again, it is unlikely that by that point in their second innings Australia would have had any reviews left.

Despite bowling the Strauss Ball, Warne was on the losing side, and Man of the Match went to Flintoff for his 68, 73, seven wickets, two catches and incalculable contribution of inspiration. The press, not surprisingly, drew comparisons with Botham and the Headingley Test of 1981. I leave you to decide for yourself which Test you think was the greatest. There are good arguments for both. Or perhaps you have another Test in mind that I have neglected to mention. It may depend, understandably, on which national team you support.

The Laker Ball

Critics will argue that this delivery is called 'Cricket Ball Fame', yet, so far, it has not been about famous cricket balls, other than certain famous deliveries, but rather about famous cricketers, cricket performances, matches and series. Well, maybe so, but none of the above achievements would have been possible without the not-so-humble cricket ball at the heart of the action.

Anyway, there are in fact certain individual cricket balls that have been fetishized; cricket balls that have become famous, sacred, iconic objects, lucky charms and talismans. Why? Because these balls were centrally involved in historical acts of cricket sorcery; magic that now permanently haunts the physical object itself.

The whereabouts of some of these cricket balls is known. They have reliable provenance. Others are still being searched for and fakes eliminated, as though they were the Holy Grail. Others are surely lost forever. What happens to all the old cricket balls, the millions that have been? Do they slip through the fabric of time-space into another dimension, along with pens, paperclips and single socks?

One iconic cricket ball with a reliable provenance, a ball that is still very much in this spatio-temporal dimension, is the J. C. Laker commemorative ball. It resides in the MCC Museum at Lord's as part of the world's finest collection of cricket memorabilia. Originally an ordinary Surridge cricket ball, Jim Laker endowed it with timeless magic and the essence of his greatness when he used it to take all 10 Australian Test wickets for 53 runs at Old Trafford in 1956. Recall that he took nine wickets for 37 runs in the first innings, giving him 19 wickets in total for the match. Laker's nine-wicket ball also resides in the MCC Museum.

One wonders what Laker's 10-wicket ball, the most successful ball ever bowled in a Test match, would fetch if it ever came up for auction, but of course, the MCC Museum are about as likely to part with this prized exhibit from their permanent collection – a sacred relic, second only to the Ashes urn itself – as anyone is to better Laker's bowling figures.

The engraved, circular silver plaque on top of the ball states: 'Presented by the Lancashire County Cricket Club to J. C. Laker who with this ball took ten wickets for fifty three runs for England v Australia at Old Trafford July 26th to 31st 1956.' The display caption that accompanies the ball is also worthy of note, as it makes it clear that Laker's achievement was assisted by pitch conditions that are now unlikely ever to occur again in a Test match:

Laker spun the ball fiercely on a drying pitch when taking his record wicket haul. Pitches were left uncovered during the hours of play at the time and pitches drying out after a soaking were notoriously difficult to bat on. Uncovered pitches remained in use in England later than anywhere else, being used in Test cricket until 1972 and in county cricket until 1981. In the first innings at Old Trafford in 1956 Laker took 9 for 37, long before the wicket became 'sticky'.

The Sobers Six Sixes Ball

A cricket ball can be sanctified by either a remarkable bowling performance or a remarkable batting performance. For a batsman, nothing can surpass hitting six sixes in an over that contains no no-balls. The perfect score has not so far been achieved in a Test match, the closest to perfection being Brian Lara's 28 runs in one over off the bowling of Robin Peterson in the first Test between South Africa and the West Indies at Johannesburg in December 2003.

The feat has been achieved four times so far in non-Test professional cricket. As already mentioned, Garry Sobers hit Malcolm Nash for 36 runs in one over at Swansea on 31 August 1968, and Ravi Shastri punished Tilak Raj in the same way in a match between Bombay and Baroda at Bombay in January 1985. South Africa's Herschelle Gibbs also maxed out off the bowling of Daan Van Bunge in a World Cup ODI against the Netherlands at St Kitts in March 2007. Finally, India's Yuvraj Singh spanked

England's Stuart Broad for 36 runs in one over in an international Twenty20 match at Durban, also in 2007. Clearly, more top-class, short-format cricket, combined with improved bat technology, has made the six sixes phenomenon slightly less rare than it once was, but however common it becomes, Sobers will forever have the honour of being the first.

Now, a ball purporting to be the Sobers Six Sixes Ball – I think Nash would be happy for it not to be called the Nash Ball – was auctioned at Christie's in 2006 for a whopping £26,400. The ball was put up for auction at Christie's by Jose Miller, a former secretary of Nottinghamshire Supporters' Association, who said it had languished in her make-up drawer for nearly 40 years. The ball, she said, was given to her by her predecessor, John Gough, who received it from Sobers in 1968.

Richard Lewis, a 17-year-old youth, had proudly presented the ball to Sobers at the Glamorgan ground of St Helen's a couple of days after the legendary over took place. Lewis had retrieved the ball after Sobers smashed the final delivery of the over out of the ground. As BBC commentator Wilf Wooller said at the time, 'My goodness, it's gone way down to Swansea'.

Judging from the meticulous detective work of Grahame Lloyd, as detailed in his book *Howzat? The Six Sixes Ball Mystery*, it seems certain beyond all reasonable doubt that Lewis did indeed retrieve the Six Sixes Ball, that Sobers received it and that it travelled to Trent Bridge in his kitbag. The ball was displayed in the window of a Nottingham building society for about a year before it was returned to Trent Bridge where, like the One Ring, it fell into obscurity.

Bowler Malcolm Nash, who has every reason to recall the ball, insists it was a Surridge ball, and certainly, as several people associated with Glamorgan have confirmed, the club used only Surridge balls at that time and had done so for years. The Surridge balls were supplied by the sports shop of Glamorgan scorer Bill Edwards.

Nash and others also insist that there was only one ball used in the over and not several as some have argued. The footage of the over on YouTube is somewhat clipped and therefore not conclusive, but Grahame Lloyd kindly showed me the *full* BBC Wales footage of the over that he obtained directly from the BBC. That the ball was not replaced during the over is confirmed by this footage. There is clearly only one ball used in the over. The ball is returned each time except after the sixth and final delivery, and importantly there is no sign of the umpires going through the rigmarole of selecting a replacement ball. Anyway, had the ball been replaced it would have been replaced by a Surridge. It is very suspect indeed, therefore, that the ball sold at Christie's in 2006 for £26,400 was a Dukes ball.

Perhaps the magical powers imparted to the ball by Sobers caused it to miraculously transform from a Surridge ball into the most traditional and legendary make of cricket ball, a Dukes ball. Far more likely, there was a catalogue of errors that led to the Dukes ball being auctioned as the Sobers Six Sixes Ball, or possibly even fraud on the part of certain individuals involved. The evidence for deliberate deception, however, falls short of legal proof and lack of scepticism is not in itself a crime.

Christie's lot notes mistakenly state that Glamorgan were using Dukes balls during the 1960s and that the ball sold was the

last of three used in the over, the first two having been hit out of
the ground. Interestingly, Lloyd later discovered footage, filmed
six months before the Christie's sale, of Sobers stating that only
one ball had been used in the over. Clearly, Christie's did not
investigate the facts of the famous over for themselves by looking
at the unedited BBC TV footage or consulting with central
figures such as Nash.

Christie's also ignored pre-auction concerns expressed by
former England and Glamorgan player Peter Walker regarding
the authenticity of the Dukes ball. It appears Christie's allowed
themselves to be entirely convinced by a certificate of provenance
signed by no less a figure than Sir Garfield Sobers himself.

Perhaps evidence provided by a cricket legend should be enough
to convince anyone; it was certainly enough to convince Christie's.
Upon speaking to Sobers, however, Lloyd discovered that Sobers
had no recollection of the make of the ball he had hit for six sixes all
those years ago – he was too busy hitting it to read it – and that he
had signed the certificate on trust after questioning Miller. Sobers
insisted that he did not profit in any way from the sale of the Dukes
ball. It appears that Sobers signed the certificate without asking too
many questions because he trusted Miller and was keen to help her
pay for alterations to her house that her declining health required.

Sobers' agent at the time, Basharat Hassan, who was
instrumental in the signing of the certificate, admitted profiting
from the sale of the Dukes ball, but insisted that a cheque for
nearly £4,000 pounds sent to him by Miller was unsolicited. She
said he had demanded payment. He denied having any part in
the erroneous Christie's lot notes.

The Dukes ball was bought by Indian art impresario Neville Tuli, but financial difficulties in his organization meant that he was unwilling or unable to pay customs charges. As a result, the ball was placed in an airport online auction and purchased by Ashish Singhal. In 2012, Singhal put the ball up for sale at Bonhams in Chester. It would presumably have sold again as authentic had Lloyd not intervened.

After he threatened to go public with his evidence, Lloyd was granted an interview with an initially resistant Bonhams in which he eventually managed to persuade them that the ball was a wrong'un. Describing his evidence as 'compelling and conclusive' Bonhams withdrew the ball from sale. Bonhams belief that the ball was genuine had been largely based on Christie's catalogue notes.

Stubborn, obtuse and haughty, Christie's, in 2015, were continuing to insist that the ball they sold in 2006 was genuine. Also in 2015, Nash requested a meeting with the chairman of Christie's, the Queen's cousin, Lord Linley, to clear the matter up. Nash wished, he said, to remove any suggestion that he was in any way involved in what some perceive to be a fraudulent act. Ignoring his request to meet, Linley replied reservedly that he would refer the matter to Christie's legal department.

The controversy continues, with Singhal owning a ball that Christie's claim is genuine but that no self-respecting auction house would sell as the Sobers Six Sixes Ball, and no self-respecting collector would buy. It would be interesting to see if Christie's actually had the temerity to sell the Dukes ball again as the Six Sixes Ball if asked to do so.

In an article that appeared in the *Independent* on 13 May
2015, 'Riddle of the £26,400 Ball Garry Sobers May Not Have hit',
John Parkin, the batsman at the other end from Sobers, offered
an innocent explanation that more or less absolves everyone
involved. Sobers inadvertently pulled the wrong ball, a Dukes
ball, out of his kitbag when he returned to Trent Bridge and
handed it to John Gough. The root of all future error lies in that
simple mistake. Has anyone got a photograph of a Nottingham
building society window 1968–9 with a cricket ball sitting in it?
What make?

According to Christie's own lot notes, the Dukes ball in
question is stamped 'Duke & Son, Nottingham'. Dukes, as we
know, are based in southern England, originally Kent and certainly
not Nottinghamshire, but it was their practice to stamp their balls
with the name of the county club they were supplying. The Dukes
ball in question is very much a Nottingham Dukes ball.

If Sobers did mistakenly give Gough this ball when he returned
to Trent Bridge in 1968, it is odd that nobody at Nottingham ever
thought to question why on earth Glamorgan would be using
a Nottingham Dukes ball in a home match when it is the
responsibility of the host team to provide the match balls. Anyway,
the fact that the Dukes ball is a Nottingham Dukes ball is further
strong evidence that it is not the Six Sixes Ball.

There is another Surridge ball associated with the Six Sixes
Match, signed by Sobers, which now resides in the Cricket
Legends of Barbados Museum in the West Indies. This is not the
ball Sobers hit for 36 runs, but a ball Sobers gave to Richard Lewis
as a thank-you for retrieving and very honestly returning the

actual Six Sixes Ball. When Bonhams withdrew the Dukes ball from sale in 2012, Lewis decided to auction his ball. That ball, which made Lewis £1000, was sold on to the museum for £3000.

As to the real Six Sixes Ball, who knows where it is. Perhaps the Six Sixes Ball is the Surridge ball in the Barbados museum after all, a theory I am proposing on no stronger basis than another mix-up in Sobers' kitbag. Perhaps Sobers gave Lewis the Six Sixes Ball back thinking he was giving him a different one. Perhaps the Six Sixes Ball has transcended to a higher plain of existence as befits its divine, Holy Grail status in the folklore of cricket, or perhaps it was simply stolen one drunken evening from the Eddie Marshall Bar where, according to some, it resided for a time.

Who knows, and as some may be inclined to argue, who cares. Perhaps what matters is that the ailing Jose Miller got her house refit paid for by a wealthy Indian who, at least at the time of purchase, had £26,400 to spare on a cricket ball.

Some years ago the Sobers Six Sixes Bat, a short-handled Slazenger, was auctioned by Christie's in Melbourne for a staggering £54,257. Hope that was genuine.

Finally, it is worth noting that the Dukes ball in question has now become famous in its own right as perhaps the most *infamous* cricket ball in cricket history. Perhaps it could be auctioned for thousands of pounds on that basis. Singhal should give it a try.

Seventh Delivery

Umpire Miscounting and Other Ball Stories

These days an over contains six deliveries. So what is this seventh delivery doing here? None of the previous deliveries was a no-ball. It must, therefore, simply be a mistake on the part of the umpire who has failed to keep count correctly with his pebbles or coins.

According to Law 22.5: Umpire Miscounting, 'If the umpire miscounts the number of balls, the over as counted by the umpire shall stand'. So this book may remain a seven-ball over. The call of 'Over' is the responsibility of the bowler's-end umpire but it helps if the striker's-end umpire counts as well. Umpires are advised to unobtrusively signal one another after five legitimate deliveries to confirm that only one delivery remains in the over. Such precautions mean that miscounted overs are rare in top-class cricket. They are not, however, unheard of.

Anyway, there used to be eight balls in an Australian over – the Aussies took the idea from the Californians of all people – and you may recall the ancient Stonyhurst over with its 21 balls bowled as fast as possible in quick succession. Since the late nineteenth century the number of balls in an over has varied between four and eight, but it has never been seven. There was a brief period in England in the very late nineteenth century when it was five balls, although the overriding preference around the world has always been for even-numbered batches. Eight-ball overs were still being bowled in various parts of the globe, New Zealand and Pakistan as well as Australia, up to the end of the 1970s. ICC rules allowed for both six- and eight-ball overs in different parts of the world.

The advantage of eight-ball overs was that more balls could be bowled in a day because there were less changeovers. The disadvantage was that bowlers tended to slow down in order to pace themselves through a long over. Six-ball overs have been the standard in England since 1900, except for a brief experiment with eight-ball overs beginning in 1939 that was soon scuppered by the Second World War. The six-ball over finally became the ICC worldwide standard in 1979, the happy medium in an increasingly commercialized game. In case there is any doubt, Law 22.1: Number of Balls, now clearly states, 'The ball shall be bowled from each wicket alternately in overs of 6 balls'.

Actually, to be honest, this seventh delivery or chapter is here not because the umpire miscounted, or because I wanted to bang on about the fascinating history of the over, but because this book needs to have something approaching or resembling a conclusion. At the very least, it needs to have a neat if not eloquent polishing off. Therefore, by way of conclusion, I have decided on a shortish chapter of various odd cricket ball anecdotes, musings and tall tales, or, rather, ball tales.

It is interesting that a book ostensibly about a single object should have become quite so sprawling, but as I said in my first delivery, 'every sustained consideration of any object soon begins to drag the whole universe in'. Cricket is, of course, an entire, infinite universe in itself, so how could a consideration of the cricket ball not drag *that* universe in? You probably sussed out this book long ago. It is really a book about cricket that by turns, loving and merciless, relentlessly exploits the cricket ball as its guiding thread and driving force.

I could have written a book about cricket with the cricket bat as its guiding thread, or the stumps, or even the bails. I am sure it could be done and perhaps one day I will do it. Writing about cricket beats working for a living, or rather it is a joyful, absorbing, myopic sort of work that distracts the mind from metaphysical anxieties, current affairs – other than cricket current affairs of course – and even concerns about the state of the roof. Unlike you, probably, I do not really want this book to end.

Wisden. It is amazing that this name, so famous in cricket circles, has only cropped up a couple of times, in passing, so far in this book. *Wisden* is best known now as the title of the world-famous, yellow-jacketed *Cricketers' Almanack*, the bible of cricket. Wisden, however, was not originally an almanack, but John Wisden, born in Brighton in 1826. Less than 5 feet 6 inches tall and weighing just 7 stone, John Wisden was dubbed 'The Little Wonder' for his fast and accurate bowling. He made it into the All-England Eleven before leading a rebellion against its dictatorial and somewhat tight-fisted manager, William Clarke. As a consequence Wisden formed his own England, the United England Eleven.

That was Wisden, one of cricket's first great entrepreneurs. In partnership with Nottinghamshire-born cricketer George Parr he established The Parr and Wisden Cricket Ground in Royal Leamington Spa in 1849. Located in central England with easy access by train from north and south, the ground was a great success, hosting many of the biggest teams of the day. The following year, Wisden established a sports shop in Leamington under the name of John Wisden & Co.

Apart from playing cricket for several professional teams and running his various cricket-related businesses, Wisden also found time to coach bowling at Harrow School in his capacity as professional bowler there from 1852 to 1855. A man of boundless energy, he teamed up with fellow player Fred Lillywhite and in 1855 they opened a cricket and cigar emporium in Coventry Street in the West End of London. In those good old, bad old days, before people finally worked out that constantly drawing smoke into their lungs was terribly bad for them, smoking was synonymous with the healthy, outdoor, sporting life.

Actually, down through the years, more than a few cricketers have enjoyed an anxious puff behind or within the pavilion before going out to bat, or a sorrowful or celebratory one on returning to it. C. L. R. James tells how the great West Indian batsman George Headley, 'the black Bradman', always chain-smoked in the dressing-room while anticipating his innings, and all the time between matches while on tour. It was as though any other activity except smoking was a distraction from his obsessive, artistic preoccupation with batting (*Beyond a Boundary*, pp. 189–90).

For his part, legendary Yorkshire and England fast bowler Fred Trueman is pictured on the front of his authorized biography by Chris Waters menacingly blowing a huge cloud of tobacco smoke from the side of his grimacing mouth.

Then there is that iconic photograph of a sweaty, padded-up, grim-faced, steely-eyed Ian Botham in a classic three lions cricket jumper, sitting in the Headingley dressing room in 1981 enjoying a well-deserved cigar following his Homeric slaughter of the Australian bowling. Like those other assassins, the Hashishin, Botham, by his own admission, also liked to partake of a weed that was considerably more psychoactive than tobacco. Bet John Wisden never sold that.

Wisden later moved his cricket and cigar business a short distance across London to Cranbourn Street, where an attractive terracotta 'J Wisden & Compy' sign, featuring a wicket, two bats and a ball, is still visible to this day above the door of the fast-food outlet at number 21, a part of the Leicester Square tube station building.

Fred Lillywhite, in partnership with his brother John, went on to found the world-famous Lillywhites sports department store, which trades to this day in Piccadilly Circus, just behind the statue of Anteros. Wisden founded *Wisden* in 1864 to compete with *Lillywhite's Guide to Cricketers*, which folded in 1900. Wisden died a childless bachelor in 1884, in his flat above his Cranbourn Street shop, and his business was bought by his manager, Henry Luff.

This book has detailed several serious disputes surrounding the cricket ball, and certainly Luff was instrumental in bringing about perhaps the earliest; a dispute that ended up in the High Court and threatened to bring the good name of Wisden into disrepute.

Ten years after John Wisden died, Luff was selling the Luff and Week's Patent Marvel ball. It is not clear which company actually made this ball, but during Wisden's lifetime his shop had sold Twort balls and Dukes balls legally badged as Wisden balls. The Luff ball, rather oddly, was marketed as being 'less hard than most balls' (*Quilt Winders and Pod Shavers*, p. 78). It was entirely Luff's prerogative to sell his own-label balls in his own shop, but rumour began to reach the Dukes factory in Kent that Luff was badmouthing the peerless Dukes ball, the brand leader, in order to sell more of his own. In 1896 Henry Edgar, a Wanstead vet, reported that according to Luff the quality of Dukes balls had deteriorated. 'Duke's were bad and Dark's very bad' (*Quilt Winders and Pod Shavers*, p. 78).

This was enough to turn Dukes the colour of their product with anger and indignation, but it was only half the story. Acting as something of a spy for Dukes, Edgar established as true the rumour that when customers asked Luff to sell them Dukes best ball – the 7s.6d Dukes Number 1 Best – he was fobbing them off with the inferior Dukes Number 4 ball, which should have cost only 5s. With their products being mis-sold by a leading London sports retailer and their reputation for excellence under threat, Dukes decided to sue. In 1898 they had Luff brought before the Lord Chief Justice, Charles Russell, Baron of Killowen.

Luff insisted that he understood the Dukes Royal Crown ball to be their best. An easy mistake to make, perhaps, as one has to scrutinize the small print of Dukes advertising of the time – the Victorians certainly liked to embellish their ads with small print – to establish that while the Dukes Number 1 Best ball was best, the Dukes Royal Crown ball was more durable. None of this explained, however, why Luff was selling the Dukes Number 4 ball for the price of the Dukes Number 1 Best ball to customers who specifically asked for the Dukes Number 1 Best ball. Luff's excuses would have had some credibility only if he had been selling the Dukes Royal Crown ball to customers requesting the Dukes Number 1 Best ball, but he had not been, shenanigans evidenced by the testimony of his former manager of 12 years, William Smith.

The game was up for Luff. Lord Russell duly found in favour of the plaintiffs, Dukes, who wanted only justice and their good name restored rather than financial compensation. Luff was required to give a solemn undertaking that in future he would sell Dukes cricket balls 'under their proper denomination' (*Quilt Winders and Pod Shavers*, p. 79).

To his credit, Luff was instrumental in keeping the famous *Wisden Cricketers' Almanack* afloat during a difficult period following the death of John Wisden. Ironically, without Luff, Wisden would probably be a footnote in cricket history, rather than the name given to the legendary publication that has documented cricket's magnificent story since 1864.

A final twist in relations between John Wisden & Co. and Duke & Son was the formal merger of the two businesses in

1920. Wisden cricket balls, or at least many of them, had been made by Dukes for decades.

Cricket ball stories can be found in almost any direction one cares to look. In *Birds Without Wings*, a novel about the founding of the modern Turkish nation, perhaps the last place you would expect to find a reference to the cricket ball, Louis de Bernières claims that playing cricket made the troops of the British Empire – Brits, Aussies, Kiwis and Indians – very good at expelling grenades from their trenches at Gallipoli.

Some cricket was certainly played at Gallipoli and the Turks had a ball grenade made of cast iron that came to be known as a 'cricket ball' grenade. In his book *Victoria Cross: Australia's Finest and the Battles They Fought*, historian Anthony Staunton tells the story of Corporal Leonard Keysor who won a Victoria Cross at Gallipoli for repeatedly catching bombs in flight 'as if fielding at cricket' (*Victoria Cross*, p. 23) and throwing them back to the sender if the fuse showed there was time.

Their cricketing skills, however, were not enough to win the troops of the British Empire the Gallipoli Campaign. De Bernières' harrowing account of the Gallipoli Campaign, 1915–16, written from the point of view of a soldier of the Ottoman Empire, has the following to say about the 'Franks', the Ottoman Turk name for Western Europeans, their descendants and those who fought alongside them:

> These grenades were turned against us, because some of the Franks, but not the French Franks, would catch them and toss them back to us. We never knew how this was possible until we

realised from observing the Franks on the beach that they had a game which involved waving a plank, running backwards and forwards, and frequently throwing and catching a ball. The consequence of this was that all the Franks, except for the French Tangos, were very good at catching and throwing, and I believe that they had men on the alert whose job was to catch the grenades as they came in, or scoop them up straight away and throw them back. After a time we got wise to this and we let the fuses burn for longer before we threw them.

Birds Without Wings, p. 369

From fact to fiction is always a short step in cricket and, as I said in my first delivery, cricket writing is a thoroughly respectable branch of English literature. There is so much scope for exploring character, introducing humour and concocting a delightful theatre of the absurd that great writers are time and again drawn to producing a fictional match report in their own inimitable style, either as a set-piece chapter in a novel or as a standalone short story.

Vet turned bestselling author James Herriot gives us an exquisitely well-observed and highly amusing description of a 1930s Yorkshire cricket match between the villages of Hedwick and Rainby, in which even the stage itself is preposterous.

The strip stood on the only level part of the field, and that was a small part. Within twenty yards it swept up steeply to a thick wood that climbed over the lower slopes of the fell. On the other side it fell away to a sort of ravine where the rank grass ended only in a rocky stream.

Vet in Harness, p. 166

The ravine is so deep that the central strip cannot be seen from it and the team have to call to the man fielding down there that the ball is on its way. A good arm is required to return the ball from this literal deep. Not surprisingly, the Yorkshire men favour bludgeoning the ball in that direction rather than uphill. The ball can only be bludgeoned through the air because of the rank state of the playing surface. Elegant strokeplay along the ground is useless. 'I leaned across the rough stones and stared in some bewilderment at a wildly undulating field almost knee deep in rough grass among which a cow, some sheep and a few hens wandered contentedly' (*Vet in Harness*, p. 166). Herriot, in his dry manner, adds that, 'A massive oak tree sprouted from somewhere around mid-on' (p. 166). The field is also liberally strewn with cow pats. The ball, of course, finds its way into the thick of a cow pat during the course of the match.

The Yorkshire men play a rip-roaring game of cricket that soon disabuses Herriot, with his cinema newsreel images of Hobbs and Sutcliffe clad in white on 'the wide sweep of smooth turf' (*Vet in Harness*, p. 165), of the romantic notion that cricket is a soft and gracious game.

Old Len, with his crabbed features, his bracered trousers nearly up to his armpits, his single pad and dangling cigarette, takes strike and immediately thumps the ball within inches of the rear end of the aforementioned cow.

'By gaw, vitnery,' he said, looking at me, 'ah damn near made a bit of work for tha there.' He eyed me impassively for a moment. 'Ah reckon tha's never took a cricket ball out of a cow's arse afore, eh?'

Vet in Harness, p. 169

A hundred years or so earlier, Charles Dickens had Mr Pickwick attend a somewhat more elegant and well-provisioned match between Dingley Dell and All-Muggleton. The match is beautifully pictured in miniature on the reverse of the Dickens £10 note. Dingley Dell are completely overwhelmed by 'the superior prowess of All-Muggleton' (*The Pickwick Papers*, p. 87), who bat first and set a considerable target. Dingley Dell struggle to 'regain the ground' (p. 87) until they eventually accept that All-Muggleton's advantage is too great and concede defeat. The prize for All-Muggleton and the price for Dingley Dell is a plain dinner at the Blue Lion Inn, Muggleton, where all present get extremely drunk.

In the refreshment marquee, Pickwick comes across the fast-talking rogue Alfred Jingle, a thin, shabby young man he has encountered on previous occasions. A master of imposture, Jingle has wheedled and charmed his way into the company of the All-Muggleton team and their supporters. He has been stuffing his face with food and drink, all the while vociferously praising good play and criticizing bad in a manner that 'seemed to establish him in the opinion of all around, as a most excellent and undeniable judge of the whole art and mystery of the noble game of cricket' (*The Pickwick Papers*, p. 88).

Such is Dickens's inventive genius that within his tale of a cricket match he manages to provide a ridiculously far-fetched tale of another cricket match that the opportunistic, loquacious but undeniably entertaining Jingle claims took place once upon a time in the West Indies. In his rapid and disjointed manner of speaking, Jingle tells how he single-handedly took on Colonel Sir Thomas Blazo and his servants in the sweltering heat of the tropics.

Jingle wins the toss, of course, and elects to bat. 'Natives' field until they all faint with the heat. Blazo and two more natives bowl without joy until Blazo also faints and is cleared away. Blazo's faithful attendant, Quanko Samba, takes over the bowling. 'Quanko Samba – last man left – sun so hot, bat in blisters, ball scorched brown' (*The Pickwick Papers*, p. 88). With Jingle on 570 runs, Quanko gathers his 'last remaining strength' (p. 88) and finally bowls Jingle out, after which Jingle takes a bath and goes out to dinner.

An old gentleman dares to enquire what became of Quanko Samba.

> 'Poor Quanko – never recovered it – bowled on, on my account – bowled off, on his own – died, sir.' Here the stranger buried his countenance in a brown jug, but whether to hide his emotion or imbibe its contents, we cannot distinctly affirm.
>
> *The Pickwick Papers*, p. 88

One of the finest and funniest short stories ever written on the subject of cricket is to be found in Herbert Farjeon's *Cricket Bag*, a classic collection of cricket tales, musings, poems and plays. 'Herecombe v. Therecombe' is an exquisitely farcical account of the ultimate grudge match; a match that is played in accordance with the basic Laws of Cricket, very debatably, but is as far from the spirit of the game as could ever be achieved. Indeed, the pursuit of victory at all costs by one team, and the pursuit of not losing at all costs by the other, not only reduces the match to a farce, it virtually annihilates anything approaching actual play.

> I question whether any match has ever been conducted in a more thoroughly unsportsmanlike manner than a certain officially 'friendly' match between the old-world villages of Herecombe and Therecombe. In the annals of the game it will, I imagine, stand for all time as the only match in which, although there was not a drop of rain, although play continued uninterrupted through the whole afternoon, and although both sides had a knock, only two balls were bowled.
>
> 'Herecombe v. Therecombe', *Cricket Bag*, pp. 120–1

Herecombe win the toss – an event viewed with suspicion by Therecombe – and elect to bat. The captain opens. The first ball strikes a flint and skids away at right angles to square leg with more turn than Shane Warne ever achieved in the opposite direction. The Herecombe captain exclaims, 'Well, I declare!' (*Cricket Bag*, p. 121). The Therecombe captain insists the umpires consult the Laws of Cricket and it is eventually decided that the Herecombe captain has 'inescapably, if unintentionally, declared' (p. 122).

With one run required to beat the Herecombe score of 0–0 declared, Therecombe commence what they anticipate will be a brief but glorious innings. The Herecombe captain, however, deploys a devious strategy. He hands the ball to little Smith, who is not a bowler of any experience but a marathon runner. Smith begins a long zigzag approach to the wicket but before he reaches the crease he starts to run in circles. The umpires consult the Laws of Cricket once again, but can find nothing in them limiting the length of a bowler's run-up.

> Hour after hour little Smith kept up his capering – a noble effort – the batsman sternly refusing to leave the wicket lest he should be bowled in his absence. The fieldsmen lay down at full length on the ground. Spectators went away and then came back again, to find little Smith still running. Longer and longer grew his shadow as the sun travelled into the west. The clock on the old church tower chimed five, then six, then seven.
>
> *Cricket Bag*, p. 123

By prior agreement, the stumps are to be drawn when the clock strikes seven, but a match cannot end mid-ball. Smith finally delivers the ball at ten o'clock in almost total darkness, the harvest moon having disappeared behind a cloud. Unable to pierce the gloom, the Therecombe batsman misses the ball which is somehow fielded by one of the seven men, wicket-keeper included, who have gathered behind the stumps to prevent a bye.

The Herecombe captain shouts that the match is drawn. The Therecombe batsman protests that stumps cannot be drawn mid-over. As the umpires begin to consult yet again, the Herecombe captain appeals against the light, 'a rare thing indeed for a fielding side to do' (*Cricket Bag*, p. 124). The umpires allow the appeal and the protracted, ill-tempered, two-ball match finally ends in a draw.

The result was not, as some have suggested, a tie. Although the scores were level at the finish, Therecombe had not completed their innings. 'The result of a match shall be a Tie when the scores are equal at the conclusion of play, but only if the side batting last has completed its innings' (Law 21.4).

With his tongue firmly in his cheek, Farjeon concludes by saying:

> Whether the umpires were right in all their rulings may be open to question. I think they were. In any case, it must be conceded that they had some very knotty points to solve, and that on the whole they appear to have discharged their duties conscientiously.

> *Cricket Bag*, p. 124

In truth, the umpires failed to apply various sections of Law 42: Fair and Unfair Play, concerning 'the spirit and traditions of the game'. Not least, Law 42.9: Time wasting by the Fielding Side clearly states, 'It is unfair for any member of the fielding side to waste time'. But of course, long before little Smith began wasting time with his several hour long run-up, it is highly unlikely that the umpires would have obliged the Herecombe captain to declare the innings of his team on the basis of an exclamation that clearly meant something quite different.

It is a great story all the same, certain features of which remind me of the controversy, considered earlier, surrounding the last underarm ball ever bowled in formal cricket. That incident happened back in what we all like to call reality, but does anything about cricket ever quite happen in reality? Cricket is surreal. It is pure escapism. A life-enriching sideshow that persuades our hearts, while the game is afoot, to place it centre stage, above personal, social and political concerns.

> The foreigner is naturally baffled. He arrives in London and sees a newspaper poster: 'England's Danger'. An international crisis has occurred behind his back, during his journey from the continent! No; but almost as important, six wickets have fallen at Lord's, including that of Hammond, to the invading Australians.
>
> *English Cricket*, p. 8

Cricket can be valued so highly because it is, in a sense, a religion. Certainly it is a religion to those lovers of the game who find in its complex rituals more inspiration, emotion, morality, dignity, rationality, wisdom, philosophy and mysticism than is offered to them by church or temple.

As a strange, earthbound yet otherworldly institution, rich in symbols, rituals, customs and traditions that are certainly quasi-religious if not entirely so, it was inevitable that cricket would find its way into science fiction, even comedy science fiction.

The central characters of Douglas Adams's novel *Life, the Universe and Everything*, Arthur Dent and Ford Prefect, materialize on the hallowed turf of the sacred centre of world cricket, having journeyed there from prehistoric earth on a time-travelling Chesterfield sofa.

> They fell through a sickening nothingness, and emerged unexpectedly in the middle of the pitch at Lord's Cricket Ground, St John's Wood, London, towards the end of the last

Test Match of the Australian Series in the year 198–, with England needing only twenty-eight runs to win.

Life, the Universe and Everything, p. 322

We know this is fiction because the last Test of an English series is always played at the Kennington Oval.

To travel from prehistoric times to the height and centre of human civilization is a quantum leap indeed. Shortly after, robots from the planet Krikkit arrive, wreak havoc and steal the Ashes urn. Reconstituted, the ashes inside the urn form a cricket stump, a component of a special key called the Wikkit Gate. The Wikkit Gate will unlock the Slo-Time envelope surrounding the planet Krikkit. Krikkit was imprisoned in Slo-Time aeons ago to prevent any resumption of the Krikkit Wars in which its population attempted to destroy the entire universe beyond the Krikkit solar system.

The game of cricket, as invented by Englishmen and played on planet Earth, is a distant echo of the Krikkit Wars, a ritual that dimly recalls the horrors that took place.

'The game you know as cricket,' he said, and his voice still seemed to be wondering lost in subterranean passages, 'is just one of those curious freaks of racial memory which can keep images alive in the mind aeons after their true significance has been lost in the mists of time. Of all the races in the Galaxy, only the English could possibly revive the memory of the most horrific wars ever to sunder the Universe and transform it into what I'm afraid is generally regarded as an incomprehensibly dull and pointless game.'

Life, the Universe and Everything, p. 368

After many adventures in pursuit of the Krikkit robots, Arthur and Ford finally regain the Ashes and return them to Lord's. They return to Lord's at that moment in time when the robots are wreaking havoc. Seeing one wicket still standing and intact, despite the destruction, Arthur is unable to resist taking advantage of the madness and mayhem. He simply has to have a bowl. 'The air was disturbed with the sound of police and ambulance sirens, and people screaming and yelling, but he felt curiously happy and untouched by it all. He was going to bowl a ball at Lord's' (*Life, the Universe and Everything*, p. 446).

It turns out that the cricket ball is actually a supernova bomb that was planted in Arthur's bag earlier. 'It was emitting a deep red glow and flashing intermittently' (*Life, the Universe and Everything*, p. 447), not unlike something that might be used in the Indian Premier League. The bomb-ball will destroy the universe if struck by the Krikkit robot batsman standing ready at the wicket. Fortunately, Arthur never gets to release his killer delivery and the universe is saved.

Like Adams, I feel that cricket somehow holds the key to life, the universe and everything. Like life, the meaning of cricket is totally accessible, yet at the same time totally elusive. Cricket makes sense within its context, within its boundary, but viewed from a detached perspective, a perspective without love or appreciation, it is pointless and absurd. Like every sphere, cricket is a language game complete in itself. As the great philosopher Ludwig Wittgenstein once said, '*The limits of my language* mean the limits of my world' (*Tractatus Logico-Philosophicus*, 5.6).

The one millionth delivery in Test cricket in England was bowled at Trent Bridge on 7 August 2015 by England's Ben Stokes and hit for four by Australia's David Warner. Only until the end of human civilization on Earth will the cricket ball go on being delivered and hit across the globe, unless humankind can export the game throughout the universe as the English one exported it throughout their empire.

Life on other planets seems almost certain, even intelligent life on other planets is statistically likely, but that cricket could have developed elsewhere in the universe, in quite the form it has on Earth, with quite the ball it has on Earth, is surely impossible; an absurd suggestion. Cricket is too peculiar, too unique, too human and, above all, as Adams makes clear, too English to have evolved twice.

I have to stop delivering this book, even though the rich life of the cricket ball, in and out of its ownmost context, would easily allow me to double or quadruple its length ...

A cricket ball is struck into the air. It splits in half. A fielder catches one of the halves. Is the batsman out caught? As recently confirmed during 'Ask the Umpire' on BBC *Test Match Special*, the answer is no. The moment the ball splits in half it becomes a dead ball. Cricket must be played with the ball, the whole ball and nothing but the ball, so help me God.

Out of darkness, through fire, into light.

I Zingari

'Over.'

Bibliography

Books

Adams, Douglas, *Life, the Universe and Everything*, in Adams, *The Hitchhiker's Guide to the Galaxy: A Trilogy in Four Parts* (London: Pan Macmillan, 1992).

Arlott, John, *Book of Cricketers* (London: Lutterworth, 1979).

Atherton, Mike, *Opening Up* (London: Hodder, 2002).

Austin, J. L., *Sense and Sensibilia* (Oxford: Oxford University Press, 1979).

Barty-King, Hugh, *Quilt Winders and Pod Shavers: The History of Cricket Bat and Ball Manufacture* (London: Macdonald & Jane's, 1979).

Berkeley, George, *Principles of Human Knowledge* (London: Penguin, 2005).

Bernières, Louis de, *Birds without Wings* (London; Secker & Warburg, 2004).

Boswell, James, *Life of Johnson* (Oxford: Oxford University Press, 1980).

Brearley, Mike, *The Art of Captaincy: What Sport Teaches Us About Leadership* (London: Channel 4 Books & Macmillan, 2001).

Brown, Harry, *Golf Ball* (New York: Bloomsbury Academic, 2015).

Cardus, Neville, *English Cricket* (London: Collins, 1946).

Cardus, Neville, *Good Days: A Book of Cricket* (London: Rupert Hart-Davis, 1948).

Chesterton, G. K., *Lines on a Cricket Match*, in *G. K. Chesterton: Collected Works, Vol. 10, Collected Poetry, Part 1* (San Francisco, CA: Ignatius Press, 1994).

Descartes, René, *Discourse on Method and The Meditations*, trans. F. E. Sutcliffe (London: Penguin, 2007).

Dickens, Charles, *The Pickwick Papers* (Ware: Wordsworth Classics, 1993).

Farington, Joseph, *The Farington Diary*, ed. James Greig (London: Hutchinson, 1927).

Farjeon, Herbert, *Cricket Bag* (London: Sportsman's Book Club, Pelham Books, 1969).

Goldwin, William, *In Certamen Pilae* (*On a Ball Game*), in *Musae Juveniles* (Detroit, MI: Gale Ecco Print Editions, 2010).

Haigh, Gideon, *Silent Revolutions: Writings on Cricket History* (Melbourne: Black Inc., Schwartz, 2006).

Heidegger, Martin, *Being and Time*, trans. John Macquarrie and Edward Robinson (Oxford: Blackwell, 1993).

Herriot, James, *Vet in Harness* (London: Pan, 2006).

Holding, Michael, *Whispering Death: The Life and Times of Michael Holding* (London: André Deutsch, 1993).

Hughes, Simon, *And God Created Cricket: An Irreverent History of the Greatest Game on Earth* (London: Black Swan, Random House, 2010).

Hume, David, *A Treatise of Human Nature*, ed. L. A. Selby-Bigge (Oxford: Oxford University Press, 1978).

James, C. L. R., *Beyond a Boundary* (London: Yellow Jersey Press, Random House, 2005).

James, Steve, *The Art of Centuries* (London: Bantam, Transworld, 2015).

Lloyd, Grahame, *Howzat? The Six Sixes Ball Mystery* (Cardiff: Celluloid, 2013).

Lloyd, Grahame, *Six of the Best: Cricket's Most Famous Over* (Cardiff: Celluloid, 2008).

Locke, John, *An Essay Concerning Human Understanding* (London: Everyman, J. M. Dent, 1993).

Low, Robert, *W. G.: A Life of W. G. Grace* (London: Richard Cohen Books, 1997).

Moorhouse, Geoffrey, *The Best Loved Game: One Summer of English Cricket* (London: Faber and Faber, 2013).

Nyren, John, *The Young Cricketer's Tutor* (London: HarperCollins, 1974).

O'Neill, Joseph, *Netherland* (London, HarperPerennial, 2009).

Plato, *The Republic*, trans. Desmond Lee (London: Penguin, 2007).

Ranjitsinhji, K. S., *The Jubilee Book of Cricket* (Edinburgh: Blackwood, 1897).

Sartre, Jean-Paul, *Being and Nothingness: An Essay on Phenomenological Ontology*, trans. Hazel E. Barnes (London: Routledge, 2003).

Sellars, Wilfrid, *Science, Perception and Reality* (Atascadero, CA: Ridgeview, 1991).

Smith, Tom, and MCC, *Cricket Umpiring and Scoring: Laws of Cricket, 2000 Code, Fourth Edition* (London: Weidenfeld & Nicolson, 2011).

Staunton, Anthony, *Victoria Cross: Australia's Finest and the Battles They Fought* (Victoria, Australia: Hardie Grant, 2005).

Steen, Rob and McLellan, Alastair *500–1: The Miracle of Headingley '81* (London: Wisden, 2010).

Tennyson, Alfred Lord, *Selected Poems* (London: Penguin, 2007).

Trescothick, Marcus, *Coming Back to Me* (London: HarperSport, 2009).

Trueman, Fred, *Ball of Fire: An Autobiography* (London: J. M. Dent, 1976).

Waddell, Dan, *The Wit and Wisdom of Test Match Special* (London: BBC Books, 2015).

Waters, Chris, *Fred Trueman: The Authorised Biography* (London: Aurum Press, 2011).

Wells, H. G. *Experiment in Autobiography: Discoveries and Conclusions of a Very Ordinary Brain (Since 1866)* (New York: Lippincott, 1967).

Wilde, Oscar, *The Picture of Dorian Gray* (Ware: Wordsworth Classics, 1992).

Wittgenstein, Ludwig, *Tractatus Logico-Philosophicus*, trans. D. F. Pears and B. F. McGuiness (London: Routledge, 2001).

Woodcock, John, *The Times One Hundred Greatest Cricketers* (London: Pan Macmillan, 1998).

Other media references

10CC, 'Dreadlock Holiday', Track 1, *Bloody Tourists* (Mercury, 1978).

'Bancroft Caught on Cam Pocketing Sugar During Ashes' (India Today, YouTube, 2018).

BBC Sport: Cricket Website: www.bbc.co.uk/sport/cricket

'Brisbane Heat's Deandra Dottin and Laura Harris Collision' (Jiurra Wroshyr, YouTube, 2016).

'Cricket Balls 1956' (British Pathé, YouTube, 2014).

Duckworth Lewis Method, 'Jiggery Pokery', Track 5, *The Duckworth Lewis Method* (Divine Comedy Records, 2009).

ESPN Cricinfo Website: www.espncricinfo.com

Fire in Babylon, Director: Stevan Riley (Cowboy Films, Passion Pictures, 2010).

'Garfield Sobers Six Sixes in an Over' (BBC Wales, 1968 & EOMA's Cricket Compilations, YouTube, 2010).

'I Just Cut Open a $120 USD Kookaburra Cricket Ball – See What's Inside' (Jason Mellet, YouTube, 2013).

'Jacques Rudolph Kills a Pigeon – Cricket Ball Air Strike' (Desi-Link, YouTube, 2009).

Lord's Website: www.lords.org

Padding Up With Sachin (Aviva, YouTube, 2013).

'Shane Warne: King of Spin – Leg Spin Tutorial' (Rob Lanchbury-Thomas, YouTube, 2010).

Index

10CC 1

Abbott, Sean 183
Abbott, Tony 184
absurdity 11–12, 54, 75, 240, 263,
    272–3
Abu Dhabi 50, 195
Achong, Ellis 'Puss' 147
Adams, Douglas 14, 270, 272–3
adversity 202, 211–12, 217, 219
Aeroball 58
aerodynamics 38–9, 56, 92
aesthetic 4, 49, 93, 187, 207, 209,
    211
Afridi, Shahid 100
agility 133, 160, 206, 208
Agnew, Jonathan 54
agricultural 7, 57
air resistance 97, 123 *see also* drag
Akhtar, Shoaib 121–3, 127
Alderman, Terry 213–14
Ali, Moeen 52
All-England Eleven 11, 171, 209,
    223, 257
alum 43, 78
Americans 8–9

Amiss, Dennis 178
Anand & Anand ball 60
ancient Greeks 21
Anderson, James 52, 96, 194–5,
    221
anecdote 14, 75, 161, 167, 257
aniline leather 55
animism 3, 26, 182
Antigua 200
Apartheid 103
apartheid 5–6, 142
aristocracy 68–9
Arlott, John 18, 205, 209–10
arm ball 151–2
arms race 156, 226
artefact 39
Ashes 16, 44, 115, 139–40, 142–3,
    167, 184, 192, 194, 196, 207,
    212, 217, 219, 227, 232–3,
    237–8, 246, 271–2
asymmetrical ball 94, 98
Atherton, Mike 50, 103–7, 233
atmospheric conditions 39, 97,
    102, 123

atoms 25–6, 28–9
attentiveness 156–7
Austin, J. L. 26
Australia 16, 44, 49–50, 85–6,
    95–6, 112, 114–19, 122, 125,
    140–3, 183, 193–4, 196, 199,
    203–4, 207–8, 213–18, 222, 224,
    227, 232, 237–9, 242, 244, 246,
    256
Awaskar, Hillel 189
Aziz, Abdul 186

back foot 24, 68, 128–9
back-spinner 154
bad light 46, 50–1, 56–7, 108, 195
Baggy Greens 244
bails 65, 109–10, 181–2, 197, 236,
    241, 257
Ball from Hell 232
Ball of the Century 232
ball tampering 38, 98, 100–4,
    107–10, 112, 114–16, 118
ball-in-action 164
Baluch, Kiran 204
Bancroft, Cameron 112–13, 115–18
bandsaw 27, 40
Bangladesh 187, 198
Barnes, Julian 14
Barnes, Sydney 200
Barty-King, Hugh 63, 65, 67, 71–2,
    169, 188
baseball (ball) 60
baseball (game) 7–8
baseball bat 7
Bat and Ball Inn 67
bat handle 171, 174, 176–7, 225,
    235, 244

bat width 75–6
batsman 4, 6–7, 11, 19, 22–3, 38,
    48–9, 52, 55, 58, 60, 66–8, 71,
    74, 83–5, 90–6, 98–9, 100–1,
    107–8, 112, 119, 121–4, 126–40,
    142, 144–5, 147, 149–56, 160–1,
    165, 168, 172–4, 176–80, 182–6,
    195–8, 201, 208–9, 211, 220,
    223–6, 228–32, 237, 240–4, 247,
    252, 258, 268, 272–3
batting crease *see* popping crease
batting side 53, 90, 99, 101, 135,
    139, 198
battle 3, 9, 119, 131, 177, 213, 226,
    238, 262
BBC 15–18, 54, 177, 184, 193, 207,
    209, 234–5, 248–50, 273
BBC Sports Personality 207
BBC Test Match Special (TMS)
    17–18, 54, 193, 273
beamer 131
Beauclerk, Lord Frederick 174–5
beautiful 4, 20–1, 23, 34, 36,
    210–11, 225–6, 265
beautiful game 4
Benaud, Richie 17, 86, 234–6, 243
Berkeley, George 24–5
Berkeley, George Fitz-Hardinge 24
Betjeman, John 14
big bang 182
black power 125–6
Blackwash series 126
Blackwood, Jermaine 52
blade throw (of bat) 176
block hole 96
blood 11, 34, 93, 169, 178, 183, 187,
    207

blood red ball 11, 34, 207
bodyline 139–44, 181
Bombay 247
bone jarring 176, 225
Bonhams 251, 253
Border, Allan 170, 214, 216, 220, 233
boring 6, 13, 51, 84, 91, 198, 271
Bosanquet, Bernard 153
bosie 153
Boswell, James 25
Botham, Ian 194, 212–19, 245, 259
Botham's Ashes 212, 219
Boucher, Mark 181, 197
bouncer 89, 125, 129–31, 134, 170, 178, 183
boundary 5, 12, 90, 140, 157–8, 170–1, 181, 190, 214, 216, 231, 233, 242, 244, 272
bowled around legs 151
bowler 7, 11–12, 17, 19, 23, 28, 30–1, 38–9, 48, 51, 55–8, 61, 65–9, 83–96, 98–9, 102, 111, 116, 121–2, 124–32, 134–40, 144–50, 154, 156–7, 165, 171, 173–7, 183, 187–9, 191, 194, 198–203, 208–10, 212, 220, 226, 228–9, 232, 237–8, 241, 249, 255–6, 258–9, 267–8
bowling 19, 22–4, 44, 46, 52, 55, 58, 61, 68–9, 83–90, 95, 97–8, 100, 111, 120–1, 125–7, 131–3, 135–6, 138, 140–2, 144–8, 153–6, 172–3, 178, 181, 187, 199–201, 204, 206, 209–10, 214–15, 217–19, 224, 226–7, 230, 232–4, 237, 244–7, 257–9, 266

bowling crease 68
bowling side 22–3, 90, 97
box (guard) 161, 168, 173–4, 177, 180
Boycott, Geoffrey 107, 109, 193, 213
Bradman, Donald 16, 139–40, 143, 194, 204, 221, 258
Brand, Henry 185
bravado 179, 193, 231
Bravo, Dwayne 52
brazilwood 78
Brearley, Mike 162, 178, 202, 212, 215, 218, 220
Bridgetown 178
Bright, Ray 216
Brittin, Janette 204–5, 222
Broad, Stuart 52, 102, 194, 248
Broadhalfpenny Down 67
Brown of Brighton 171
Brown, Harry 40–1
bruises 19, 25, 34, 140, 161, 169
Bull, Charles 186
Buller, Syd 186
Burge, Peter 103–4, 106–7
Burton, George 229
byes 268

cakes 11, 17
cane handle bat 171, 176–7, 225
captain 5, 50, 52, 67, 85–6, 92, 103–5, 107, 110–13, 115, 117, 119, 125–6, 140–2, 160–2, 167, 178, 181, 184, 189, 196–7, 204–5, 209, 212–13, 215, 221, 224, 226, 233, 235–6, 238–40, 267–9

carbon fibre 177, 179

carbon fibre shaft bat 177

Cardus, Neville 7, 34, 84–5, 137, 159, 170–2, 175, 181, 209, 211, 221, 226, 231

Caribbean Premier League (CPL) 52

carnage 181

Cat in the Hole 63, 65

catching 22, 36, 44, 65, 69, 93, 113, 133, 137, 150, 152, 156–7, 159–60, 162, 180, 182, 185, 187, 195, 197–8, 208, 216–17, 241, 245, 262–3, 273

Chadwick, Henry 7

Champagne 213, 215, 218, 242

champion 221, 240

Chappell, Greg 85, 119

Chappell, Trevor 85

character 3–4, 6–7, 13–14, 193, 200, 263

Chase, Roston 52

cheating 100, 106, 108–9, 111, 114, 117, 119, 139, 229

cherry 21, 35, 37

chess 9

Chester-le-Street 135, 195

Chesterton, G. K. 14

children 37, 59, 63

Chinaman (delivery) 147

Christie's 248–53

chucking 88

civilization 8, 10, 17, 76, 169, 271, 273

Clarke, Charles Cowden 67

Clarke, Michael 184, 243

Clarke, William 209, 258

class discrimination 5, 142

Close, Brian 162, 167

close-in fielder 140, 161–2, 168, 180

cloud 27, 207, 259, 268

club (bat) 7

Code of 1744 67, 69, 185

collection of appearances 24–5, 32

Collingwood, Paul 108

colonialism 5, 76

colour blindness 29

coma 183, 187

comedy 13–14, 167–8, 270

commentary 14, 17–18, 54, 86, 89, 107, 178, 190, 234, 243, 248

Compton, Denis 202, 220

concept 28, 99

conduct 8, 75, 109, 117, 120, 141, 228

conker 21, 37, 60

consistency 19, 49, 52, 80–1, 136, 139, 198

conventional swing 97–8

Cook, Alastair 52–4, 167, 194–7, 208, 210

core of ball 39, 42–3, 57–8, 70–3, 76, 79

coriaceus orbis *see* leathern orb

cork 43, 57–9, 61, 70, 72–3, 76, 79, 175

cork/rubber 42–3, 57

corridor of uncertainty 137

County Championship 45–6

county cricket 20, 45–6, 73, 101, 192–3, 228, 247, 252

cover drive 225

Coverdale, Brydon 51, 56
cowhide (leather) 37, 55
cranberry 34–5
Cricket Australia 44, 114–18
cricket field *see* field of play
Cricket Tennis Ball 60–1
Cricket World Cup 62, 121, 205–6, 247
cricketer 16, 24, 37, 44, 67, 73–4, 81, 89, 101, 107, 143, 153, 158, 160, 168, 173, 182, 184, 186–7, 191, 193–4, 199–200, 202–12, 216, 218, 220–1, 225, 245, 258
crimson rambler 34
Croft, Colin 178
Cromwell, Oliver 68
crooked bat 76, 84
croquet 11
culture 3, 14, 116
curved bat 76, 84

Da Vinci, Leonardo 196
Daft, Richard 173
danger 9, 61, 96, 136, 140, 144, 149, 153, 171–3, 175–6, 178, 181, 185, 190, 270
Dark ball 75, 260
Dark, James Henry 75
Dark, Robert 75, 77–8, 81, 175–6, 260
David, Neetu 204
Davies, Stephen 189
day-night matches 46, 49–51, 54, 56, 192
De Villiers, AB 197
dead ball 89–90, 273

death 8, 12, 58, 90, 130, 140, 165, 167–9, 173, 181–91, 235, 261
Decision Review System (DRS) 230, 244 *see also* Hawk-Eye
deep long-on 159
Delhi 187, 200
delivery 9, 16, 19–20, 24, 28, 38–9, 61, 76, 83–91, 94–6, 98–9, 119, 121–5, 127–9, 131–7, 140, 144–55, 161, 163, 171, 173–4, 178, 181, 186–7, 208, 210, 215–16, 232–43, 245, 248–9, 255–7, 263, 268, 272–3
Descartes, René 32–3
Dev, Kapil 220
diamond 27, 42, 61–2, 226
diamond-studded ball 61–2
Dickens £10 note 265
Dickens, Charles 12, 14, 21, 227, 265
Dilley, Graham 213–14, 216
Din, Asif 101
dip 149, 151, 234–5, 240
diplomacy 2, 103, 110, 141, 143, 226
dirt 48–9, 55, 70, 103–6
Dirt in the Pocket affair 103
dismissal 50, 65–6, 84, 90–1, 95–6, 131, 136, 150, 156, 169, 181, 186, 197–8, 212–13, 215, 222, 228–30, 242
Doctrove, Billy 108
dog (canine) 84, 171, 222, 189
dog (primitive bat) 63–6
doosra 152–4, 156
dot ball 89, 98–9
Dottin, Deandra 170

Downton, Paul 181
drag 94, 97–8, 123
drama 4, 14, 18, 206
Dravid, Rahul 197–8
draw (result) 12, 51, 56, 99, 109, 195, 201, 218, 268
drift 149, 151, 234–5, 240
drive 132–3, 188–9, 225
drying of ball 101, 105
drying pitch 202, 247
duck (0) 212–13, 215, 218
Duckworth Lewis Method (pop band) 236–7
Duke & Son 44–5, 47, 72–7, 80–1, 252, 260–2 *see also* Dukes ball
Duke, John 73
Duke, Timothy I 73
Duke, Timothy II 73
Dukes (Duke & Son) ball 20, 41, 44–5, 47, 51, 54, 59, 72–7, 80–1, 102, 249–53, 260–2
Durban 200, 248
dye 28, 55, 67, 70, 78
Dyson, John 216

Edam 40
Edgar, Henry 260
Edgbaston 16–17, 51, 53, 56, 186, 197, 218, 238–9
Edwards, Bill 249
Edwards, Charlotte 205
eight ball over 255–6
elegance 52, 196, 208–9, 225, 264–5
elitism 192
Elizabethan Cricket 71

empire 6, 10, 76, 262, 273
empirical 12, 34
Engel, Matthew 235
England 15–16, 44–5, 50–4, 56, 62–3, 69, 71, 74–5, 81, 85–7, 96, 101–3, 106–9, 115, 121, 125–7, 130, 135, 139–43, 154, 162, 167, 177–8, 181, 187, 193–201, 203–7, 209, 211–14, 116–18, 222, 224, 226, 232–3, 237–9, 241–4, 246–8, 250, 252, 256–9, 270–1, 273
English literature 13, 70, 263
ergonomic 7
ESPN Cricinfo 51, 122, 182, 204, 209, 224, 230, 235
ethics 4, 5, 8, 35, 106, 120, 229
Essex CCC 122, 186, 229
Eton 9
existential 34, 62, 163–4
extension (in space) 27–8, 32
external world 32–3

fair play 5, 76, 269
Fairbrother, Neil 107
Farington, Joseph 73–4
Farjeon, Herbert 266, 269
fast bowling 17, 19, 22, 38–9, 58, 61, 71, 81, 93–4, 98, 120–3, 125–8, 130–1, 136–7, 140, 143–6, 148–9, 160, 170, 172–4, 177–8, 183, 186, 194, 200, 203, 212–15, 226, 229, 232–3, 239, 243, 256–7, 259
field of play 8, 10–11, 24, 46, 86, 90, 95, 101, 106, 109–10, 112–13, 118, 126, 135, 142, 157–9, 168,

170, 173–4, 181–2, 186–8, 198,
207, 218, 227, 263–4

fielders 11, 24, 66, 87, 89–93, 95,
132, 134, 139–40, 144, 155–62,
168, 180, 182, 185, 188–9, 191,
198, 231, 240, 273

fielding 11, 18, 52, 84, 90, 95, 101,
112, 156–7, 160–2, 168, 171,
180, 187, 189–90, 197, 244, 262,
264, 266, 268–9

fielding side 24, 49, 53, 92–4, 99,
134–5, 139, 173, 229, 268–9

fine leg 153, 171

finger spin 147–8

fingers 35–6, 41–2, 137, 147–55,
179, 180, 208

first-class cricket 45–6, 48, 122,
181, 186, 202, 224

Fitzpatrick, Cathryn 203

Fitzpatrick, Paul 214

flat-spinner 154

flight 38, 57, 84, 98, 123, 149, 151,
234

Flintoff, Andrew 242, 244–5

flipper 153

floodlights 46–7, 49–50, 54

flying saucer ball 154

Folley, Ian 187

follow-on 213, 216

Fonzie 30

football (ball) 60, 92

football (game) 6–7, 226

footballer 102, 206

foreigners 10, 270

formal cricket 44, 57, 59–60, 62,
85, 87, 121, 171, 269

forward defensive stroke 132

French cricket 59

front foot 68, 128, 132

Fry, C. B. 226

full-length delivery *see*
full-pitched delivery

full-pitched delivery 123–4, 132–3

future (of cricket) 2, 56, 192

Gallipoli Campaign 262

gambling 67–9

gamesmanship 108, 228–9, 231

Garner, Joel 125, 178

Gatting Ball 232–3, 235, 237, 240

Gatting, Mike 216, 232–7

Gayle, Chris 52

genius 13, 137, 193, 202, 208, 222,
226, 240, 265

Gentlemen and Players 142, 223

George Avery (company) 78

George Prince of Wales (later
George IV) 72

Gibbs, Herschelle 247

Gilchrist, Adam 239

gladiatorial 169

Glamorgan CCC 219, 248–50,
252

glass ceiling 205, 207

Glitter Windball 59–60

Gloucestershire 222, 224

Gloucestershire CCC 122, 222

gloves 59, 90, 93, 175–6, 179–80,
236, 244

God 24, 32–3, 39, 53, 57, 173–4,
182, 192, 210, 227, 273

gold leaf 35, 38

gold-flecked ball 207

Goldwin, William 70

golf 63
golf ball 40–1
Gooch, Graham 196, 213, 233, 236
good light 57
good-length delivery 128–9, 132–3
googly 152–3, 156, 242
Gough, Darren 209
Gough, John 248, 252
Gower, David 209
Grace, E. M. 222
Grace, Fred 222
Grace, Henry 222
Grace, Martha 222
Grace, W. G. 122, 172, 206, 221–31
graceful 163–4, 207–8, 210
grass 11, 24, 30, 70, 172, 212, 263–4
Gray-Nicolls ball 45, 58
Great Exhibition (1851) 77
greeny-yellow ball 50–1
Greig, Tony 125–6, 178, 234, 243
grenade, cricket ball 262
grenades 9, 262–3
grub bowling 84, 86
grudge match 266
gully 95, 132, 162
Guptill, Martin 49
Guy, Joe 209

hacksaw 40–1
Hadlee, Richard 220
Haigh, Gideon 168, 177, 209
Hair, Darrell 108–11
Hambledon Club 66–7, 69, 74–5, 203

Hammond, Walter 220–1, 270
handful 27, 34, 36
handmade ball 58, 81
hands 7, 24, 90, 103, 105, 145, 152, 158–60, 164, 168, 174, 176, 179–80, 216, 235
hard hands 160
hardness (of ball) 21–2, 24, 35–7, 47–8, 61, 71, 94, 145, 160–1, 260
Harmison Ball 243
Harmison, Steve 243–4
Harris, Laura 170
Harrow 258
Hashishin 259
Hassan, Basharat 250
Hawk-Eye 150, 241
Hayden, Matthew 201
Hazlewood, Josh 50
Headingley 53, 137, 189, 197, 212, 214, 218–19, 245, 259
Headley, George 258
Healy, Ian 233, 236
heart 2–3, 21, 37
heart attack 186, 189
Heidegger, Martin 164–5
helmet 59, 130, 140, 161–2, 173, 177–81, 183–4, 187–8, 213
Hendren, Patsy 177
Henry Parker (company) 78
Herriot, James 14, 263–4
Heyhoe-Flint, Rachael 205–6, 222, 224
history 2, 18, 20, 39, 44, 62–3, 70, 75, 86, 100, 108–9, 113, 122, 137, 139, 152, 168, 173, 177, 183, 186, 193–7, 200–1, 207,

216, 219, 224, 226, 233, 237, 241, 243, 253, 256, 261
hit the ball twice 185–6
Hobbs, Jack 202, 220, 264
Holding, Michael 58, 122, 125–6, 194
home counties 69, 81
hook shot 130, 183, 208, 225
hops (flowers) 78
Howarth, Geoffrey 86
Hughes, Kim 215
Hughes, Merv 233
Hughes, Phillip 183–5, 189
Hughes, Simon 54–5, 173, 209–10, 241
Hume, David 33–4
Hutton, Leonard 220

I Zingari 273
iconic ball 1, 245–6
ideal ball 21, 58
idealism 24–6
ideology 6
illegal polishes (of ball) 56, 97–8, 100–2, 105, 108
impenetrability 27
impressions 33
inanimate objects 1–3, 26
Incrediball 58, 61
India 16, 44–5, 60, 117, 126, 145, 187, 196–7, 200, 203–4, 206, 224, 247, 251, 253, 262
India rubber 71, 174–5
Indian gum lac 78
Indian Premier League (IPL) 115, 117, 272
infielders 157, 160

infinite 2, 4, 9, 15, 23, 61, 91, 192, 230, 257
injury 19, 130, 133, 140–1, 144, 160, 168–70, 179, 181–2, 184–7, 191, 214
inside (of ball) 39–43 *see also* core of ball
inside edge 95, 137
instrument (ball as) 164–5
inswinger 19, 58, 94–6
International Cricket Council (ICC) 9, 45–6, 50–1, 56, 61–2, 88, 109, 111–16, 118, 135, 152, 256
Inzamam-ul-Haq 111

Jajodia, Dilip 44
jalebi 154
James, C. L. R. 4–6, 8, 208, 210, 227, 258
James, Steve 228
Jardine, Douglas 140–3
Jayawardene, Mahela 197
Jenkins, Alcwyn 189
Jessop, Gilbert 122
jingoistic 10
Johannesburg 116, 200, 247
John Martin & Son 78
John Sales (company) 78
John Wisden & Co 258–9, 261 *see also* Wisden
Johnson, Martin 236
Johnson, Samuel 25, 34
Johnston, Bill 16
Johnston, Brian 17
Jones, Geraint 244
justice 5, 15, 142, 261

Kallis, Jacques 196–7, 221
Kasprowicz, Michael 244
Keats, John 67
Kennington Oval 16, 108, 218, 222–3, 227, 271
Kent CCC 66, 73
Keshri, Ankit 182, 185
Kevlar 179
Keysor, Leonard 262
Khan, Imran 110, 220
Khan, Javeria 170
Khan, Shaiza 204
Khan, Younis 195
kitbag 19, 58, 248, 252–3
Knight, Nick 127
Kookaburra ball 40, 43–5, 47, 49–51, 59–61, 76, 80, 102
Kortright, Charles 122, 229
krickstoel 64
Kumble, Anil 145, 200, 221
Kwik cricket 59

lac dye 78
lacquer (of ball) 43, 55
Lahore 80
Laker Ball 245–7
Laker, Jim 199–200, 246–7
Lamba, Raman 187
laminations (of bat) 177
Lancashire CCC 107, 187, 189, 246
language game (of cricket) 12, 272
Lara, Brian 200–1, 247
Larwood, Harold 140, 142–3
late cut 225
Latter, Thomas 185

Laws of Cricket 11, 35, 45–6, 57, 60, 66–8, 74–5, 83, 86–7, 100, 102, 104–6, 110, 117, 134–5, 141–2, 144, 155, 185, 228, 230, 255–6, 267–9
Lawson, Geoff 214
lbw 50, 52, 96, 133, 135–6, 150, 153–4, 213, 229
leadership 6, 9, 113, 117, 162
leather 4, 21, 30–1, 35, 37–9, 41–3, 47, 54–5, 57–9, 61, 64, 70–4, 77–9, 81, 92–3, 101, 108, 164, 179
leathern orb 4, 68, 70, 77, 81
Lee, Brett 127, 244
left-arm orthodox 147–8
left-arm unorthodox 147–8
leg break 147–8, 150–4, 230, 235–6, 242
leg glance 225
leg side 94, 134–5, 139–40, 144, 149–50, 152–3, 211, 231, 234–5, 239, 241
leg spin 58, 147, 150–3, 200, 232, 234–7
leg stump 140, 150–1, 233, 235, 241
leggings 174–5
Lehmann, Darren 116
length (of delivery) 84, 96, 127–9, 132–3, 136, 144–5, 149, 151, 172, 226, 234–5
length (of pitch) 66–7, 71, 76, 154, 240
Lewis, Richard 248, 252–3
light meter 56
Lillee, Dennis 213, 216
Lillywhite, Fred 258–9

Lillywhite, John 223, 259

Lillywhites 223, 259

Lindwall, Ray 16, 177

line (of delivery) 38, 94, 121, 124, 127, 133–41, 144–5, 148, 150–1, 153, 226, 233, 235 *see also* bodyline

linguistics 106

Linley, Lord 251

Lion Cricket Ball Works 77

little devil 182

live ball 89–90

Lloyd, Clive 126

Lloyd, Grahame 219, 248–51

lob *or* lobster bowling 85

Lock, Tony 199–200

Locke, John 26–7

lofted ball 132, 159

logo 35, 59

London CC 67, 71, 188

long barrier 158

long hop 131, 225

long stop 171

Lord's 10, 59–60, 75, 77, 85, 103, 141, 172–3, 175, 202, 205–7, 212, 223, 227, 238, 246, 270, 272

Lord's slope 173

lost ball 24, 89–90, 92, 246

Low, Robert 172, 229

Luff and Week's Patent Marvel ball 260

Luff, Henry 259–61

Lycra 179

Lyons, Joseph 141

Machiavellian orb 175

machine-made ball 80–1

Mad Hatter's tea party 4, 11

magenta ball 50

maiden 137

Major, John 143

malfunction 165

Man of the Match 19, 195, 216, 245

Mars 37

Marsh, Rodney 86, 216

Martin, John 77–8

Marxist 5

Marylebone CC (MCC) 10–11, 35, 51, 60–2, 67, 71, 74–5, 85, 87, 109, 135, 141–3, 173–4, 177, 205, 227, 246

Marylebone CC (MCC) Museum 246

Mason, Peter 205

match ball 57, 100, 252

match-fixing 139

mathematics 12, 15, 18, 212

McGrath, Glenn 136–7, 145, 194, 221, 238

McKechnie, Brian 85–6

McLellan, Alastair 219

meaning of cricket 99, 272

means 163, 165

meat of bat 178, 214

Meeks, Alan 184

Melbourne 43, 85, 170, 193, 204, 224, 253

metaphysical 22–3, 32, 257

Miandad, Javed 195

middle stump 66, 74, 134, 147, 216, 241

Middlesex CCC 59, 181

Miller, Jose 248, 250, 253

Miller, Keith 177

mind 24–6, 33, 118, 143, 145, 147, 159, 164, 229, 231–2, 236, 245, 257, 271

mixing it up (bowling) 132

modern game 49, 67–8, 74, 81, 85, 127

Molony, Trevor 85

Mondal, Sourabh 182

money 14, 40, 43–4, 47, 57, 62, 75, 78, 104, 110–11, 117, 122, 200, 202, 228, 248–50, 252–3, 265

Moorhouse, Geoffrey 74

moral obligation 107, 229–30

morals 107, 217, 225, 229–30, 270

motion 2, 5, 11, 21, 27–8, 32, 39, 83, 88, 146–7, 164, 189, 207–9, 211

movement 28, 38–9, 58, 147, 149, 151, 155–6, 158, 163, 179, 207–8, 210

Muldoon, Robert 86

Muralitharan, Muttiah 145, 152, 194, 220–1

Murray Mints 101–2

muscle memory 158

Mushtaq, Saqlain 152, 154

Mynn, Alfred 174–5, 194

mysticism 28, 144, 270

Nash, Malcolm 219, 247–51

natural variation (of spin) 149, 155, 234, 242

Neale, Phil 101

Netherlands 247

nets 19, 58

Nevill, Peter 49

new ball 22–3, 34, 37, 40–1, 43, 56, 89, 92–4, 124–5, 145

New Zealand 49, 85–6, 135, 203, 206, 221, 233, 256

newspapers 14, 100, 107, 143, 170, 197, 220, 230, 245, 270

Nichol, Maurice 186

no-ball 83, 85, 88–90, 131, 144, 247, 255

Noblemen's and Gentlemen's Club 67

nurdling 127, 176, 231

Nyren, John 67

Nyren, Richard 67

object (ball as) 1–3, 20–3, 26–9, 35–7, 39, 44, 46, 59, 62–3, 92, 163–5, 245, 257

obstructing the field 185–6

ODIs 47–8, 85, 95, 130, 135, 183–4, 193, 205, 247

off break 147–53, 186, 242

off drive 225

off side 94, 134–5, 137, 139, 149–51, 153–4, 183, 233, 236, 239–41

off stump 137–8, 235

old ball 20, 22–3, 40–1, 89, 246

Old Trafford 107, 199, 218, 232, 246–7

Old, Chris 214, 216

Oldfield, Bert 140

omnipresence 24

on drive 225

O'Neill, Joseph 8, 34

one-piece bat 176

orange ball 29, 48, 59, 61

outfield 90, 157

outside edge 95, 137, 150, 152

outswinger 58, 94–6

over 20, 28, 48, 71, 89, 130, 172, 219, 239, 243, 247–50, 255–6, 268, 273 *see also* overs

overarm bowling 83, 85, 87

overs 46, 50–1, 53–4, 56, 61, 92, 97, 99, 108, 137, 139, 145, 157, 206, 215, 219, 231–2, 237, 239, 255–6

Oxbridge ball 45

pace bowling *see* fast bowling

pads 11, 59, 96, 112, 140, 171, 174–5, 177, 179–81, 196, 241, 259, 264

pain 20, 25, 34, 157, 165, 167–9, 171, 176, 182

Pakistan 44, 50, 61, 80, 100, 108–11, 121, 152, 154, 170, 195, 200, 204, 256

Pakistan Cricket Board (PCB) 111

Palmer, Ken 236

Pandey, Shikha 206

Parker & Mercer 78

Parkin, John 252

Parr, George 258

patience 9, 158, 193, 198, 231

pavilion 13, 56, 215, 228, 236, 241, 258

Penshurst 72, 77

perception 3, 24–9, 31–2, 47, 251

perfect ball 22–3, 32, 34, 145

periscope bat 130

Perth 201

Peterson, Robin 247

phenomenology 32, 163

philosophy 1, 3–5, 19, 21–6, 29, 32–4, 46, 62, 100, 106, 148, 158, 162–4, 192, 210, 230, 270, 272

physical properties 31

physical things 22, 24

physical world 22, 25–6, 33

Pietersen, Kevin 108, 135

pigeon 188–90

pigmented leather 55

pigments 55, 78

pila lubrica (greased ball) 70

Pilch, Fuller 171

pink ball 29, 44, 49–57, 192, 195

pitch (cricket pitch) 8, 23, 38–9, 46, 62, 66–7, 71, 74, 76, 86, 89, 94, 97, 121, 123–4, 128–9, 134, 137, 145–6, 149–50, 154, 171–3, 201–2, 215, 222, 231, 233–4, 239–40, 246–7, 270

pitch (of ball) 15, 38, 84, 96, 98, 121, 123–4, 128–9, 131–3, 138, 140, 144, 146, 149–54, 174, 216, 235, 240–1

Plato 21–4

Platts, John 173

Platypus Speedball 61–2

playing conditions 11, 23, 29, 39, 46–7, 49, 52, 93, 97, 123, 125, 137, 182, 202, 246

Pocock, Alfred 222

polishing (of ball) 21, 30, 35, 44, 55–6, 93–4, 100–2, 105, 108

politics 2, 5, 14, 103, 110, 141, 143, 168, 205, 226, 270

polymer topcoat (of ball) 55

Ponting, Ricky 160, 196–7, 208, 221, 239, 242
popping crease 66, 68, 76, 96, 123, 133, 140, 144, 176, 189, 241
practice ball 57–8
Pradhan, Snehal 203
precision instrument (bat) 7
present-at-hand (vorhanden) 165
pressure game 9, 52, 99, 201, 216–17, 226
primary qualities 26–8, 31
primary seam 37–43, 45, 51, 57–9, 62, 70–2, 80–1, 94, 98, 107, 121, 123–4, 148–50, 154–5, 240, 242
Prince of Wales, Frederick Louis 188
private parts 161, 168, 174
protective gear 59, 125, 144, 168, 171, 173–5, 177–82, 185
psychological 4, 9, 14, 48, 91, 151, 162, 240
pundits 14, 17, 55, 114, 122, 152, 154–5, 192, 203, 209, 243

quantum physics 33, 271
quarter seams 37–8, 41, 72, 79, 103, 107–9, 111
quilt (of ball) 42–3, 73, 79–80
quilt hammer 79

race 5, 111, 125, 271
racism 5, 109, 111, 125–6
radio 14–15, 17, 206
rag ball 65
Raj, Tilak 247
Ramprakash, Mark 209
Randall, Darryn 188

Ranjitsinhji, K. S. 224, 226
rational 11, 35, 270
Readers ball 45, 59
ready-to-hand (zuhanden) 164–5
realism 26
rearguard action 99
red and white ball 57–8
red and yellow ball 57
red ball 11, 20, 29, 34–5, 44–9, 51, 53–8, 60–1, 70, 77–8, 207, 272
reflexes 4, 160, 206
Reid, John Richard 221
release speed (of delivery) 123, 126–7
religion 49, 81, 270
replacement ball 108, 249
replay (play back) 112, 155, 208, 232, 244
reverse swing 97–8
Richards, Vivian 220
Roach, Kemar 52
Roberts, Andy 178
Roberts, Fred 122
roller 171
rolling globular body 62–3
romanticism 17, 122, 209, 264
Ronaldo, Cristiano 92
Ronay, Barney 112
Root, Joe 52, 197
roughening of ball 55–6, 93–4, 97, 105, 108, 112, 116, 118, 120
roundarm bowling 83–5, 87, 171–2, 174–5
rounders ball 60
rounders bat 7
roundness (of ball) 24, 68
Rowan, Eric 177

Rudolph, Jacques 189–90, 206
rugby 13, 16, 206
run-out 66, 90, 189, 206
run rate 52, 139, 239
run-up 46, 58, 90, 121, 135, 147,
    157, 215, 233, 240, 268–9
Russell, Baron Charles 260–1

sacred 9, 35, 110, 245–6, 270
saliva 30, 55–6, 92–3, 97, 101–2,
    108
Sami, Mohammad 121, 127
Samuels, Marlon 52
sandpaper 106, 112, 116, 118, 120
Sandpaper Gate 116
Sanspareils Greenlands ball (SG)
    45
Sartre, Jean-Paul 163
Saturn 37, 72
science 3, 33–4, 47, 81, 102, 144,
    210, 225
science fiction 270
scorecard 12, 16, 99
scuffing (of ball) 93, 102
seam bowling *see* fast bowling
seamer *see* fast bowling
seams *see* primary seam *and*
    quarter seams
second bowler 65–6
secondary qualities 26–9, 31, 100
segregation 5, 142
Sellars, Wilfrid 3
serial killer 169
sexual discrimination 203–4, 205
Shastri, Ravi 247
shine (of ball) 23, 37, 39, 43, 52,
    55–6, 94, 97, 100–1, 145

shooters 172
short-length delivery *see* short-
    pitched delivery
short-pitched delivery 124, 129,
    131, 140, 144, 215–16
showbiz 199
Shrubsole, Anya 206–7
sightscreen 13
silly mid off 161
silly mid on 161
silly point 11, 152, 161
Singh, Yuvraj 247
Singhal, Ashish 251, 253
size (of ball) 26–7, 35–6, 46, 68, 79,
    92
skull 19, 140, 162, 178, 183, 190
Slazenger ball 45
slider 153–4
slips 95, 132, 150, 152, 160, 162,
    215–16, 237
slogging 90, 138, 231
slow bowling 121, 181, 231
Small, John 66, 74–5, 77, 81, 175,
    194
Small, John (junior) 75
smell (of ball) 27, 30–2, 100
Smith, Graeme 208
Smith, Robin 237
Smith, Steven 112–19
Smith, William 261
smoking 258–9, 264
Smollett, Tobias 188
snobbery 142–3, 192
snooker ball 60
Snow, John 130
Sobers Six Sixes Ball 247–53
Sobers Six Sixes Bat 253

Sobers, Garry 219–20, 247–53
sociological 4
soft hands 159, 235
Soft Impact ball 59
Softaball 59
solidity (of ball) 27–8, 32
solipsism 33
Somerset CCC 181
sound (of ball) 27, 31–2
South Africa 102–3, 106, 112,
    114–15, 125–6, 177, 181, 188–9,
    196–7, 200, 247
Southborough 77
spectators 8, 16, 31, 47, 50, 86, 99,
    111, 125, 143, 164, 169, 206,
    210, 268
speed gun 121
speed records (bowling) 121–2,
    127, 203
sphere 21–2, 27, 29, 35, 63, 94
spin bowling 23, 57–8, 88–9,
    92, 120–1, 144–56, 181, 194,
    200, 226, 231–2, 234–7,
    240–2
spirit of the game 87, 111, 120,
    267, 269
spiritual 3–4, 10, 26, 57, 87, 211–12
split ball 273
Spofforth, Frederick 226–7
Spooner, Reginald 211–12
spot-fixing 139
square cut 225
square drive 225
square leg 11, 48, 140, 162, 236,
    267
Stapley, Ms 169–70, 182
Staunton, Anthony 262

Steen, Rob 219
steerhide (leather) 43
stemguard 184
Stevens, Lumpy 66
sticky wicket 124, 137, 201, 247
stiff upper lip 76
stitching (of ball) 37, 41–5, 54,
    57–8, 72, 77, 107 *see also* seams
Stokes, Ben 52, 273
Stonyhurst ball 71–2, 74
Stonyhurst Cricket 70–2, 256
stool ball (game) 64–5
straight drive 188, 225
strategy 7, 9, 206, 267
Strauss Ball 155, 238, 241–3, 245
Strictly Come Dancing 209
strike bowler 145
strokeplay 48, 209, 264
stuffed ball 64
stumped 66, 90, 197
stumps 31, 66, 74, 76, 123, 137, 189,
    208, 228–9, 241, 243, 257, 268
    see also leg, middle *and* off
    stump
subarachnoid haemorrhage
    (SAH) 183
summer 16, 18, 25, 34, 74, 120, 126,
    172, 233, 237
Summers, George 173, 182, 185
Surrey CCC 85–6, 172, 202
Surridge ball 45, 246, 249, 252–3
Sussex CCC 73, 172, 202
Sutcliffe, Herbert 264
Sutherland, James 116, 119
Swann, Graeme 154
sweat 30, 55–6, 92, 97, 101, 103,
    178–9, 259

swing 19, 21, 23, 47, 51, 55–8, 89,
     92, 94–8, 101, 120–1, 133, 138,
     152
swirling ball 159
switch-hitting 135
Sydney 143, 183

tactics 7, 9, 130, 189, 206, 240
Tait, Shaun 127
tape ball 61
tapered splice (of bat) 176
taste (of ball) 27, 29–30, 32
Tate, Maurice 209–10
Taunton 181
Taylor, Bob 213, 218
tea 4, 11, 54, 108–10, 213, 239
team game 6, 217
team-spirit 159
teesra 154
teeth 19, 58, 181
Tendulkar, Sachin 196–7, 220
tennis ball 60–1, 92, 188
Tennyson, Alfred Lord 190
Test cricket 16, 46, 50, 54, 56, 109,
     177–8, 193, 195–6, 200–1,
     203–5, 243, 247, 273
That Ball 232
theory of forms 22–4
Thomson, Jeff 122
throwing 36, 83, 87–9, 100, 152,
     155–6, 189, 262–3
tie (result) 85, 268–9
timeless Test 13
Tingley, Charlie 79–80
Titmus, Fred 202
Tonbridge 77
top-spinner 153

tragedy 13, 167, 184, 187, 189
transcendental ball 162–4, 253
treble-sewn ball 72, 76
Trescothick, Marcus 101–2, 239
Trueman, Fred 17, 142, 259
Trumper, Victor 220
Tuli, Neville 251
turf 45, 137, 171–2, 264, 270
turmeric 78
turn 23, 92, 149–50, 154, 233–5,
     240–1, 267
Turnbull, Malcolm 114
Twenty20 47–8, 52, 100, 111, 130,
     170, 184, 189, 192, 195, 205, 248
Twort & Martin 77
Twort ball 77–9, 260
Twort process 78–80
Twort, Thomas 77–9, 81, 175
Tye, Edward 185

umpire 11, 44, 48, 56, 62, 85–6,
     88–9, 92, 101, 103–5, 108–13,
     129, 135, 144, 150, 169, 188–9,
     228–30, 236, 244, 249, 255–6,
     267–9, 273
umpire miscounting 255–6
underarm bowling 83–7, 111, 119,
     171, 269
uniqueness (of cricket) 273
United England Eleven 258
universe 1–2, 58, 71, 104, 182, 257,
     270–3
unplayable 24, 92, 200, 231, 235
unsportsmanlike 141, 143, 228,
     267
Upfront ball 45, 58
USA 7–8

Van Bunge, Daan 247
Vaughan, Michael 115, 239
vertebral artery dissection 183
very fine leg 171
vibrations 31, 176
Victoria Cross 262
village green 69
Vinall, Jasper 185
Voce, Bill 140
Voges, Adam 139
Voltaire, François Marie Arouet de 192

Waddell, Dan 17
Walker, Peter 250
Walker, Thomas 'Old Everlasting' 84
walking 228–30
walking in 11, 157, 190
Walsh, Courtney 194
war 9, 17, 141, 256, 262–3
Ward, Earnest 72
Warne, Shane 145, 149–50, 153–5, 194, 231–4, 237–45, 267
Warner, David 113, 115–19, 273
Warwickshire CCC 101
Waterloo 9
Waters, Chris 259
wear and tear (of ball) 22–3, 48, 92–3, 97, 102, 121
weather 11, 23, 46, 137
weed (marijuana) 259
weed killer 171
weight (of ball) 21, 35–6, 46, 60–1, 68–70
Wellington, Duke of 9
Wells, H. G. 73–4

Wells, Joseph 73–4
West Gloucestershire Club 222–3
West Indies 5, 8, 44, 51–4, 58, 122, 125–6, 129, 147, 170, 178, 194, 197–8, 200–1, 204, 247, 252, 258, 266
West Kent Club 73
Whispering Death ball 58
white ball 46–9, 190
White, 'Shock' (of Brentford) 75
White, Thomas 'Daddy' (of Reigate) 75–6
whites 11, 21, 49, 93, 159, 203, 207, 264
whole ball 273
wican 64
wicker ball 64
wicket 14, 18–19, 23, 48–53, 60, 64–8, 71, 74–6, 89, 91, 95–9, 122, 124, 128, 131, 133–9, 145, 151–3, 163, 176, 180, 183, 189, 194–5, 198–204, 206, 208, 215–18, 223–4, 227–8, 230–1, 233–7, 239–47, 256, 259, 268, 270, 272
wicket-keeper 66, 86, 90, 93, 95, 144, 150, 171, 175, 180–2, 187–8, 195, 197, 213, 216, 233, 239, 244, 268
Wilde, Oscar 237
Willes, Christiana 84
Willes, John 84–5
Willis, Bob 212, 214–17
willow 11, 14, 30–1, 176
Wilson, Betty 204
windball 59–61
Wisden (publisher) 111, 207, 257, 259, 261

Wisden ball 260, 262
Wisden, John 257–61
Wittgenstein, Ludwig 272
women's cricket 9, 35, 45–6, 170, 202–7
Wonderball 58
Wood, Graeme 215
Woodcock, John 199–200, 202, 216, 218–21
wooden ball 70
Woodhams, Leonard 77
Woodruff, Bill 141
wool ball 64
Wooller, Wilf 248

Worcestershire CCC 186
World Test Championship 192
wrist spin 147–8, 154
wrong'un 153–4, 251

Yallop, Graham 178, 215
yellow ball 48, 50
yips 187
yorker 19, 34, 96, 123, 128, 133–4
Yorkshire CCC 107, 162, 189, 259
Yorkshire grit 167

Zimbabwe 95, 201
zooter 154